PENGUIN

T0200791

THE JOYOUS SCIENCE

FRIEDRICH NIETZSCHE was born near Leipzig in 1844, the son of a Lutheran clergyman who died when Nietzsche was four. He attended the famous Pforta School, then went to university at Bonn and at Leipzig, where he studied philology and first became acquainted with Richard Wagner. When he was only twenty-four he was appointed to the chair of classical philology at Basel University; he stayed there until his health forced him into retirement in 1879. While in Basel, he participated as an ambulance orderly in the Franco-Prussian War and published *The Birth of Tragedy* (1872), *Untimely Meditations* (1873–6) and the first volume of *Human, All Too Human* (1878). From 1880 until 1889, except for brief interludes, he divorced himself from everyday life and, supported by his university pension, lived mainly in France, Italy and Switzerland. Works published in the 1880s included *Dawn, The Joyous Science, Thus Spoke Zarathustra, Beyond Good and Evil, On the Genealogy of Morals* and *The Case of Wagner*. In January 1889, Nietzsche collapsed on a street in Turin and was subsequently institutionalized in Basel and Jena. He spent the remaining years of his life in a condition of mental and physical paralysis, cared for by his mother and later his sister Elisabeth. The last works published during his lifetime were *Twilight of the Idols* (1889), *The Anti-Christ* (1895) and *Nietzsche contra Wagner* (1895). After Nietzsche's death in 1900, Elisabeth assembled *The Will to Power* based on her brother's notebooks and published it the following year; a greatly expanded edition appeared in 1906. *Ecce Homo*, Nietzsche's autobiography, was published in 1908.

R. KEVIN HILL is Associate Professor of Philosophy at Portland State University. From 1994 until 2001 he taught in the Philosophy Department at Northwestern University. He is the author of *Nietzsche's Critiques: The Kantian Foundations of his Thought*, published by Oxford University Press (2003), and the editor and co-translator of Nietzsche's *The Will to Power*, published by Penguin Classics (2017).

Nietzsche in Penguin Classics

FRIEDRICH NIETZSCHE

The Joyous Science

('la gaya scienza')

Translated and edited by
R. KEVIN HILL

PENGUIN BOOKS

PENGUIN CLASSICS

UK | USA | Canada | Ireland | Australia
India | New Zealand | South Africa

Penguin Books is part of the Penguin Random House group of companies
whose addresses can be found at global.penguinrandomhouse.com

This edition first published in Penguin Classics 2018

012

Translation © R. Kevin Hill, 2018
Editorial material © R. Kevin Hill, 2018
All rights reserved

Set in 10.25/12.25 pt Sabon LT Std
Typeset by Jouve (UK), Milton Keynes
Printed and bound in Great Britain by Clays Ltd, Elcograf S.p.A.

A CIP catalogue record for this book is available from the British Library

ISBN: 978-0-141-19539-1

www.greenpenguin.co.uk

Penguin Random House is committed to a
sustainable future for our business, our readers
and our planet. This book is made from Forest
Stewardship Council® certified paper.

Contents

Chronology

1844 Birth of Friedrich Wilhelm Nietzsche on 15 October in Röcken, Prussian Saxony, to the pastor Karl Ludwig Nietzsche and his wife Franziska, née Oehler.

1846 Birth of Elisabeth Nietzsche on 10 July.

1848 Birth of Joseph Ludwig Nietzsche on 27 February.

1849 Death of Karl Ludwig Nietzsche on 30 July.

1850 Death of Joseph Ludwig Nietzsche on 9 January. Family moves to cathedral city of Naumburg.

1855 Nietzsche enters school associated with the cathedral.

1858 Accepted at prestigious boarding Pforta School, where he receives a traditional classical education.

1864 Matriculates at Bonn University to study theology and classical philology.

1865 Transfers to the University of Leipzig, where he becomes Friedrich Ritschl's favourite student. First acquaintance with the philosophy of Arthur Schopenhauer.

1866 Friendship with Erwin Rohde. Reads Friedrich Albert Lange's *History of Materialism*.

1867 First publication in classical philology. Enters military service in October.

1868 Riding accident in March leads to discharge from military service on 15 October. First meeting with Richard Wagner in November.

1869 Appointed to special professorship in Basel in classical philology (January). Awarded doctorate by Leipzig (23 March). Gives up Prussian citizenship. Holds inaugural lecture on 'Homer and Classical Philology' (28 May). Meets colleagues:

the historian Jacob Burckhardt and the theologian Franz
Overbeck.

1870 Professorship regularized. Public lectures on 'The Greek
Music Drama' (18 January) and 'Socrates and Tragedy' (1 February). Serves as an orderly in Franco-Prussian War with
Prussian army; contracts dysentery and diphtheria. Discharged
in October.

1871 Granted leave of absence from Basel due to ill-health.

1872 Publication of *The Birth of Tragedy* (January), which was
largely ignored by the academic world. Series of five public
lectures on education ('On the Future of Our Educational
Institutions'). Present at laying of foundation stone for Bayreuth opera house (22 May).

1873 Publication of first *Untimely Meditation: David Strauss,
the Confessor and Writer*. Befriends Jewish student and moral
philosopher Paul Rée.

1874 Publication of second and third *Untimely Meditation:
On the Uses and Disadvantages of History for Life* and
Schopenhauer as Educator.

1875 Meets Heinrich Köselitz (to whom Nietzsche gives the
pseudonym Peter Gast in 1881). Elisabeth moves to Basel and
sets up home for herself and her brother.

1876 Publication of fourth *Untimely Meditation: Richard
Wagner in Bayreuth*. Attends first Bayreuth festival (July).
Granted one-year leave of absence from the university. Lives
in Sorrento with Rée and Malwida von Meysenbug. Sees
Wagner for last time.

1877 Returns to Basel and resumes teaching. Lives with Elisabeth and Gast.

1878 Publication of *Human, All Too Human*, which finalizes
break with Wagner.

1879 Publication of sequel to *Human, All Too Human* (*Mixed
Opinions and Maxims*). Resignation from professorship due
to ill-health; granted pension. Travels in Switzerland, then to
Naumburg.

1880 Publication of *The Wanderer and His Shadow*. Travels
to Riva, Venice, Marienbad, Naumburg, Stresa and Genoa,
where he spends the winter.

1881 Publication of *Dawn: Thoughts on Moral Prejudices*. Travels to Recoaro Terme and Riva with Gast; alone to St Moritz and Sils-Maria. Winter in Genoa.

1882 Publication of *Idylls from Messina* and *The Joyous Science*. Meets Lou Andreas-Salomé in Rome at the home of Malwida von Meysenbug (May). Returns to Naumburg; visits Berlin and Tautenburg, where Lou joins him. With Lou and Rée in Leipzig (October). Break with Lou and Rée; leaves for Rapallo (November).

1883 Publication of *Thus Spoke Zarathustra*, I. Death of Wagner (13 February). Travels to Genoa, Rome, Sils-Maria, Naumburg, Genoa and Nice. In Naumburg learns of Elisabeth's engagement to anti-Semite Bernhard Förster, a member of the extended Wagner circle.

1884 Publication of *Zarathustra*, II and III. Stays in Venice, Sils-Maria, Zürich and Nice.

1885 Publication of *Zarathustra*, IV (published privately). Travels to Venice, Sils-Maria, Naumburg and Nice. Marriage of Elisabeth and Förster, who leave together for the colony Nueva Germania in Paraguay.

1886 Publication of *Beyond Good and Evil*. Stays in Naumburg, Leipzig, Genoa and Nice.

1887 Publication of *On the Genealogy of Morals*. Travels to Sils-Maria, Venice and back to Nice. Publication of new editions of *The Birth of Tragedy*, *Human, All Too Human*, *Dawn* and *The Joyous Science*.

1888 Publication of *The Case of Wagner*. Stays in Turin and Sils-Maria; returns to Turin in September. Composition of last sane writings.

1889 Publication of *Twilight of the Idols* (completed in 1888). Collapses on street in Turin (3 January). Retrieved by Overbeck. Enters clinic in Basel (10 January). Transferred to clinic in Jena (17 January). Förster commits suicide in Paraguay after embezzling colony's funds.

1890 Franziska Nietzsche takes her son to Naumburg, where he remains in her care. Elisabeth returns from Paraguay.

1892 Plan for first edition of Nietzsche's published works (discontinued after volume 5), edited by Köselitz but arranged by Elisabeth, who then returns to Paraguay to clear up business of the colony.

1893 Elisabeth returns from Paraguay for good.

1894 Founding of the Nietzsche Archive.

1895 Publication of *The Anti-Christ* and *Nietzsche contra Wagner* (both completed in 1888). Elisabeth acquires all rights to Nietzsche's writings.

1896 Archive transferred to Weimar.

1897 Death of Nietzsche's mother. Elisabeth takes Nietzsche to Weimar.

1900 Death of Nietzsche (25 August); buried in Röcken.

1901 First version of *The Will to Power* (second, expanded edition 1906), edited by Elisabeth and Köselitz; based on Nietzsche's notebooks and plans in his notebooks.

1908 First publication of *Ecce Homo* (written in 1888).

Introduction

When Nietzsche published *Human, All Too Human* in 1878, the first volume in his 'Free Spirit' trilogy (of which *The Joyous Science* is the triumphant conclusion), it was a declaration of independence from many things to which he had previously been committed, especially independence from German Romanticism in general and from the Wagner cult in particular, as well as from academic scholarship in classical literature. The effect on Wagner, his friend and ally, was immediate and overwhelmingly negative. Nietzsche's resignation from his position at the University of Basel would come but a year later. The book was followed by two sequels, *Mixed Opinions and Maxims* in 1879 and *The Wanderer and His Shadow* in 1880, and a further entry, *Dawn: Thoughts on Moral Prejudices*, in 1881. Following the model of *Human, All Too Human*, Nietzsche then began to work on what was initially conceived as an addition to *Dawn*. It was this text which ultimately became *The Joyous Science* and was published in 1882.

That Nietzsche himself regarded the book in 1882 as the culmination of his authorship which had only truly begun with *Human, All Too Human*, is indicated by the blurb he wrote for its back cover, which read: 'With this book we arrive at the conclusion of a series of writings by FRIEDRICH NIETZSCHE whose common goal it is to erect *a new image and ideal of the free spirit*. To this series belong: *Human, All Too Human. With a Supplement: Mixed Opinions and Maxims*; *The Wanderer and His Shadow*; *Dawn: Thoughts on Moral Prejudices*; *The Joyous Science.*' Nietzsche then relegates *The Birth of Tragedy* (1872) and *Untimely Meditations* (1873–6) to 'earlier writings by the same author'.

From *Thus Spoke Zarathustra* (1883–5) onwards, Nietzsche entered his mature period, and the 'Free Spirit' trilogy subsequently came to be regarded as (or consigned to) Nietzsche's 'middle' or 'positivistic' period. However, *The Joyous Science* was to become more than just the third part of a trilogy. After completing *Zarathustra* and *Beyond Good and Evil*, Nietzsche turned to the task of bringing out new editions of the middle works in 1886. *Mixed Opinions and Maxims* and *The Wanderer and His Shadow* were consolidated into volume 2 of *Human, All Too Human*. New Prefaces were written for both volumes, as well as for *Dawn* and *The Joyous Science*. But the modifications of *The Joyous Science* were to prove far more extensive. First, Nietzsche added a fifth part to the original four, containing forty new aphorisms he had written in 1886 after the completion of *Beyond Good and Evil*. As a result, the book now came to straddle his middle and late phases, reflecting both his middle style and his final views. Second, although the original edition had a 'prelude in German rhymes' (sixty-three short poems), in the second edition Nietzsche appended fourteen more poems, six of which had previously appeared in his only published collection of verse, *Idylls from Messina* (1882), making the book into more of a synthesis of his analytical and lyrical sides than it had been before, and an epitome of his writing both in prose and in poetry. The end result contains the most important ideas that he would ever discuss in print in his lifetime, as well as some of his most ravishing prose (especially the Preface, of which he was so fond that he reused it for the conclusion of the last book he worked on, *Nietzsche contra Wagner*).

The title of the book has been the subject of some discussion. 'Die fröhliche Wissenschaft' has been variously translated as 'The Joyful Wisdom' (by Thomas Common), 'The Gay Science' (by Walter Kaufmann), 'The Joyous Science' (by Laurence Lampert) and 'The Joyful Science' (in the forthcoming Stanford University Press edition). It is now generally agreed that the implications of rigorous knowledge strongly suggest 'science' rather than wisdom, even if the German word for science is much broader than the English term would suggest (the sense of the German word would have it that Nietzsche was a 'scientist' by

virtue of being a professor of classical languages and literature).
Although these implications of rigour are fully intended, there is
also an element of irony mixed with them. The phrase 'die fröhliche Wissenschaft' had been used in German to refer to the art
of poetry since at least the eighteenth century, while 'la gaya scienza', which Nietzsche took as his subtitle, also historically
referred to the art of poetry, especially as practised by the Provençal troubadours of the Middle Ages. Many other indications
in the text show that Nietzsche intended the title not only to
point forwards to his new conception of philosophical enquiry,
but also backwards to the art of poetry. And there had always
been a tinge of irony in referring to poetry as 'the gay science' or
'the joyous science', one slightly reminiscent of the expression
'the sweet science' for the sport of boxing (neither poetry nor
boxing seem particularly 'scientific'), an irony doubled by
Nietzsche's suggestion that philosophical enquiry *can* be both
scientifically rigorous *and* poetic. One might have been encour-
aged to translate the title as 'The Gay Science' by the fact that the
English usage contemporaneous with Nietzsche would also have
referred to the art of poetry as 'the gay science', or, somewhat
less frequently, as 'the joyous science' (it is almost never referred
to in English as 'the *joyful* science').[1] However, the term 'gay' is
apt to mislead today. When Kaufmann's translation was published in 1974, the English word was only just beginning its
career as a more positive replacement for the adjective 'homosex-
ual'. Interestingly, Kaufmann regarded this association, which
was clearly never a part of Nietzsche's intention, as a strength, in
so far as being 'gay' suggested to him 'light-hearted defiance of
convention'. Several decades later, the word has become a victim
of its own success, and a living metaphor has become a dead one;
'gay' effectively denotes at least male homosexuality, and in a
world in which widespread acceptance has replaced an older big-
otry, for many people 'gay' no longer connotes 'light-hearted
defiance of convention' at all.

But what is this book actually about? In the first place, it is one
of Nietzsche's 'aphoristic' works, and thus draws on the models
of French moralists like La Rochefoucauld, and their German
imitator Schopenhauer (in his *Parerga and Paralipomena*, 1851).

One can gain a sense of the topics and concerns of Nietzsche's aphoristic works by a glance at the chapter titles of the first volume of *Human, All Too Human*: 'Of First and Last Things' (i.e. metaphysics and epistemology), 'On the History of Moral Feelings', 'Religious Life', 'From the Soul of Artists and Writers', 'Signs of Higher and Lower Culture', 'Man in Society', 'Woman and Child', 'A Look at the State', 'Man Alone with Himself'. However, in the sequels to volume 1, as well as in *Dawn* and *The Joyous Science*, Nietzsche abandons any attempt to organize his remarks under rubrics in this way. But the superficial appearance of chaos is misleading, for beneath it there is both an underlying theory and something of a 'narrative arc'. In fact, there is something of a protagonist of this narrative with whom we are meant to identify: Nietzsche himself.

The underlying theory is one which Nietzsche had expressed clearly enough some years before, in *Schopenhauer as Educator*, the third part of *Untimely Meditations*. In its first few pages, Nietzsche articulates a virtue ethic, but with some twists which distinguish it from its ancient Greek antecedents. The first is that, instead of emphasizing a kind of human essence which all human beings share and which must be actualized (and from which one might derive ethical standards), Nietzsche stresses the *uniqueness* of each individual, almost as if each of us is a species unto ourselves. Accordingly, the conditions for flourishing and self-actualization will vary widely from one person to the next. This in turn means that individuals cannot rely unthinkingly on their own socialization or inherited traditions in order to determine how best to actualize their own potential, since the customs and traditions in question are not sufficiently tailored to the individual case. Consequently, the discovery of the means to self-actualization must be left to the individual's own experimentation. Second, precisely because social customs and inherited traditions are geared to collective flourishing, they tend to demand self-sacrifice from the individual and can even be quite harmful. Finally, since Nietzsche from the beginning abandons any justification for interpersonal morality couched in terms of religion, intrinsic rights or collective interests, leaving him with no normative standard at all other than the desirability of individual self-actualization, a better understanding of the ways society obstructs this development acquires some urgency – an urgency only intensified by the fact that in our age of democratization, the suffocating character of public life and public opinion has made matters for the individual even worse. As an aside, it is striking that this overall picture closely resembles the concerns John Stuart Mill expressed in chapter three of *On Liberty*, 'Of Individuality, as One of the Elements of Well-Being', despite Nietzsche's frequent condemnations of Mill in his notebooks and later writings.

In the text of *The Joyous Science* itself, the critique of religion, morality, the arts and modernity proceeds as if we are on a voyage of discovery, accompanying Nietzsche as his insights occur to him, for Nietzsche is not merely adopting the stance of the cold and cynical outsider who stands above or apart from society, as a too-rigorous adherence to the French moralist model might have suggested. Rather, he develops his criticisms with an eye to his own self-emancipation, and the self-emancipation of others who, though they may have very different individual 'essences', share a common enemy in the things being critiqued. However, with each new discovery, with each new toppled idol, the personal dangers of this voyage increase as well. In particular, the terrifying realization that God is 'dead', announced for the first time in Nietzsche's writings in *Joyous Science* § 108 and discussed more fully in §§ 125 and 343, poses profound dangers not only for the culture in which the beliefs and precepts of Christianity are thoroughly intertwined, but for aspiring individuals as well, given the ways in which they remain formed by and dependent upon it.

Yet the overall message of *The Joyous Science* remains a positive one. At the climax of Book III, Nietzsche offers a bracing but hopeful catechism of sorts for his self-emancipating individuals:

268
What Makes You Heroic?

To face at the same time your greatest suffering and your greatest hope.

269
What Do You Believe?

In this: that the weights of all things must be determined anew.

270
What Does Your Conscience Say?

'You shall become who you are.'

271
What Is Your Greatest Danger?

Pity.

272
What Do You Love in Others?

My hopes.

273
Whom Do You Call Bad?

Those who always want to put others to shame.

274
What Is Most Humane?

To spare someone shame.

275
What is the Seal of Liberation?

To no longer be ashamed of oneself.

As we turn the page from the end of Book III to the beginning of Book IV, we notice that something important is afoot, because for the first time the Book has its own title: 'Sanctus Januarius'. This is a reference to the miracle of St Januarius, a sample of whose blood was allegedly saved in a vial after his martyrdom and stored as a holy relic in Naples Cathedral. For centuries the blood is said to have miraculously liquified. Nietzsche's suggestion, implied by the title and its accompanying poem, and carefully spelled out in the Preface of 1887, is that

during his middle phase he had experienced a kind of inner fro-
zenness, lifelessness and rigidity as he turned his back on the
things that had formerly moved him and took up the stance of
the cynical observer of common life from the outside, the solitary 'wanderer' whose only friend is his own shadow. But as
Nietzsche's pursuit of self-emancipation begins to reach fulfilment, he feels his 'blood', his inwardness and emotional life,
'liquifying', warming into a new hopefulness. It is in part this
new zest for life that leads him to use the phrase 'the *joyous* science' to title his book. This new fulfilment is accompanied, and
perhaps occasioned, by a new discovery which sets *The Joyous
Science* apart from its aphoristic predecessors: the doctrine of
the eternal recurrence.

   The final four sections of Book IV represent the climax of the
book as a whole and, in its first edition of 1882, its conclusion. In
'*Vita Femina*' Nietzsche mourns the fact that while the world is
rich in beautiful things, it is poor in 'beautiful moments' in which
these things are revealed to us. A part of this mourning is contained in the observation that the best things reveal themselves
only once. This claim is contrasted with the Greeks' prayer that
beautiful things be *repeated* 'twice, or three times!', laying the
foundation for the idea that, ideally, these 'beautiful moments'
should be repeated *an infinite number of times*. Nietzsche then
eroticizes the notion of beautiful things being veiled, and 'beautiful moments' rarely revealing themselves to us with the striking
claim that 'life is a woman'. The implication is clear: life is not to
be observed from without, dutifully borne or vitriolically condemned. Life is to be *loved*.

   The next section, 'The Dying Socrates', takes a figure who
previously in the middle works had been celebrated for his
independence and rationality (in part to make up for being
accused of killing Greek tragedy in Nietzsche's early *The Birth
of Tragedy*) and, by interpreting a stray remark attributed to
him from Plato's *Phaedo*, concludes that even Socrates for all
his virtues did not truly love life. The contrast to '*Vita femina*'
is unmistakable: Socrates' seemingly heroic embrace of death is
born of weakness, a failure to love, a wish for annihilation rather
than repetition. And this is why it isn't enough for Nietzsche to

become pagan, to return to antiquity in his attempt to transcend both Christianity and modernity, for Socrates was the best pagan antiquity had to offer. For this reason, Nietzsche says that 'we have to surpass even the Greeks!'.

It is at this point that Nietzsche gingerly introduces the thought which had first occurred to him 'at the beginning of August 1881, in Sils-Maria, 6,000 feet above the sea and much higher above all human things' (*Kritische Studienausgabe*, volume 9, p. 494). In *The Joyous Science* it is presented hypothetically: suppose that you learned (from a 'demon') that your life was to be repeated an infinite number of times without the slightest variation. Would you be horrified? Or would you be ecstatic? Nietzsche seems to think that only these extreme reactions make sense in the face of infinite repetition. The first point to make here is that Nietzsche's emphasis is simultaneously on the aforementioned 'beautiful moments' which are so very rare that they never repeat themselves within a single lifetime, and the amount of suffering involved even in a life well lived. While we may imagine that a life which ends in death may be less than fully satisfying for that reason (at least the believers in an afterlife seem to think so), there is some consolation in knowing that one's *suffering* will be at an end by virtue of annihilation. This, Nietzsche thinks, is the 'Socratic' reaction (despite the fact that Socrates in the *Phaedo* argues extensively for the existence of an afterlife). If instead of death there were infinite repetition of *this* life, this nihilistic solace would be as unavailable to us as the solace of a happy afterlife. We might also add that, since Nietzsche's metaphysics is completely naturalistic and deterministic, in order for one human life to be exactly repeated, all of the history of the cosmos within which it was embedded would also have to be exactly repeated. And with that, any solace one might experience at the thought of posthumous reputation, heirs, the success of future generations, indeed, future progress of any kind, would be made a mockery of by the endless cycling of the cosmos and human history. In a sense, Nietzsche radicalizes a common secular thought that, in the absence of an afterlife, we must make the most of this life, for this life is all we have. Matters for him are more extreme: this life is *inescapable*. If its ending provides any solace to the weary, that solace is illusory, for as soon as you end this life you must (subjectively speaking) start it over again from the beginning.

The idea that this *could* be true, and that we must test our fundamental attitude towards life as affirming it or negating it by contemplating our reaction to this thought, is the idea as it is presented in *The Joyous Science*. However, the evidence of Nietzsche's notebooks suggests that he regarded the eternal recurrence not only as a terrifying or exhilarating thought experiment, but as actually true, indeed, *provably* true. This colours the idea in a very different way than those who regard Nietzsche's notion as purely hypothetical have thought. In fact, it is hard to imagine why Nietzsche would have placed such an enormous emphasis on the idea if he thought it was merely a challenging hypothetical with which we might reconsider our fundamental attitudes. This point can be seen more clearly if we imagine that Nietzsche's great rival, Christianity, were to present itself in the following words. '*Suppose* that after you die, if you have sinned in this life and have not properly received the atoning death of Jesus Christ, then you will continue to exist in a non-physical form, subjected to horrible tortures for all eternity. If that were the case, wouldn't you want to renounce sin and accept Jesus to avoid such a horrible torment? Not that any of this is true of course! Thank God for that! But you should act *as if* it were true.' But why should we? Most of the vivacity of the idea of damnation dissipates into a sigh of relief that it is *merely* hypothetical, and with it, all motivating force as well. Why should I act as if something is true when it is precisely *not* true?

It does seem to be the case, once we take Nietzsche's unpublished remarks into account, that he actually believed this mad idea, and found not only challenge in it, but consolation and a sense of mission as well. For the infinite repetition of your life means that, in a certain sense, you will never truly die, and that those 'beautiful moments' shimmer with the radiance of eternity. The sense of mission comes from the fact that Nietzsche, in asking himself what life he wishes to lead, now that he knows

his life is subject to and must become worthy of infinite repetition, answers that he is to become the teacher of the doctrine of
the eternal recurrence.

At which point we come to the final section of Book IV,
'*Incipit Tragoedia*'. This section introduces the character of Zarathustra by giving us an almost verbatim anticipation of the
opening of Nietzsche's next work, *Thus Spoke Zarathustra*. In
it, Zarathustra, modelled on the ancient Iranian prophet and
founder of Zoroastrianism, grows weary of his solitude and
decides to descend from his mountain cave to return to humanity with new teachings. What new teachings? Nietzsche explains
in *Ecce Homo* that one of the reasons why he chose Zarathustra
for his fictional persona is because Zoroaster's original teaching
was that the cosmos is to be understood as a great battleground
between the forces of good and evil, light and darkness.[2] In this
battle, human beings must freely choose a side on which to fight;
this idea eventually finds its way into Christianity. But, Nietzsche
imagines, the genius who first thought up this false conception
of things must surely have been the first to see through it? And
so by using Zarathustra as a mouthpiece, Nietzsche styles himself as the first teacher of the fact that the cosmos is precisely *not*
a battleground between the forces of good and evil, and the
teacher of all the implications of this fundamental criticism. But
as we learn in reading *Thus Spoke Zarathustra*, most of the text
is concerned not just with Nietzsche's new ethic, but with Zarathustra's own struggle to accept, affirm and ultimately teach the
doctrine of the eternal recurrence itself. Thus *The Joyous Science* in its original form ends by announcing that Nietzsche can
no longer continue as the aloof outsider who criticizes humanity, society and modernity. He must achieve a higher form of
joyous affirmation, and must become the quasi-religious teacher
of this doctrine to the humanity he had formerly left behind.

If *The Joyous Science* has a protagonist of sorts, and a story-
line, it even more clearly has a setting. Although the idea of the
eternal recurrence came to Nietzsche in Sils-Maria, Switzerland,
most of the book was written on and near the Mediterranean,
in northern Italy, in such cities as Genoa (the birthplace of Christopher Columbus, a figure often alluded to in the text), Recoaro

Terme and Cannobio. The poems in the Appendix were written in Messina, Sicily. Some of Book V was written in Nice. Throughout the text, Nietzsche contrasts the warm, cosmopolitan and life-affirming spirit of the South to the cold, parochial and stultifying spirit of the North. Finally, the book opens and closes with references to Provence, the coastal region of the South of France which is not far from Genoa. The first reference, as mentioned above, is the title *The Joyous Science* ('*la gaya scienza*'), with its associations with the poetry of the medieval troubadours of Provence. The final reference is the last poem, 'To the Mistral Wind', in which Nietzsche likens himself and his free spirit to a cold, north-westerly wind that blows across Provence, and is strongest during the transition between winter and spring. The Mistral brings with it exceptionally clear and fresh weather and plays an important role in creating the conditions which give the region the qualities Nietzsche so appreciated, and whose sunlight attracted artists like Cézanne, Monet, Van Gogh, Picasso and Matisse.

Provence itself has a peculiar history which resonates in surprising ways with Nietzsche's personality and his conception of philosophy. Until the thirteenth century, Provence was an autonomous region with its own culture and language (Occitan, or 'langue d'oc') which were much closer to Latin influences than France proper, with its Frankish-Germanic origins. Its social character was dictated by the effects of Mediterranean trade rather than agriculture, and as a result Provence was for much of its history a bastion of the rising middle class, and an environment more friendly to merchants, lawyers and gnostic heretics (the Cathars) than to the aristocracy or clergy. Given Nietzsche's staunch opposition to anti-Semitism, it is significant that it also possessed a flourishing and well-received Jewish community. It is in this cosmopolitan, almost Italian setting that the troubadours emerged. And because in such a community wealth is valued more than birth, the intelligence required to succeed in commerce or law came to be valued more than mere position or ecclesiastical credential. The troubadours thus represented not merely the local entertainment, but a new model of the independent intellectual, beholden to no one and prized for his or her talents and wits. Interestingly, given the meritocratic spirit of the region, the troubadours themselves displayed as a group a remarkable indifference to social class, with people of noble birth who had taken up the art out of passion mixing freely with people of the middle and lower classes. This remarkable degree of social freedom gave rise to a small renaissance of sorts and produced a body of poetry containing over two thousand separate compositions.

Ultimately, northern France, the Church and the French monarchy had enough of this luxuriant and permissive society, and in 1209 Pope Innocent III initiated the Albigensian Crusade in an attempt to stamp out the Cathar heresy which was largely present in the South, and the process of subjugation and assimilation began in earnest. Most of the troubadours eventually fled to the more tolerant climes of northern Italy or Moorish Spain. It was a foreshadowing of many later developments throughout Europe in which national cultural identities consolidated themselves at the expense of individual and regional ones. In this, the character and fate of the South of France at the hands of Christianity and nationalism served as an apt analogue for the very qualities and types of person Nietzsche thought were similarly threatened by the new forces of modernity.[3]

I mentioned above that *The Joyous Science* straddles Nietzsche's middle and late periods, and thus provides us with an unusually comprehensive exposition of his themes, problems and proposed solutions. As a result, it is a treasure trove of philosophical suggestions and insights, and for intellectual content few of Nietzsche's works are its equal. It is, however, more than just a philosopher's book. With its unique voice and prose style, its playful combination of poetry and prose, its implied Mediterranean setting, its authorial persona's quest for self-emancipation, *The Joyous Science* is a literary tour de force. It is quite possibly Nietzsche's best book.

I am indebted to the support and assistance of numerous people, but most notably and in no particular order: Tom Seppalainen at Portland State University; Iain Thomson at the University of New Mexico for his stylistic suggestions; Jessica Harrison at

Penguin; Gerald Simon of the Nietzsche Channel for providing me with his own renditions of the two *Idylls from Messina* poems; Ruth Pietroni, Michael Brown and Linden Lawson for editorial assistance; and my wife, LisaMary, for her continued patience and generosity.

NOTES

1.   It is merely felicitous that Emerson, whom Nietzsche read closely while writing this book, also referred to the art of poetry as 'the joyous science' (though there is no indication that Nietzsche himself was aware of this fact).

2.   *Ecce Homo: How One Becomes What One Is*, trans. R. J. Hollingdale, reprinted with an Introduction by Michael Tanner (London: Penguin Classics, 1992), pp. 97–8.

3.   I am especially indebted to Rolando Pérez's 'Towards a Genealogy of the Gay Science: From Toulouse and Barcelona to Nietzsche and Beyond', *eHumanista*, vol. 5, pp. 546–703 (2014) for this historical background.

Note on the Text and Translation

The textual foundation of this translation is Friedrich Nietzsche, *Die fröhliche Wissenschaft ('la gaya scienza'), Neue Ausgabe mit einem Anhange: Lieder des Prinzen Vogelfrei* (Leipzig: E. W. Fritzsch, 1887) and *Idyllen aus Messina*, published in *Internationale Monatsschrift. Zeitschrift für allgemeine und nationale Kultur und deren Litteratur*, vol. 1, no. 5 (May 1882), pp. 269–75 (Chemnitz: Ernst Schmeitzner). I have also consulted Nietzsche, *Kritische Gesamtausgabe: Werke*, ed. Giorgio Colli and Mazzino Montinari (Berlin: Walter de Gruyter, pp. 1967ff.).

Although the translation of a book Nietzsche himself saw to press not once but twice scarcely poses the philological difficulties which were involved in the translation of *The Will to Power* (a text controversially assembled by editors from Nietzsche's notebooks after his death), the same methodology of translation has been applied here as well. Translation is somewhat freer than is often the case with Nietzsche's books, in part out of a commitment to the notion that the unit of meaning is the sentence and not the word. The overarching goal has been to present Nietzsche's thought as clearly and as gracefully as possible, while striving to avoid anachronism. Also, considerable freedom has been needed to render the many poems in a manner which preserves both their sense and their prosody. Finally, no attempt has been made to foist a language of gender neutrality upon Nietzsche which would be alien to both his time and his own sensibility.

Further Reading

Ruth Abbey, *Nietzsche's Middle Period* (Oxford: Oxford University Press, 2000).

Paul Franco, *Nietzsche's Enlightenment: The Free-Spirit Trilogy of the Middle Period* (Chicago: University of Chicago Press, 2011).

Laurence Lampert, *Nietzsche and Modern Times: A Study of Bacon, Descartes and Nietzsche* (New Haven: Yale University Press, 1995).

William H. Schaberg, *The Nietzsche Canon: A Publication History and Bibliography* (Chicago: University of Chicago Press, 1996).

Julian Young, *Friedrich Nietzsche: A Philosophical Biography* (Cambridge: Cambridge University Press, 2010).

THE JOYOUS SCIENCE

I live here in my own house,
I copy no one's craft,
And laugh at every master,
Who at himself can't laugh.

OVER MY FRONT DOOR

'To the poet and sage, all things are
friendly and sacred, all experiences profitable,
all days holy, all men divine.'

Emerson[1]

[Epigraph to the first edition]

Preface to the Second Edition

Perhaps more than one preface would be necessary for this book; and after all it might still be doubtful whether anyone could be brought nearer to the *experiences* in it by means of prefaces, without having himself experienced something similar. It seems to be written in the language of the thawing wind: there is exuberance, restlessness, contrariety and April showers in it; so that one is as constantly reminded of the proximity of winter as of the *victory* over it which is coming, which must come, which has perhaps already come . . .

Gratitude continually flows forth, as if the most unexpected thing had happened, the gratitude of recovery – for to *recover* was most unexpected. 'Joyous Science':[1] that implies the Saturnalia of a spirit which has patiently withstood a long, terrible pressure – patiently, strictly, coldly, without submitting, but without hope – and which is now suddenly overcome with hope, the hope of health, the *giddiness* of recovery. What wonder that much that is unreasonable and foolish thereby comes to light, much mischievous affection is lavished even on problems which have a prickly hide, and are therefore not meant to be caressed and courted. The whole book is really nothing but a revel after a long privation and sense of powerlessness: a rejoicing in the return of strength, in newly awakened belief in a tomorrow and day after tomorrow, in sudden sentiment and presentiment of a future, in approaching adventures, in seas open once more, and aims once more permitted and believed in. And consider what I had just passed through, what I had left behind! This wasteland of

8

exhaustion, disbelief and freezing up in the midst of youth, this premature onset of old age, this tyranny of pain, surpassed, however, by the tyranny of pride which repudiated the *conclusions* of pain – and conclusions are consolations – this absolute seclusion, as defence against a contempt for mankind become abnormally clairvoyant, this restriction on principle to all that is bitter, harsh and woeful in knowledge, as prescribed by the *revulsion* which had gradually resulted from an imprudent intellectual diet and self-indulgence – it is called Romanticism – oh, who could share these feelings of mine! Whoever could do so would surely forgive me more than a little folly, high jinks and 'Joyous Science' – for example, the handful of songs which are given along with the book on this occasion – songs in which a poet mocks all poets in a way not easily forgiven.

Alas, it is not only on the poets and their fine 'lyrical sentiments' that this convalescent must vent his spleen: who knows what kind of victim he is seeking, what kind of beastly stuff he will soon be provoked into parodying? *Incipit tragoedia*, it is said at the conclusion of this scrupulously unscrupulous book; one must be on one's guard! Something exceedingly naughty and wicked announces itself here: *incipit parodia* no doubt . . .

2

But let us leave Herr Nietzsche; what is it to us that Herr Nietzsche has been restored to health?

Few questions are more attractive to the psychologist than those concerning the relation of health to philosophy, and in the case where he himself falls ill, he will bring with him into the illness all his scientific curiosity. For assuming that he is a person, of necessity he also has his own personal philosophy: there is, however, an important distinction to be made. In some, their deficiencies philosophize, in others, their wealth and strength. The former have *need* of their philosophy, whether as support, reassurance, medicine, deliverance, exaltation or depersonalization; the latter merely regard it as a fine luxury, or at best the voluptuousness of a triumphant gratitude which in the end must inscribe itself in cosmic capitals on the heaven of ideas. In the more common case, when exigencies impel a man to philoso-phize, as is always the case with ailing thinkers – and perhaps in the history of philosophy the greater part of the thinkers *are* ill – what will become of thought itself when it is subjected to the *pressure* of illness? This is a question for the psychologist: and here an experiment is possible. Just like a traveller who under-takes to rouse himself at an appointed hour and then calmly abandons himself to sleep, we philosophers, should we become ill, may for a time surrender ourselves to the illness body and soul – and close our eyes to ourselves, as it were. And just as the traveller knows that something does *not* sleep, that something counts the hours and will awaken him, we also know that the critical moment will find us awake – that just then something will pop up and catch the intellect *in the very act*, I mean in weakness, or repentance, or resignation, or rigidity, or gloom, or whatever the morbid intellectual conditions are called, which in better times have intellectual *pride* opposed to them (for it is as in the old rhyme, 'The spirit proud, peacock and horse, are the three proudest things on earth, of course'). After such self-interrogation and self-examination one comes to view all that has ever been philosophized with a keener eye; one more readily discerns the involuntary wrong turns, side streets, resting places and *sunny* spots of thought to which suffering thinkers, pre-cisely as sufferers, are led and misled: from now on, one knows where the sickly *body* and its needs unwittingly urge, prod and entice the intellect – to sunlight, tranquillity, gentleness, patience, medicine, balm in some sense. Every philosophy which puts peace above war, every ethic with a negative conception of hap-piness, every metaphysic and physic that knows an end, a final state of any kind, every predominantly aesthetic or religious longing for some means to get away from, outside of, above or beyond the world, all these raise the question of whether illness has not inspired the philosopher. The unconscious disguise of physiological needs under the cloak of the objective, the ideal, the purely intellectual, occurs to an alarming extent – and I have often wondered whether on the whole philosophy has thus far really been only an interpretation of the body, and a *misunderstanding of the body.* Concealed behind the most exalted value judgements that have governed the history of thought so far lie misunderstandings of physicality, either of individuals, classes, or entire races. One may consider these bold absurdities of the metaphysicians, and especially their answers to the question as to the *value* of existence, first and foremost as symptoms of different bodily constitutions; and although not one iota of significance inheres in such affirmations and denials of the world when scientifically measured, they nevertheless furnish valuable hints to historians and psychologists, and, as I have said, serve as symptoms of the bodily constitution which flourishes or fails, of its plenitude, power and imperiousness in history, or else of its inhibition, fatigue and depletion, its premonition of the end, its desire for the end. I still await a philosophical *physician*, in the exceptional sense of the word – one who will apply himself to the problem of the overall health of peoples, periods, races and mankind – who will some day have the courage to push my suspicions to their extreme and venture the following suggestion: in all philosophizing so far it has not been a question of 'truth' at all, but of something else – namely of health, futurity, growth, power, life . . .

3

One might surmise that I do not wish to take my leave of that period of severe infirmity ungrateful for the profits it afforded me, which are far from spent: I am well aware of the advantages over sturdier intellects conferred by my capricious health. A philosopher who has repeatedly passed through many conditions of health has also passed through just as many philosophies: he really *cannot* do otherwise than invariably convert his condition into the most intellectual form and distance – this art of transfiguration just *is* philosophy. We philosophers are not at liberty to separate body and soul, as the people do; and we are still less at liberty to separate soul and intellect. We are not thinking frogs, we are not coolly objective recording instruments, frigid and barren – we are mothers whose thoughts are born from our pain, and we must lavish on them all that we have of blood, heart, fire, joy, passion, torment, conscience, destiny and doom. Life – for us that means the continual transformation of all that affects us and all that we are into light and flame; we simply *cannot* do otherwise. And as for the illness, are we not almost tempted to ask if it is not indispensable? In the end, it is great pain only which liberates the spirit;[2] for it teaches a *great suspicion* which reveals the apparently genuine to be counterfeit, makes a known quantity into an unknown one, and, in solving that equation, prepares us for an ultimate decision[3] ...

It is great pain only, the long, slow pain which takes its time, by which we are burnt, as it were, with green wood, that compels us philosophers to descend into our deepest depths and put aside all confidence, everything good-natured, dressed-up, mild, middling, which perhaps formerly constituted our humanity. I doubt whether such pain 'improves' us; but I know that it makes us *profound*. Whether we learn to oppose to it our pride, our scorn, our force of will, and do as the Indian does, who, howsoever horribly tortured, requites himself on his torturer with his malicious tongue; whether we withdraw from the pain into that Oriental nothingness – also known as Nirvana – into deaf, mute, numb resignation, oblivion, annihilation: one emerges from such long, dangerous exercises in self-mastery as another person, with a few more question marks, above all *determined* to keep questioning, more profoundly, strictly, sternly, wickedly and discreetly than ever before. Trust in life is gone: life itself has become a *problem*.

One should not infer that this is inevitably a dismal condition! Even love of life is still possible – only one loves differently. It is the love for a woman who inspires doubts ...

But with such more intellectualized men, the attraction of the problematic, the delight in an unknown quantity, is too great not to spark a bright blaze of delight again and again over all the distress of the problematic, over all the risk of uncertainty, and even over the jealousy of the lover. We know a new happiness ...

4

Finally, that the most essential may not be left unsaid: one comes back out of such abysses, out of such severe infirmity, and out of the infirmity of strong suspicion – *reborn*, with skin shed; more ticklish, more mischievous, with a finer taste for delight, with a more delicate palate for all good things, with a more blithesome disposition, with a second and more dangerous innocence in delight, at the same time more childish and a hundred times more sophisticated than before. Oh, how repugnant to us now is pleasure, coarse, dull, drab pleasure, as the pleasure-seekers, our 'educated' classes, our rich and ruling classes, usually understand it! How mischievously we now listen to the great festive tumult of 'educated people' and city folk today, as they allow themselves to be violated by art, books and music for the sake of 'spiritual pleasures', with the aid of distilled spirits! How the theatrical cry of passion now hurts our ears, how foreign to our taste all this romantic riot and confusion of the senses which the educated riff-raff love, along with their aspirations to the illustrious, the exalted and the eccentric! No, if we convalescents still need an art at all, it is *another* art – a mocking, light, fleeting, divinely serene, divinely artificial art which blazes up like a bright flame into cloudless skies! Above all, an art for artists, only for artists! Afterwards, we understand better that such an art first requires cheerfulness, *any* sort of cheerfulness, my friends! also as artists – I should like to prove it. There are some things we now know too well, we knowledge-seekers: oh how well we artists now learn to forget, learn *not* to know! And as to our future, you are not likely to find us again on the paths of those Egyptian youths[4] who break into temples at night, embrace statues and want to unveil, uncover and bring into the light of day everything which is with good reason concealed. No, this bad taste, this desire for truth, this love of truth, for 'truth at any cost', this madness of youth has been spoiled for us: we are too experienced, too serious, too blithe, too burnt, too profound for that . . .

We no longer believe that truth remains truth when her veil

is withdrawn; we have lived too long to believe this. Nowadays we regard it as a matter of common decency not to be eager to see everything naked, or be present at everything, or understand and 'know' everything. 'Is it true that the good Lord is present in all things?' asked a little girl of her mother: 'I think that is indecent' – a hint to philosophers! One should cherish the *modesty* with which nature has concealed herself behind enigmas and iridescent uncertainties. Perhaps truth is a woman who has reasons for not showing her reasons? Perhaps her name (to speak in Greek) is *Baubo*?[5]

Oh, those Greeks! They knew how to *live*: for that one must boldly stay on the surface, the fold and the skin, to worship appearance, to believe in forms, tones and words, in the whole Olympus of appearance! Those Greeks were superficial – *from profundity*! And are we not returning to just this, we daredevils of the spirit, who have scaled the most perilous heights of contemporary thought and have looked around up there, have *looked down* from up there? Are we not exactly in this respect – Greeks? Worshippers of forms, of tones, of words? And for that very reason – artists?

Deruta, near Genoa,
Autumn 1886

'Jest, Trick and Revenge'[1]
Prelude in German Rhymes

1
Invitation

Would you try this dish I offer?
Later it will taste much better,
And later still, taste good enough!
Should you want more of this porridge,
Buckle down, screw up your courage,
And try some of my older stuff.

2
My Happiness

Since the quest now wearies me,
I much prefer the grail.
Since the winds all fought with me,
These days I trim the sails.

3
Undaunted

Where you stand you must dig deep,
Below you is the well!
Let the superstitious shout,
That down there's only hell!

4
Dialogue

A: I was sick and then got better?
I don't even know my doctor!
How could I forget all that!
B: Only now do you recover:
Health returns when you forget.

5
To the Virtuous

Our virtues ought to dash, and so,
Like Homer's verse, should come *and go*!

6
Worldly Wisdom

Don't stay on the solid ground,
The peaks you should forswear,
Gorgeous vistas are all found,
Before you get up there.

7
Vademecum – Vadetecum²

Attracted by my style and voice,
You would follow after me?
Walk your own path faithfully,
And – bit by bit – become like me.

8
The Third Moulting

My skin already bends and breaks,
From all the earth which I've devoured,
And yet the snake within me craves
More earth with every passing hour.

On crooked trails, hungering,
I creep between the rocks and turf
Seeking what I'm always seeking,
Food for snakes,[3] delicious earth!

9
My Roses

My delight wants to delight you,
Does my garden not invite you?
Won't you take some roses with you?
You must crouch 'twixt rock and hedges,
Grasping at the thorny branches,
Often pricking fingertips!
My delight – she loves her tricks!
My delight would love to tease you!
Won't you take some roses with you?

10
The Scornful

I spill much of what I pour,
And so you say I'm filled with scorn.
And yet whoever's cup is full
Will find that when he drinks, he spills –
Without despising wine the more.

11
The Proverb Speaks

Incisive, gentle, crude, refined,
Familiar, foreign, pure and vile,
A tryst of sage and imbecile:
All this I seek and claim as mine,
To be at once dove, snake and swine!

12
To a Friend of Light

Lest your eyes be blinded,
And your mind prostrate,
You should follow sunlight,
While you walk in shade!

13
For Dancers

Smooth ice
Is paradise
For those whose dancing can suffice.

14
The Brave and True

Sooner whole hostility
Than pieced-together amity!

15
Rust

There should be rust on a blade so keen,
Lest they all say that you're too green!

16
Upwards

'What's the best way to the summit?'
Climb! Don't think too much about it!

17
Maxim for the Violent

Never ask! Leave off this pleading!
Seize whatever's there for seizing!

18
Narrow Souls

Narrow souls are odious:
Good or bad, they scarce possess.

19
The Involuntary Seducer

He shot vain words into the air,
And thereby felled a maiden fair.

20
Consider

Shared pain is not as hard to bear,
As lone pain: do you take my dare?

21
Against Arrogance

Self-inflation's ill-advised,
You'll pop when pinpricks are applied.

22
Man and Woman

'Ravish the woman, if that's what you feel!' –
Men think like robbers, but women just steal.

23
Interpretation

My soul is in my work, I will admit,
But I myself cannot interpret it.
If you climb up your own path, then you might
My image carry with you to the light.

24
Antidote to Pessimism

You say that life's unsavoury?
My friend, renounce that ancient grievance!
By ranting, raving endlessly,
You break my heart and try my patience!
Take a tip from me, my friend,
And wisely follow this suggestion,
Every morning eat a toad[4] –
I'll bet that cures your indigestion!

25
Request

My grasp on others' minds is sure,
But to myself I am obscure!
My eye is far too close to me –
I am not what I saw and see.
For introspection, it might help
To get more distance from myself.
Though not as distant as my foe,
Or closest friend, for neither know
Me. Something halfway would be best!
Can you guess what I request?

26
My Hardness

I have to climb a hundred stairs.
I hear a voice cry in despair:
'Tread lightly! Am I made of stone?' –
I have to climb a hundred stairs,
But no one would be tread upon.

27
The Wanderer

'No path! Abysses! Isolation!'
Wasn't straying your decision?
Eyes ahead, and do not frown:
For all is lost if you look down.

28
Consolation for Beginners

Among the pigs, a child is crawling
Never rising to his feet.
Listen to his endless bawling!
When will he get up and stand?
No, he won't admit defeat!
Soon the child will learn to dance!
First he walks on his two feet,
But in the end walks on his hands.

29
Planetary Egoism

Were I not, in empty space,
A barrel ever turning,
How could I endure to chase
The hot sun without burning?

30
The Neighbour

My neighbour is too close to me:
To height and distance banished, he
May yet become a star to see! –

31
The Holy Mask

Lest your happiness depress,
Wrap yourself in wickedness,
In wicked wit, in wicked dress.
But in vain! Your eyes exhibit
All your hidden holiness!

32
The Unfree

A. Is he deceived in what he hears?
What's that ringing in his ears?
What struck him down and laid him low?
B. If chains were once all he did know,
Then chains are all he'll ever hear.

33
The Recluse

How I detest to lead and to be led.
I won't command! And nor will I obey!
Only the fearsome make others afraid;
Only the frightened let themselves be led.
I hate still more the task of self-command!
I love to play like beasts of sea and land,
I love to lose myself for just a day,
To sit and muse, to lead my thoughts astray,
And when at length my home I yearn to see,
I coax myself and then return to me.

34
Seneca et Hoc Genus Omne[5]

They scribble their insufferably
Noble dreck and folly,

As if to *primum scribere,*
deinde philosophari.[6]

35
Ice

Yes! At times I make some ice,
It helps me to digest!
If you had all this to digest,
You too would love my ice!

36
Early Writings

All my wisdom's A and O[7]
resounded from them. What I hear
now doesn't sound wise any more.
Perennial youth's Ah! and Oh!
of suffering is all I hear.

37
Caution

Sojourning in those parts is rather hard,
If you have brains, you must be on your guard!
First they adore you, then tear you to shreds,
Devotees haven't a brain in their heads!

38
The Pious Speak

God loves us, and that's *why* He made us! –
'We made God', the wits reply.
Should *we* not love what we have made?
What we've made we should *hence* deny?
The devil's hoof[8] that thought displays.

39
In the Summer

In fields, by the sweat of our brows,[9]
They say we should eat our bread?
In fields you should not eat and plough,
Or so the physician said.
With what are we still not endowed?
The Dog Star with its fiery sign,
In fields, by the sweat of our brows,
Tells us we should drink our wine!

40
Without Envy

His unenvious eyes you all greatly admire,
But he never sought that to which you all aspire;
His eagle eye seeks only that which is far,
He does not see you! He sees only stars.

41
Heraclitism

All happiness on earth, my friends,
Only comes from struggle!
Yes, to be a faithful friend,
It takes the smoke of battle!
Only one in three are friends:
Brothers to their final breath,
Equals before enemies;
Free – in facing death!

42
Principle of the Too Well-Mannered

Rather on one's tiptoes
Than crawling on all fours!

Best to peep through keyholes
Than gape at open doors!

43
Encouragement

Have you now set your sights on fame?
To what I teach take heed:
In due course, you must waive all claim
To honour, if you would succeed.

44
The Thorough

You call me a scholar? You are far too kind! –
I'm just *heavy-laden* with many a pound!
Tumbling downwards, I draw ever closer,
But sooner or later, I do hit the ground!

45
For ever

'I come today, it's opportune' –
Thinks one who won't be leaving soon.
What's it to him if they all prate:
'You come too soon! You come too late!'

46
Judgements of the Weary

Against the sun they remonstrate,
And love trees only for their shade!

47
Sunset

'He sinks, he falls,' they ridicule,
In truth he condescends to you.
Overjoyed, he sought his doom,
Overbright, he pierced your gloom.

48
Against Laws

From now on, around my neck,
A little clock hangs by a thread:
The sun and stars stop in their tracks,
No cock crows, shadows are not cast,
And what was once declared by time,
To me is now deaf, dumb and blind –
Despite our steady old tick-tock,
Nature knows no law or clock.

49
The Sage Speaks

Strange to the crowd but of use to the crowd,
I go my own way, under sun, under cloud –
But always above and beyond that same crowd!

50
Lost His Head

She's had some brains ever since she was wed,
Recently she made a man lose his head,
Before this diversion, with thoughts he was rife:
His mind's gone to hell – no! no! to his wife!

51
Wishful Thinking

May all the keys that still exist
Come to be mislaid,
And for the empty keyholes
Some brand-new pick-locks made.
That's how every era talks,
Which finds it's good at picking locks.

52
Writing with Feet

Pen in hand, all my writing begins,
But my feet, they would like to join in,
Running free, they're so fleet and so brave,
Crossing fields and crossing the page.

53
Human, All Too Human. A Book

As long as you dwell on the past,
    you're filled with doubt and sorrow.
As long as you trust in yourself,
    then you trust in tomorrow:
Bird, do you belong
    among the eagles taking flight?
Or are you just Minerva's pet[10] –
    spreading wings at fall of night?

54
My Readers

May my readers be granted strong stomachs,
May my readers be granted sharp teeth.
If this book is one that they can stomach,
Then surely they can stomach me!

55
Realist Painters

'Be true to nature!' – That's how they began:
How *could* one exhaust her in art made by man?
The world's inexhaustible, in every piece!
All that they do is to paint what they *please*.
And what gives them pleasure? To paint what they *can*!

56
Poetic Vanity

All I need is glue; I find
I've got the wooden fragments!
Making sense from silly rhymes:
It is no mean achievement!

57
Picky Taste

If I could pick my favourite spot,
I think the place I'd cultivate,
Is in the midst of Paradise,
Or better still – outside the gate!

58
The Broken Nose

His nostrils are always flaring with scorn,
This proud little man, this rhino *sans* horn.
He turns up his nose at the whole human race,
And therefore he always falls flat on his face!
Thus the one with the other invariably goes:
An arrogant posture, and oft-broken nose.

59
The Pen Scribbles

The pen keeps scribbling: this is hell!
To scribble, am I now condemned? –
I boldly reach for my inkwell,
And let the ink flow forth again.
The quantity's considerable,
And everything goes brilliantly.
But while it's not quite legible –
Who cares? What I write, no one reads!

60

Higher Man

His climb towards the heights is justly acclaimed;
The other, he nobly descends.
He has dispensed with the need for acclaim,
The base he already transcends!

61

The Sceptic Speaks

Half of your life is now over,
The hour hand moves as you tremble with fear!
Over the earth you have wandered,
And though you found nothing you still tarry here.
Half of your life is now over,
It was suffering and error, day in and day out.
What more do you hope to discover?
Just this: to know what the whole thing was about!

62

Ecce Homo[11]

Yes! I know from whence I came!
An insatiable flame,
Glowing and consuming me.

Everything I touch burns brighter,
All I leave are dying embers;
Flame I am assuredly.

63
Star Morals

To a star's path preordained,
How could the darkness leave you pained?
So pass right through this age in bliss,
A stranger to its wretchedness!
For the farthest world you shine:
The sin of pity you abjure!
Your sole commandment is: be pure!

BOOK I

BOOK I

I
The Teachers of the Purpose of Life

Whether I look upon men with a good or evil eye, I always find them engaged in but one task, each and every one of them: the preservation of the human race. And certainly not from any great love for it, but simply because nothing in them is older, stronger, more inexorable or invincible than that instinct – because this instinct is precisely the *nature* of our species and herd. With our usual short-sightedness, we are quick to divide our neighbours rather neatly into beneficial and injurious, into good and evil men; however, upon a great reckoning, when we further consider the whole, we become suspicious of this neat division, and in the end abandon it. Even the most injurious man may still be the most beneficial of all, with respect to the preservation of the human race; for he preserves in himself, or by his effect on others, impulses without which mankind might long since have languished or decayed. Hatred, malicious glee, rapacity and ambition and whatever else is called evil belong to this remarkable economy of preservation; to be sure, a costly, extravagant and on the whole rather foolish economy – but one which has thus far been *proven* to preserve our kind. My dear neighbour and fellow man, I doubt whether you even *can* live to the detriment of your species, that is to say 'unreasonably' and 'badly'; perhaps that which could have damaged it died out thousands of years ago, and is now among things which are no longer possible even for God. Indulge your best or worst desires, and above all perish! Either way, you're probably still somehow the patron and benefactor of mankind, and thus entitled to your eulogists – as well as your detractors! That said, you will never find anyone who could give you, the individual, even at your best, the ridicule which you deserve. You will never find anyone who could impress upon you how frog-like, how gnat-like, how boundlessly paltry you are, enough as is consistent with the truth! To laugh at yourself as you would have to laugh, to laugh *out of the whole truth* – so far, for that the best had not enough of a faculty for truth and the gifted far too little genius! Perhaps even laughter still has a future! Then, when mankind has subscribed to the proposition 'the species is everything, the individual is always nothing' – and for every man, the way is open at all times to this final liberation and irresponsibility – perhaps then laughter will be allied with wisdom, perhaps then there will be nothing but 'Joyous Science'. For the time being, things are quite different; for the time being, the comedy of life has not yet 'become conscious' of itself; for the time being, it is still the age of tragedy, the age of moralities and religions. What does it indicate, this endless procession of moral and religious founders, authors of strife over moral standards, teachers of remorse and religious war? What does it indicate, this succession of heroes on the stage? For thus far they have been its heroes, and everything else that is alone visible and in the limelight for a time has only served to set the stage for these heroes, whether as theatrical machinery and backdrop, or in the role of confidants and valets. (The poets, for example, have always been the valets of some morality or other.)

It goes without saying that these tragedians also work in the interest of our species, even though they may believe themselves to be promoting the interest of God and serving as His emissaries. They also contribute to the life of the race *by encouraging belief in life*. 'Life is worth living' – they all cry – 'there is something about this life, something behind and beneath it: beware!' That impulse, which prevails in the highest and the basest alike, the impulse to preservation, breaks forth from time to time as reason and intellectual passion; it has about it then a brilliant host of reasons, and tries with all its might to make us forget that at bottom it is impulse, instinct, folly and baselessness.

Life *should* be loved, *because*! Man *should* help himself and his neighbour, *because*! And what do all these 'shoulds' and 'becauses' mean, and what might they mean in the future! In order that whatever happens, necessarily and always, of its own accord and without purpose, may from now on appear to be done on purpose, and may be intelligible to men as rational and obligatory – to that end, the ethical teacher arises who teaches the purpose of life; to that end, he devises a second and different life, and by means of this new mechanism he lifts the old common life off its old common hinges. He certainly does not want us to *laugh* at life, at ourselves – or at him; to him an individual is always an individual, something first and last and tremendous, to him there are no species, no sums, no zeroes. However foolish and rapturous his inventions and enthusiasms may be, however much he may misunderstand the course of nature and deny its conditions – and all systems of ethics hitherto have been foolish and unnatural to such a degree that if any of them had taken possession of mankind, we would have perished – nevertheless! Whenever 'the hero' appeared on the stage, something new was achieved, the thrilling counterpart of laughter, the profound shock of many individuals at the thought: 'Yes, life is worth living! I am worthy of living!' Life and you and I and all of us together once again became *interesting* to us for a while.

There is no denying that *in the long run* every one of these great teachers of purpose so far has been overcome by laughter and reason and nature: in the end the brief tragedy always turned and returned to the eternal comedy of life; and the 'waves of countless laughter'[1] – to speak with Aeschylus – must eventually shipwreck even the greatest of these tragedians. Notwithstanding all this laughter serving as a corrective, human nature has been wholly transformed by the endless procession of those teachers of the purpose of life – human nature now has a further need, precisely the need for an endless procession of such teachers and doctrines of 'purpose'. Man has gradually become a fanciful animal, who has one more condition of existence to fulfil than other animals: from time to time, man *must* think he knows *why* he exists; the human race cannot flourish without periodically renewed trust in life! Without believing in the *reason in life*! And again and again humankind will decree from time to time: 'There is something at which you are henceforth absolutely forbidden to laugh!' And the canniest philanthropist will add: 'not only laughter and joyous wisdom, but also the tragic with all its sublime unreasonableness are among the necessities and means of preservation!'

And consequently! Consequently! Consequently! Do you understand me, my brothers? Do you understand this new law of ebb and flow? Our time will come!

2

The Intellectual Conscience

Experience teaches me again and again and always I resist the conclusion, not wanting to believe it even though it is palpable: *the majority lack an intellectual conscience*; indeed, it often seemed to me that one with such demands is as alone in the most populous cities as in a desert. Everyone looks at you with a puzzled expression and still holds their scales, calling this good and that evil; and no one would blush if you were to say that they use false weights – nor is there any indignation against you; perhaps they laugh at your doubts. I mean to say: *the majority* do not find it contemptible to believe this or that, and live accordingly, *without* ascertaining in advance what speaks for and against it, and without even bothering to do so after the fact – the most gifted men and the noblest women still belong to this 'majority'. But what are kind-heartedness, sophistication and genius to me, if a person with these virtues tolerates a lackadaisical sensibility in belief and judgement, and does not consider *the demand for certainty* their innermost desire and profoundest need – as that which separates the higher from the lower! Among the pious, in some I have found a hostility to reason, and was well disposed to them for it: at least this still revealed their intellectual bad conscience! But to stand in the midst of this *rerum concordia discors*[2] and all the wonderful uncertainty and ambiguity of life, *and not question*, not to tremble with curiosity and the passion for enquiry, not even to hate those who do – perhaps even to find them mildly amusing – that is what I feel to be *contemptible*, and it is this sentiment which I first look for in everyone – some foolishness never fails to persuade me that every man as such has this sentiment. This is my kind of injustice.

3
Noble and Common

To common natures all noble, magnanimous sentiments appear inexpedient and therefore incredible: they blink their eyes when they hear of suchlike, and seem inclined to say, 'there is probably some advantage to be had from them, not every wall can have a window'[3] – they are jealous of the noble person, as if he sought a clandestine advantage. When they are quite clearly convinced of the absence of selfish intentions and gains, they regard the noble person as a kind of fool: they despise him in his joy, and laugh at his shining eyes. 'How can someone enjoy being at a disadvantage, how can someone seek his own disadvantage with open eyes! The noble affection must involve a disease of reason' – so they think, and they look down on it; just as they look down on the enjoyment the madman derives from his obsession. The common person is distinguished by the fact that he keeps his advantage steadily in view, and that this thought of the practical end and advantage is even stronger than his strongest impulse: not to be misled by his impulses to acts that are inexpedient – in this does his self-respect and wisdom consist. By contrast, the higher nature is more *unreasonable* – for the noble, magnanimous and self-sacrificing person is in fact governed by his impulses, and in his best moments his reason *pauses*. An animal, which risks its life to protect its young, or in the mating season follows the female even to the death, does not think of danger and death; its reason likewise pauses, because it is preoccupied with its pleasure in its offspring, or in the female, and the fear of being deprived of this pleasure; it becomes more stupid than usual, like the noble and magnanimous person. Such people have a few feelings of pleasure and pain so intense that the intellect either falls silent before them, or lends itself to their service: the heart overtakes the head, and then one speaks of 'passion'. (Occasionally, we find what is arguably the opposite case, and what you might call the 'inversion of passion', for example with Fontenelle, on whose heart someone once laid their hand and said, 'What you have there, my good man, is also brain.')[4] It is passion's unreasonableness, its being at cross-purposes with reason, which the common despises in the noble, especially when it is directed towards objects whose value seems to be quite fantastic and arbitrary. He is irked at one who is governed by the passions of the belly, but he understands the appeal of what there plays the tyrant; but he cannot grasp how one could, for example, gamble with one's health and honour for the sake of a passion for knowledge. The taste of the higher nature is directed towards the exceptional, towards things that usually leave people cold and seem to lack sweetness; the higher nature has a distinctive standard of value. Yet he is for the most part convinced that his idiosyncrasies of taste do *not* manifest a distinctive standard of value; he takes what he regards as worthy or unworthy to be generally valid, and thus what he wants becomes incomprehensible and impracticable. It is very rare that a higher nature has enough sense to see everyday human beings for what they are and treat them accordingly: at the very most he believes in his passion as the hidden passion of all, and in this faith he is especially full of fervour and eloquence. Now if such exceptional men do not feel themselves to be exceptions, how can they ever hope to understand the common natures and obtain a fair assessment of the norm? Thus it is that they also speak of the folly, perversity and delusions of mankind, filled with amazement at how mad the course of the world is, and that it will not own up to what 'needs to be done'.

This is the eternal injustice of the noble.

4

That Which Preserves the Species

The strongest and most evil minds have thus far advanced mankind the most: they ever rekindled slumbering passions – all orderly society lulls the passions to sleep – they ever reawakened the sense of comparison, of contradiction, of the pleasure in experiment, innovation and adventure, compelling people to set opinion against opinion, epitome against epitome. By force of arms, by displacement of boundary stones,[5] by violation of the pieties most of all; but also by new religions and morals! The same kind of 'malice' which makes a conqueror infamous is present in every teacher and preacher of some *innovation*, although it expresses itself more daintily, and does not immediately set the muscles in motion, and for that reason does not make them infamous! Innovation, however, is under all circumstances *evil*, being that which wants to conquer, which wants to topple the old boundary stones and the old pieties; only the old is good! The good people of every age are farmers of the mind who dig deep into the soil of the old thoughts and get it to bear fruit. But in the end, every soil becomes exhausted, and the ploughshare of evil must come, again and again.

There is at present a fundamentally erroneous theory of morality much celebrated, especially in England, according to which the judgements 'good' and 'evil' are the accumulation of the experiences 'expedient' and 'inexpedient': whatever preserves the species is called good, whatever harms it is called evil. In truth, the evil impulses are every bit as expedient, indispensable and conducive to the preservation of the species as the good – they just have a different function.

5
Unconditional Obligations

All people who feel that they need the strongest words and tones, the most eloquent gestures and attitudes, in order to be effective at all, revolutionary politicians, socialists, preachers with or without Christianity, for whom there must be no merely partial success: all these speak of 'obligations', and indeed, always of obligations which have the character of being unconditional – without such they would have no right to their great pathos: that they know full well! So they seize upon philosophies of morality, preach some kind of categorical imperative, or help themselves to a good slice of religion, as, for example, Mazzini[6] did. Because they want to be trusted implicitly, it is first of all necessary for them to trust themselves, on the basis of some ultimate, incontrovertible, intrinsically sublime authority whose minister and instrument they would like to impersonate and feel themselves to be. Here we have the most natural, and often very influential, opponents of moral enlightenment and scepticism; but they are rare. On the other hand, there is a very extensive class of opponents wherever interest teaches subjection, while reputation and honour seem to forbid it. Anyone who feels dishonoured at the thought of being the *instrument* of a prince, or of a party and sect, or even of a moneyed power, for example the descendant of a proud, old family, but who now wishes to be or must be seen to be an instrument, in his own eyes and in the eyes of the public, has need of lofty principles which may at any time be pronounced – principles of an unconditional 'shalt' to which one may without shame bow down and make a display of subservience. A finer servility adheres to the categorical imperative, and is the mortal enemy of those who want to deprive obligation of its unconditional character: the dignity of their position requires this of them, and not only that of their position.

6
Loss of Dignity

Contemplation has lost all its dignity of form; we have made a mockery of the ceremonial and solemn bearing of the contemplative person, and would no longer abide a wise man of the old style. We think too hastily while on the go and out and about on all kinds of business, even when engaged in the most serious thought; we require scarcely any preparation or even any quiet – it is as if we had wheels inexorably turning in our heads even under the most adverse circumstances. Formerly one could tell at a glance that a man wanted to think – it was probably the exception – that he now wanted to grow wiser and prepared himself for a thought: he came to a halt and put on a prayerful countenance; indeed, one stood still in the street for hours in case a thought 'came' – on one leg or two. Such was the 'dignity of the thing'!

7
Something for the Industrious

At present, whoever wants to make a study of moral matters opens a vast field of labour for himself. All kinds of passions must be considered and pursued individually through periods, peoples, individuals great and small; the reason in them, all the appraisals they involve and the light they shed on things must themselves be brought to light! So far all that has given colour to existence still has no history: where would you find a history of love, of avarice, of envy, of conscience, of piety, of cruelty? Even a comparative history of law, or even only of punishment, is so far completely absent. Have the various ways of dividing the day, the consequences of appointing regular times for labour, rest and festival, ever been made the subject of investigation? Do we know the moral effects of foods? Is there a philosophy of nutrition? (The perpetual hue and cry for and against vegetarianism proves that there is still no such philosophy!) Have the experiences of living together, for example the experience of the monasteries, been collected? Has the dialectic of marriage and friendship ever been represented? The mores of the scholars, merchants, artists, workmen – have they yet found their thinkers? There is so much in them to think about! All that until now people have taken to be their 'conditions of existence', and all reason, passion and superstition this 'taking' involved – have they been subjected to a conclusive investigation? The observation of how variously human impulses have grown and might still grow depending upon different moral climates would, all by itself, provide more than enough work for the industrious; it would require whole generations of coordinated research just to exhaust the points of view and material. The same applies to determining the reason for the variety of the moral climates (*'why* does this sun of basic moral judgement and primary measure of value shine here – and another there?'). And it would be a further task to demonstrate the erroneousness of all these reasons, and the whole nature of moral judgement so far. Assuming all these works were done, the most delicate question of all would then come to the fore: whether science is in a position to *provide* aims for action, after it has proved that it can take them away and destroy them – and then experimentation would be in order in which every kind of heroism could satisfy itself, centuries-long experimentation which would cast into the shade all the great endeavours and sacrifices of history hitherto. Science has not yet built its Cyclopean structures;[7] for that too the time will come.

8
Unconscious Virtues

The qualities in us of which we are conscious – and especially when we assume that they are visible and evident to our milieu as well – are subject to quite different laws of development than those which are unknown or not well understood. By their subtlety the latter escape even the eye of the subtlest observer, and hide, as it were, behind nothing. So it is with the subtle bas-relief of reptile scales: it would be a mistake to suppose they are for display or defence – for they can only be seen under a microscope, and this sort of artificially enhanced vision is simply not available to similar animals for whom they might signify display or defence. The moral qualities in us that can be seen, and especially those we think *are* seen, take their course – but there are invisible qualities of the very same name, which in relation to others serve for neither display nor defence. These qualities probably take *an entirely different course*, and with lines and subtleties and bas-relief, in which perhaps a god with a divine microscope could take pleasure. For example, we have our industry, our ambition, our acumen: all the world knows of them – and, in addition, we probably also have *our* industry, *our* ambition, *our* acumen; but for these reptile scales of ours the microscope has not yet been invented! And here the friends of instinctive morality will say: 'Bravo! At least he thinks unconscious virtues are possible – that satisfies us!' Oh you are so easily satisfied!

9
Our Eruptions

Innumerable things which mankind acquired in its earlier stages, but to so slight and incipient a degree as to be imperceptible, suddenly come to light long afterwards, perhaps centuries later; in the meantime they have become strong and mature. In some ages, as in some men, this or that talent, this or that virtue, seems to be entirely lacking; but in time, what they concealed within them, their grandchildren and great-grandchildren bring into the light of day. Often, the son betrays the father, who then understands himself better for having had a son. We all contain hidden gardens and orchards; or, to vary the figure, we are all smouldering volcanoes whose time of eruption will come – but of course no one knows how soon, not even God.

10
A Kind of Atavism

I prefer to understand the best men of an age as scions of past cultures and their strengths, whose sudden emergence long after the fact is, as it were, the atavism of a people and its civilization – that way, at least there is something about them one can actually *understand*! Now, they seem rare, strange, extraordinary; and he who feels these strengths in himself has to cultivate, educate, honour and defend them in the face of opposition from another world; and he thus becomes either a great man or a strange and mad one, if he is not brought to an early grave. Formerly, these very same qualities were ordinary and therefore regarded as base: they were not a mark of distinction. Perhaps they were required, expected; it was impossible to become great with them, if only because there was no danger of becoming isolated and deranged by them.

Such grace notes of the old impulses occur principally in the *preserving* generations and castes of a people, as there is no probability of such atavism where races, habits and appraisals are rapidly changing. For among the powers of development, tempo means just as much in peoples as it does in music; in our case an andante of development is absolutely necessary, as the tempo of a passionate and steady spirit – and which is indeed the spirit of conservative generations.

I I
Consciousness

Being conscious is the last and latest organic development, and consequently also the least finished and least powerful. It gives rise to innumerable mistakes which cause a human being or an animal to perish sooner than is necessary, 'beyond fate',[8] as Homer says. Were the assemblage of instincts that contributes to our preservation not so exceedingly strong by comparison, it would not have served on the whole as a regulator: we would have inevitably perished by dint of our daydreams and misapprehensions, by our negligence and credulity, in short, by our being conscious; or rather, without these instincts, we would have long since ceased to *be* conscious! Before a function is fully formed and mature, it is a danger to the organism; it is well if something plays the tyrant over it for a good long while. Being conscious is thus much oppressed – and not least by the pride we take in it! It is thought to be the *pith and marrow* of a human being, the part that is most pristine, final, everlasting and eternal! Being conscious is held to have a determinate magnitude! Its growth and its discontinuities are denied! It is taken for the 'unity of the organism'!

This ludicrous overestimation and misunderstanding of consciousness has had in consequence the great advantage of *preventing* it from developing too rapidly. Because people believed that they already had it, they have taken no pains to acquire it – and it is no different today! It is only just dawning upon us that we have an entirely new and scarcely recognizable *task, to make what we know a part of us*, to make it instinctive – a task seen only by those who understand that so far only our *errors* have become a part of us, that being conscious pertains to nothing but errors!

12
Of the Purpose of Science

How is that? The ultimate purpose of science is to give people as much pleasure and as little pain as possible? But suppose that pleasure and pain are so intertwined that whoever *wants* as much as possible of the one *must* also have as much as possible of the other – that whoever wants to know 'rejoicing to heaven' must be prepared for 'grieving unto death'[9] as well? And such might be the case! At least so the Stoics believed, who were consistent when they sought as little pleasure as possible, that life might afford them as little pain as possible. (With the adage 'those who are virtuous are the happiest' on their lips, the school had both a billboard for the great unwashed, as well as a piece of casuistry for the subtle.) Even today you have a choice: either as little pain as possible, in short, analgesia – and in the end, socialists and party politicians cannot in all honesty promise their people more – or *as much pain as possible*, as the price of a luxuriance of subtle and seldom-tasted joys and pleasures! Should you decide in favour of the former, should you want to mitigate and assuage human suffering, well, you must also moderate and diminish the human *capacity for joy*. In fact, *science* can serve the one purpose as well as the other! Perhaps it is still better known on account of its power to kill a man's joys and make him colder, more statue-like, more Stoical. But it might also be revealed as the *great woe-bearer*! And then perhaps at the same time would its opposing force be revealed, its prodigious power to light up new starry worlds[10] of joy!

13
On the Theory of the Sense of Power

In doing others well or ill, we want no more than to exert power over them! In *doing ill*, we hurt those to whom we need to make our power palpable, for pain is a much more striking way to do so than pleasure – pain always casts about for its cause, while pleasure is inclined to look no further than itself. In *doing well* and wishing well, we help those who somehow or other already depend upon us (that is, who are accustomed to regard us as the cause of their existence); we want to increase their power, because in so doing we increase our own; or we want show them the advantages of being in our power – so they will be more satisfied with their position, and assume a more threatening and hostile aspect against the enemies of *our* power. It does not alter the final value of our actions if we make sacrifices to do well or ill; even if we lay down our lives like martyrs for the sake of our Church, it is a sacrifice made to *our* desire for power, or for the purpose of preserving our sense of power. Whoever has the feeling that says, 'I am in possession of the truth', how many other possessions would he not gladly forgo to retain it? What would he not jettison to keep 'above' water – or should I say, *above* others who lack the 'truth'! Certainly, doing ill is seldom so agreeable, so purely agreeable, as doing well; it indicates that we still lack power, or betrays that we are vexed at this privation; it exposes us to new dangers and uncertainties which threaten the power we already possess, and darkens our horizon with the prospect of revenge, scorn, punishment and failure. Only he who is most covetous of the sense of power and most susceptible to its charms, for whom the sight of an object of benevolence, that is, the already subjugated, has become tedious and burdensome, might find it more pleasurable to stamp the seal of power on more refractory material. It depends on how we are accustomed to give *spice* to life; it is a matter of taste whether we prefer a slow but sure growth of power to a sudden, dangerous and daring one – we always relish this or that spice, each according to his temperament. To proud natures, an easy prey is something contemptible; they have a sense of well-being only at the sight of an untamed man who could be an enemy, just as they do at the sight of anything difficult to acquire; they are often hard towards those who suffer as not worthy of them or their efforts – but they show themselves to be more obliging towards their *equals*, with whom strife and struggle would at least be honourable, should the occasion present itself. Imbued with the sense of well-being engendered by *this* perspective, the men of the knightly caste have accustomed themselves to an exquisite courtesy to one another.

Pity is the most agreeable sensation in those who have little pride and no prospect of great conquests: for them, easy prey – and that is what all who suffer are – is something enchanting. Pity is the much-vaunted virtue of whores.

14
What Is Called Love

Avarice and love: how differently we feel towards each of these words! And yet it could be the same impulse twice named, in the first case, disparaged by the 'haves', in whom the impulse has settled down somewhat and who now fear losing what they have, and in the other, glorified as 'good' by the discontented and the thirsty. Love of our neighbour – is it not a hankering after new *property*? And similarly, our love of knowledge, of truth and even all eagerness for news? We gradually grow weary of the old, familiar things we securely hold, and again stretch forth our hands; even the most beautiful landscape lived in for three months is no longer assured of our love, and some more distant shore excites our avarice: what is had loses much in the having. Our pleasure in ourselves thus seeks to sustain itself by continually transforming something new *into ourselves* – that is just what possession means. To grow weary with a possession is to grow weary with ourselves. (One can also suffer from an excess of possessions – and then the desire to dispose of or distribute may assume the honorific 'love'.) When we see a man suffer, we welcome the opportunity to take possession of him; for example, the charitable and compassionate do this, calling the desire for a new possession awakened in them 'love', and taking pleasure in it as in a new conquest beckoning to them. However, it is the love of the sexes that most clearly betrays possessiveness: the lover wants the unconditional and exclusive possession of the person he longs for, he wants unconditional power as much over her soul as over her body, he wants to be loved exclusively, and to live and reign in the other soul as what is highest and most desirable. When we consider that this means nothing less than to *exclude* the whole world from a precious commodity, and from the happiness and enjoyment it affords, that the lover contemplates the deprivation and ruin of all rivals, and would like to be the dragon of his golden hoard, the most inconsiderate and selfish of all 'conquerors' and exploiters, and finally that to the lover himself the rest of the world seems pale, indifferent and unprofitable, and that he is ready to make any sacrifice, disturb all existing arrangements, and put his own interests above all others – we are astonished that this ferocious avarice and injustice of sexual love has been glorified and deified to such an extent. Still more astonishing is the fact that the concept of love as the opposite of selfishness has always been modelled on it, when it is perhaps precisely the most candid expression of selfishness! Here apparently the 'have nots' and the covetous have determined usage – there were probably always too many of them. Those who have been given to enjoy possession and satiety in this area have perhaps let slip a word here and there about the 'raging demon',[11] as did the most loveable and beloved of all the Athenians, Sophocles; but the god Eros always laughed at such blasphemers – they were always his greatest favourites.

Arguably, here and there on earth one comes across a couple in whom one sees a continuation of sorts to love's avaricious appetite, in whom it has given way to a new desire and new avarice, to a *shared* thirst for an exalted ideal far above them; but who knows this love? Who has experienced it? Its proper name is *friendship*.

15
From a Distance

This mountain makes the whole landscape it dominates pregnant with meaning and attractive in every way: after saying this to ourselves for the hundredth time, our appreciation becomes so extravagant and unwarranted that we imagine the source of this attraction to be the most attractive thing in the landscape – and so we climb the mountain and are disappointed. All of a sudden we become disenchanted both with it and with the landscape around and below us; we had forgotten that much greatness, like much goodness, wants to be seen only at a certain distance, and

by all means from below, not from above – only in this way is it
effective. Perhaps you know some people around you who can
only look at themselves from a certain distance to find themselves at all tolerable or pleasing to behold and thus fortify
themselves; for them, self-knowledge is ill-advised.

16
Across the Bridge

In dealings with people who are ashamed of their feelings, one
must be able to disguise one's own; for such people take a
sudden antipathy to anyone who catches them in a moment
of tenderness, or enthusiasm, or intemperate rage, as if their
deepest secrets had been discovered. If one wants to do them a
kindness in such moments one should make them laugh, and
utter some cold, cruel witticism – then their heart turns to ice,
and they regain self-possession. But I am giving you the moral
before the story.

There was a time in our lives when we had grown so close to
one another in friendship and brotherhood that nothing seemed
to stand between us except this little footbridge. Just as you
were about to step upon it, I asked you: 'Do you want to cross
this bridge to me?' But then you no longer wanted to, and when
I asked you again, you fell silent. Since then mountains and tor-
rents and all that divides and estranges have come between us,
and even if we wanted to be reconciled with one another, it was
no longer possible. However, when you think back to that little
footbridge, you are at a loss for words – but filled with tears
and wonder.

17
To Give Reason for One's Poverty

To be sure, there is no sleight of hand by which we can make a
poor virtue into a rich and abundant one, but perhaps we can
make a virtue of necessity and reinterpret its poverty as beautiful. That way, we no longer suffer at the sight of it and feel
compelled to frown at our fate. It is the wise gardener who lets

his little brook pour from the clasped urn of a nymph; his fountain then gives a reason for his poverty – and who more than he has need of such nymphs?

18
Ancient Pride

We cannot fully appreciate the noble cast of mind in antiquity, because we have no sense of the utter degradation of the ancient slave. For a Greek of noble descent, there were so many inter-mediate strata between his lofty status and that of the slave that from such an immense social distance the slave could no longer be distinctly seen: Plato could no longer see him at all. It is other-wise with us, accustomed as we are to the *doctrine* of human equality, if not to equality itself. A human being who is not his own man and who lacks leisure is in no way contemptible in our eyes. Perhaps there is too much of that sort of slavishness in each of us, as required by our social order and activities, fundamen-tally different as they are from those of the ancients.

The Greek philosopher went through life with a lurking sus-picion that there were far more slaves than one might have supposed – to wit, everyone who was not a philosopher. His pride swelled when he considered that even the most powerful men on earth would be his slaves. This pride is also strange to us, and impossible, for we do not feel the full force of the word 'slave', not even in simile.

19
Evil

Examine the lives of the best and most fruitful men and peoples, and ask yourself: can a tree grow proud and tall without storms and inclemency? Disregard and opposition, all sorts of obstin-acy, cruelty, greed, distrust, jealousy, hatred and violence – are these not among the *favourable* circumstances without which great growth, even in virtue, is scarcely possible? The poison by which the weaker natures perish strengthens the strong – and they do not call it poison.

20

Dignity of Folly

A few more millennia down the road on which the last century set out, and all that man does will display the greatest prudence; but precisely because of this, prudence will have lost all dignity. To be sure, it will still be necessary to be prudent, but also so ordinary and commonplace that for those with a greater distaste for such things, this necessity will be regarded as *vulgar*. And just as a tyranny of science and truth could make us prize falsehood all the more, from a tyranny of prudence a new species of noble-mindedness might sprout. To be noble – perhaps then it would mean: to indulge in folly.

21

To the Teachers of Unselfishness

The virtues of a man are called *good*, not with regard to the results they have for himself, but those we expect for ourselves and for society – all along there has been very little of the unselfish, very little of the 'unegoistic' in our praise of the virtues! For otherwise one could not help but see that the virtues (such as diligence, obedience, chastity, piety, justice) are mostly *bad* for their possessors, who are too much governed by these intensely ardent impulses, impulses which refuse to be put in balance with other impulses by reason. When you have a virtue, a real and complete virtue (and not merely a slight inclination towards virtue!), you are *sacrificed* to it! But your neighbour praises your virtue for that very reason! We praise the diligent man even though he ruins his eyes, or his mind loses its freshness and originality. We honour a youth while regretting the fact that he 'worked his fingers to the bone', because we judge: 'For society as a whole, even the loss of the best individual is but a small sacrifice! What a pity that sacrifice is needed! Much worse, however, should the individual think otherwise, and regard his own preservation and development as more important than his service to society.' And so we deplore the fate of this youth, not on his own account, but because a humble *instrument* – a so-called

'good man' – through wanton self-neglect has died and been lost
to society. We might perhaps consider whether it would not have
been more useful to society if he had worked with less self-
neglect, and preserved himself longer – of course we readily
admit the advantage in that, but reply that the other advantage –
namely that a *sacrifice* has been made, and that our attitude
towards, and treatment of, the sacrificial animal has once again
been *conspicuously* confirmed – is more important and makes a
more lasting impression. Therefore when virtue is praised, what
is actually being praised is at once the instrumental character of
the virtues, and then the blind impulse which governs every virtue and which cannot be reined in by regard for the larger
interests of the individual himself: in short, the unreasonableness in virtue whereby the individual allows himself to be
converted into a function of the larger whole. The praise of virtue is the praise of some private harm – it is praise of impulses
which deprive a man of his noblest selfishness, and the strength
to take the greatest care of himself.

To be sure: we make much of a wide range of effects of virtue,
the better to promote the inculcation of virtuous habits, convey-
ing the impression that public virtue and private advantage go
hand in hand – and in fact there is a kinship between them! For
example, we represent blind and vehement diligence, the typical
virtue of an instrument, as the road to wealth and honour and as
a most salutary antidote to tedium and the passions; but we omit
mentioning the grave danger of it. For this is how inculcation of
virtue invariably proceeds: by a variety of stimuli and advantages
we seek to induce in the individual a particular way of thinking
and acting. Once it has become habit, impulse and passion, it
rules in him and over him 'for the common good', but *ultimately
to his own detriment*. How often have I observed that a man's
blind and vehement diligence does indeed create wealth and con-
fer honour, only to deprive him of the refinement he needs to
enjoy them. Thus the principal remedy for tedium and passion
simultaneously dulls the senses and renders the intellect averse to
new stimuli! (The most diligent of all ages – our age – can do
nothing with its great diligence and money, except make even
more money, and exercise even more diligence; for it requires

more genius to spend than to acquire! Well, there are always our 'grandchildren'!) If the inculcation of virtue is successful, every virtue is useful to the public while putting the individual who has it at a private disadvantage – probably some mental atrophy or even an early demise – with respect to his highest aims; consider in this light, one by one, the virtues of obedience, chastity, piety and justice. The praise of the unselfish, self-sacrificing, virtuous person – who therefore does not expend his whole energy and reason for *his own* preservation, development, ennoblement, advancement and extension of power, but who leads a humble and thoughtless life, perhaps even an indifferent or ironical one – in any case, this praise is not born of the spirit of unselfishness! The 'neighbour' praises unselfishness because *it redounds to his own advantage*! Were the neighbour's own intentions 'unselfish', he would reject this impairment of strength, this injury to others on *his* behalf, he would counteract such tendencies as they emerge, and above all he would show his unselfishness by the very fact of *not* calling them *good*!

Here we see the fundamental contradiction in the morality now held in high regard: its *motives* are opposed to its *principle*! The benefit to others with which this morality wants to demonstrate its worth is belied by its own criterion of morality! The injunction 'You shall renounce yourself and offer yourself as a sacrifice', lest it contradict its own morality, could only be decreed by a being who had renounced his own advantage and who, in the individual self-sacrifice required, perhaps even brought about his own demise. However, as soon as the neighbour (or society) exhorts us to altruism *on account of its utility*, the very opposite proposition, 'You shall pursue your advantage even at everyone else's expense', applies; and therefore 'thou shalt' and 'thou shalt not' are preached in the same breath!

22
L'Ordre du Jour pour le Roi[12]

The day begins; let us begin to arrange the day's affairs and amusements for our most gracious lord, whom it pleases to remain recumbent. His Majesty has bad weather today; we

will take care not to call it bad; we will not speak of the
weather – but we will conduct the day's affairs somewhat more
formally and the amusements somewhat more amusingly than
would otherwise be necessary. Perhaps His Majesty will even
be ill; at breakfast, we will give the good news from the night
before, the arrival of Monsieur Montaigne, who bears his illness with such good humour, joking about it – he suffers from
a stone. We will receive several personages (personages! – what
would that puffed-up old frog,[13] who will be among them, say,
if he heard this word! 'I am no personage,' he would say,
'rather, I myself am always the occasion') and the reception
will last longer than is agreeable; which is reason enough to
tell of the poet who wrote over his door: 'Whoever enters does
me an honour: and whoever does not – a kindness.'[14] Truly a
discourtesy courteously said! And for his part, perhaps this
poet is quite right to be discourteous: it is said that the verses
are better than the versifier. Well, may he make many more,
and withdraw as much as possible from the world; and that no
doubt is the point of his elegant effrontery! Conversely, a
prince is always worth more than his poetry, even when –
but what are we doing? Here we are indulging in small talk,
when the whole court thinks that we have been working and
racking our brains; no light in the window is seen burning
earlier than ours.

Hark! Was that not the morning bell? The devil! The day
and the dance begin, and we do not know what is on the pro-
gramme! Then we must improvise – as all the world improvises.
For once, let us do as all the world does! And with that my
whimsical dream this morning vanished, probably due to the
tower clock which, with its own stern significance, had just
struck five. It seems to me that on this occasion the god of
dreams wanted to mock my habits – my habit is to begin the
day by arranging it to make it tolerable *for myself*, and it may
be that I often do this too formally and in too princely a
manner.

2 3
The Signs of Corruption

Consider the following signs of that occasionally necessary condition of society called 'corruption'. As soon as corruption sets in anywhere, a motley array of *superstitions* becomes prevalent, and the earlier shared faith of a people becomes pale and powerless against it; however, superstition is a lesser species of free-thinking – he who gives himself over to it selects certain congenial forms and formulae and exercises some discretion in doing so. Compared to the religious man, the superstitious man is always much more of a 'person', and a superstitious society is one in which there are already more individuals and more delight in individuality. Seen from this standpoint, superstition is always an *advance* upon faith and a sign of the intellect becoming independent and asserting its rights. The devotees of the ancient religion and its religiosity complain then about corruption – until now they have determined linguistic usage, and have brought superstition into ill-repute even among the freest of free-thinkers. Let us learn that it is a symptom of *enlightenment*.

Second, a society in which corruption takes place is charged with *a lack of moral fibre*: its approval of and delight in war perceptibly diminish, and the comforts of life are now as ardently sought after as athletic and military honours had once been. But it is customary to overlook the fact that the old passion and energy of the people, which became splendidly conspicuous through sport and war, has now transformed itself into a multitude of private passions, and has only become less conspicuous. Indeed, the force and violence with which a 'corrupt' people expends energy is probably greater than ever; the individual squanders his own as never before – in the past, he could ill afford to do so. And so the times that 'lack moral fibre' are precisely those in which great love and great hatred are born, tragedy spreads from house to house and knowledge is set ablaze, its flame rising into the sky.

Third, as if to compensate for blaming corrupt times for their superstition and lack of moral fibre, it is customary to say that they are milder, and much less cruel when measured against the older, stronger, more credulous period. But I can no more agree with the praise than the blame: I will go so far as to admit that cruelty has become refined, and that its older forms are considered distasteful; but in such times the art of wounding with a word or a look attains perfection – it is only now that *malice* is created, and the delight in malice. The men are men of wit and slander, who know that ambush and dagger are not the only ways to kill – and that *eloquence* is always taken for truth.

Fourth, when 'morals decline', we see for the first time that peculiar being called the 'tyrant': he is the progenitor of the *individuals*, and, as it were, their harvest's unseasonable *first fruit*. A little while longer and this fruit of fruits hangs ripe and yellow on the tree of a people – and this tree stood only for the sake of these fruits! When morals descend to their nadir, and civil war between the various tyrants is brought to a head, a last tyrant and Caesar always comes to put an end to the exhausting struggle for autocratic rule, by turning exhaustion to his advantage. This is when individuals are usually at their most mature, and consequently 'culture' is at its height and at its most fruitful, but not for the tyrant's sake and surely no thanks to him, even if the most cultured men love to flatter their Caesar by pretending that he *made* them. But the truth is, they need rest from the outside, because they have their restlessness and labour on the inside. Now bribery and treason are at their greatest, for love of the recently discovered ego proves more powerful than love of the old, worn-out, talked-to-death 'fatherland'; and the need to secure oneself somehow against the terrible reverses of fortune opens even the nobler hands, once a richer and more powerful man shows himself ready to pour gold into them. The future is now quite uncertain; everyone lives for today, a state of mind in which the game of graft and swindle is played with ease – that is, it is only 'for today' that they allow themselves to be bribed and bought, while tomorrow and tomorrow's virtue they reserve to themselves! It is a well-known fact that individuals, being truly things apart,[15] care more for the moment than their opposites the gregarious do, because they consider themselves as unpredictable as the future; likewise, they readily take up with the violent, because the crowd could neither understand nor condone the actions to which they dare have recourse – but the tyrant or Caesar understands that the individual has a right even to his excesses, and has an interest in advocating a bolder private morality, and even in lending it a hand. For what he thinks of himself, and what he wants others to think of him, is what Napoleon in his classical manner at one time declared: 'I have the right to answer any complaint against me with an eternal "this is what I am".[16] I stand aloof from the whole world and accept conditions from no one. I want submission even to my fancies and regard it as a matter of course that I indulge myself in this or that diversion.' Napoleon once spoke thus to his wife, who had reasons to question her husband's fidelity.

It is during the most corrupt times that these apples ripen and fall, by which I mean the individuals who bear the seeds of the future, the intellectual pioneers and founders of causes and federations. Corruption is only an ugly word for the *autumn* of a people.

24
Various Discontents

The weak and, as it were, feminine, among the discontented, display considerable ingenuity in making life beautiful and profound; the strong ones – the masculine among the discontented, to continue the metaphor – display their ingenuity in securing and improving it. On occasion, the former, out of weakness, and as women are wont to do, readily allow themselves to be deceived, and perhaps even content themselves with a little ecstasy and enthusiasm at times, but on the whole are never satisfied, and suffer from an incurable discontent. Moreover, they promote all who are adept at providing opiate-like and narcotic consolations, and for that reason bear a grudge against those who appreciate the physician more than the priest – thereby *prolonging* the real distress! Had there not been too many of this sort in Europe since the Middle Ages, perhaps Europeans' remarkable aptitude for constant *transformation* would not have

arisen at all; for the requirements of the strong among the discontented are too broad, and at bottom too simple, not to be
rendered quiescent in the end. China is an example of a country
in which considerable discontent and the aptitude for transformation died out centuries ago; and Europe's socialists and
those who worship the idol of the state could easily bring about
Chinese conditions and a Chinese 'happiness', what with all
their measures for securing and improving life, provided that
they first eradicate the more sickly, more delicate, more feminine
discontent and romanticism which is, for the time being, still
present in abundance. Europe is an incurable invalid who owes
the deepest gratitude to her sufferings and all their endless transformations; these ever-new circumstances, and likewise these
ever-new pains, dangers and expedients, have in the end produced an intellectual fractiousness tantamount to genius, or
which in any event is the mother of all genius.

25
Not Predestined to Knowledge

It is by no means rare for a man to be burdened with a timid
humility, rendering him utterly unsuitable as a devotee of
knowledge. That is to say, the moment this kind of man notices
something striking, he immediately stops and says to himself,
'You must be mistaken! What are you thinking? That cannot
be right!' and then, instead of looking more closely or listening
more attentively, he flinches from what is striking and tries to
rid his mind of it as quickly as possible. His moral maxim reads
as follows: 'I wish to see nothing that defies conventional wisdom! Was I meant to discover new truths? There are already
too many old ones.'

26
What Does It Mean to Live?

To live – that means: to continually slough off something of
ourselves that wants to die; to live – that means: to be cruel
and implacable to all that is old and feeble in us, and not only

in us. To live – then doesn't that mean: to be without piety towards the dying, the wretched and the old? Always being a murderer? And yet old Moses said: 'Thou shall not kill!'

27
The Self-Denier

What does the self-denier do? He strives for a higher world, he wants to fly longer and further and higher than all men of affirmation – *he throws away many things* that would weigh him down on his flight, many of which are far from worthless or unpleasant to him; he sacrifices them to his longing for the heights. It is precisely this sacrificing, this throwing away, which alone is visible in him; he is accordingly called a self-denier, and as such he stands before us like a monk, the very soul of mortification. But he is well pleased with the impression he makes on us: he wants to hide from us his longing, his pride, his intention of winging his way *beyond* us.

Oh yes, he is shrewder than we thought, and so obliging towards us – this affirmer! For like us, that is what he is, even in his self-denial.

28
Doing Harm with Their Best

Our strengths sometimes impel us so far ahead of ourselves that we cannot any longer bear our weaknesses, and we perish by them; we perhaps even anticipate this outcome, and would not have it otherwise. Then we become hard with those qualities in us that want to be spared, and our greatness is also our ruthlessness.

Such an experience, which must in the end cost us our lives, is a parable of the whole effect great men have on others and on their time – it is precisely with their best qualities and singular abilities that they ruin much that is uncertain, unfinished, weak and wanting, and are thus harmful. Indeed, all things considered, it may seem that they only do harm, because their best is accepted, imbibed like strong drink, only by those who as a result lose all prudence and reason; and in the end they break their legs, stumbling on all the wrong tracks down which their intoxication impels them.

29
Corrupting the Text[17]

When people in France began to oppose the Aristotelian unities,[18] and as a result others began to defend them, something occurred which we so often see but are reluctant to acknowledge – their defenders *rationalized* these rules and why they ought to exist, for no better reason than not to have to admit that they were *accustomed* to them and their authority, and no longer wanted them otherwise. And this is what people do and have always done with every prevailing morality and religion: the reasons and intentions behind the habit are always 'interpolated' into it when some begin to deny its authority, and *ask* for reasons and intentions. Herein lies the great dishonesty of conservatives in every era – they corrupt the text.

30
The Comedy of the Famous

Famous men who *need* their fame, politicians for example, no longer choose their friends and allies without ulterior motives: from this one they want a bit of glory, the reflected glory of his virtues; from another, the awe-inspiring presence of certain of his well-known if rather dubious qualities; from yet another they steal a reputation for basking in idleness, because it serves their purpose for a time if others believe they are heedless and lie about – this conceals the fact that they lie in wait; they quickly need a dreamer in their vicinity to serve as their current persona, then they need a knowledge-seeker, then a contemplative, then a pedant, but just as quickly they do not need them any more! And thus while their periphery and surroundings are continually dying off, everyone seems to throng into them, and wants to become their 'character'; in this respect the famous resemble great cities. Their reputation is constantly in flux, as is their character, for the changing means they employ require it, and they bring now this, now that, real or imaginary quality to the fore and into the spotlight; as we have said, their friends and allies are among these theatrical qualities. On the other hand, what they want must be all the more firm and unwavering and consistently illustrious – and this too sometimes requires its comedy and stagecraft.

31
Commerce and Nobility

Buying and selling are now as common as the arts of reading and writing; now all are well practised in these arts even if they are not themselves merchants who practise them daily, just as formerly, in the age of savagery, everyone was a hunter, and day after day practised that art. At the time, hunting was common; but just as this became a privilege of the noble and powerful, and in the end lost the ordinary tone of everyday life – ceasing to be necessary and becoming a matter of whim and luxury – so might it be some day with buying and selling. Social conditions in which there is no buying and selling, in which the need for these arts is gradually lost, are entirely conceivable; perhaps individuals less subject to the rigours of the general condition will, at their own discretion, engage in buying and selling as a *sentimental luxury*. Only then would commerce be ennobled, and only then would the nobility perhaps want to concern itself with it, as it has hitherto concerned itself with war and politics; conversely, the esteem in which politics is held might have completely changed by then. Politics has already ceased to be the business of a gentleman; and it is possible that one day it may be regarded as so common, like writing for a party or for the dailies, as to fall under the rubric 'intellectual prostitution'.

32
Undesirable Disciples

A philosopher who 'corrupted' youth as Socrates had once done[19] exclaimed with dismay, 'What am I going to do with these two! Such students are most unwelcome: one cannot say no to anything, and the other wants to water everything down. Supposing they embraced my doctrine, the former would *suffer* too much, because my way of thinking requires a warrior's soul, a willingness to wound, a delight in opposition, and a thick skin – he would languish of his wounds, both open and hidden. And the other, everything he stands for he dresses up as a platitude, and to such an extent that it actually becomes a platitude – I wouldn't wish such disciples on my worst enemy.'

33
Outside the Lecture Hall

'In order to prove that man is a fundamentally benign animal, I would hasten to remind you how gullible he has been and for how long. It is only now, quite late, and after an immense self-conquest, that he has become a *suspicious* animal – oh yes! Man is now more malicious than ever.' I do not understand: why should man now be more suspicious and more malicious? 'Because now he has science – and has need of it!'

34
Historia Abscondita[20]

Every great man has a retroactive effect: on account of him, all history is weighed in the balance again, and a thousand ancient mysteries come crawling out of their hiding places – into the light of *his* sun. There is no telling what history may yet become. Perhaps the past remains as yet largely undiscovered! So many retroactive effects are still required!

35
Heresy and Witchcraft

Thinking other than is customary – that is not nearly so much the effect of a better intellect as it is of strong, evil tendencies, of antisocial, reclusive, defiant, spiteful and malicious tendencies. Heresy is the counterpart of witchcraft, and, like witchcraft, is surely by no means innocuous, much less something worthy of reverence. Heretics and witches are both people of an evil sort: what they share is that they also feel themselves to be evil, but that they cannot resist the desire to do harm to the dominant men and prevailing opinions. The Reformation, during which the medieval mind redoubled its efforts, albeit without its former good conscience, yielded both in the greatest abundance.

36
Last Words

It will be recollected that in his last words, Augustus Caesar, that terrible man who kept himself well under control and could be just as silent as a wise Socrates, let slip something about himself: for once he let his mask fall in hinting that he had worn a mask and played a comedy – representing the father of his country and wisdom on the throne with a verisimilitude that approached perfection! *Plaudite amici, comoedia finita est!*[21]

The thought of the dying Nero, *qualis artifex pereo!*,[22] was the dying Augustus' thought as well; it was the vanity of an actor who cannot contain himself, and the very opposite of the dying Socrates.

But Tiberius, that most tormented of all self-tormentors, died in silence – *he* at least was genuine and no actor! What must have passed through his mind in the end? Perhaps it was this: 'Life is but a protracted death. What a fool I was to shorten the lives of so many! Was I meant to be their benefactor? I should have let them live for ever, so that I could *watch* them *die* for ever. I had such a good eye for that: *qualis spectator pereo!*'[23] When after a long death struggle his strength seemed to rally, it was deemed advisable to smother him with pillows – he died twice over.

37
Owing to Three Errors

Science has been promoted in the last few centuries, partly in the hope of understanding God's goodness and wisdom with and by it – the chief motive of great English minds (like Newton) – partly from a belief in the absolute utility of knowledge, and especially the belief that morality, knowledge and happiness stand in the closest connection with one another – the chief motive of great French minds (like Voltaire) – partly because loving and possessing science was thought to be sufficient unto itself, selfless, innocuous and entirely innocent, a passion in which people's evil impulses played no role – Spinoza's chief motive, who as a knowledge-seeker felt himself to be divine: that is, owing to three errors.

38
The Explosive

If one considers how much the pent-up forces within the young are in need of detonation, it is no wonder that they commit themselves to this or that cause so indiscriminately and with so little sophistication: what excites them is the sight of zeal for a cause, the sight of a lit fuse, as it were – not the cause itself. The more sophisticated inveigler for a cause knows to hold out to them the prospect of an explosion, and refrains from giving reasons: it is not by reasons that these powder kegs are won over!

39
Altered Taste

An alteration of the general taste is more important than one of opinions; opinions, with the whole intellectual masquerade of evidence marshalled for and against them, are only symptoms of altered taste, and certainly *not*, as is still so often claimed, their causes. So how does this alteration come about? Through singular, powerful and influential people who shamelessly express and tyrannically insist upon *their 'hoc est ridiculum, hoc est absurdum'*,[24] and therefore the judgements of their taste and distaste – thus they impose upon many a constraint which gradually leads yet more people to be accustomed to such judgements, and in the end *everyone* to *require* them. However, such an individual's feeling and 'tasting' differently usually has its basis in some peculiarity of his mode of life, diet or digestion, perhaps in an excess or deficiency of inorganic salts in his blood and brain – in short, in his body – but he has the courage to acknowledge his body and lend an ear to the music of its demands, even in its most subtle tones: his aesthetic and moral judgements are his body's 'most subtle tones'.

40
Of the Absence of Noble Demeanour

Soldiers and their leaders always comport themselves towards one another in a loftier manner than workers and their employers. At least for the time being, culture with a military basis still stands high above all so-called industrial culture which, as presently constituted, is unquestionably the most debased form of life that ever was. Here, everything is determined by sheer need: workers want to live and have to sell themselves, but despise him who exploits this need and *buys* them. It is curious that submission to powerful, awe-inspiring and even terrible individuals, to tyrants and generals, is felt far less acutely than submission to such generic bores as our captains of industry: in the employer, workers usually see nothing but a sly dog who feeds on the misery of others, whose name, stature, character and reputation are a matter of perfect indifference to him. It is probable that in all those forms and insignia of a *superior race* which alone make a *person* interesting, industrialists and commercial magnates have thus far been woefully deficient; had they the distinction of noble birth in their look and bearing, there might not be any interest in socialism among the masses.

566 THE JOYOUS SCIENCE

For fundamentally the masses are ready for *slavery* of any
kind, provided that their betters are unfailingly legitimized as
superior and *born* to command – by their noble demeanour!
The common man feels that nobility is not to be improvised,
and that he has to honour it as the fruit of a long development –
but the absence of superior demeanour, and the blatant
vulgarity of grubby-handed industrialists, gives rise to the
thought that only luck has placed one above the other. 'Well
then,' he reasons to himself, 'for once let us try *our* luck! For
once let *us* throw the dice!' And then you have socialism.

41
Against Rue

In his own actions, the thinker sees experiments and enquiries
from which he seeks to obtain insight: to him, success and failure are, first of all, *answers*. But to be vexed at or even to rue the
fact that something goes awry – that he would leave to those
who act because someone commands them, and who expect a
beating when their gracious lord is not satisfied with the result.

42
Work and Tedium

Seeking work for the sake of the wages – in the civilized world
today almost everybody does that. Work has become a means,
not an end, which is why people are not very discerning in their
choice of employment as long as they are amply rewarded. Now
there are those rare few who would rather die than work without taking *pleasure* in it, people who are particular and hard to
please, who are not served by an ample reward if the work itself
is not rewarding. This rare breed includes all manner of artists
and contemplatives, but also men of leisure who spend their
lives hunting and travelling, or in love affairs and adventures.
All of them will endure toil and hardship if it is associated with
pleasure, and the heaviest, hardest toil, if need be. But otherwise, they are resolutely idle, even if this idleness goes hand in
hand with poverty, disgrace and danger to life and limb. It is

not tedium they fear so much as work without pleasure: they
even need a fair amount of tedium, if their own work is to succeed. For the thinker, and for any inventive genius, tedium is
that disconcerting state of a soul 'becalmed' which precedes the
happy voyage and fair winds; he must bear it and *await* its
effect on him – it is precisely *this* which lesser natures cannot
quite manage! To dispel tedium by any means necessary is
uncouth, just as working without pleasure is uncouth. The Asi-
atics are perhaps distinguished from the Europeans by their
capacity for a longer and deeper calm; even their narcotics take
effect slowly and require patience, in contrast with the appall-
ing rapidity of the European poison, alcohol.

43
Laws and What They Betray

One errs greatly in the study of a people's criminal laws, if one
regards them as an expression of its character; the laws do not
betray who they are, but rather what seems foreign, alien,
monstrous and strange to them. The laws pertain to deviations
from their traditional ethos, and the severest penalties fall on that
which is in accord with the traditions of neighbouring peoples.
The Wahhabi have only two mortal sins: having a god other
than the Wahhabi god,[25] and – smoking (which they refer to as
'the disgraceful kind of drinking'). On learning these things,
an astonished Englishman[26] once asked, 'And what about mur-
der and adultery?' 'Well, God is gracious and merciful,' the old
chief replied.

    The ancient Romans were of the opinion that there were only
two mortal sins for a woman: committing adultery and – drinking
wine. Old Cato believed that the only reason for the tradition of
kissing between relatives was to keep women under control in
this regard; a kiss meant 'Was the smell of wine on her breath?'
Women who were caught drinking wine were actually put to
death; and certainly not just because under its influence women
sometimes forget how to say 'no'; above all else, the Romans
feared something by which the women of the European South
who were then new to wine were occasionally beset, something

of an orgiastic and Dionysian nature, something foreign and monstrous that offended Roman sensibilities; to them it seemed a betrayal of Rome, the incorporation of what was foreign.

44
The Motives in Which We Believe

As important as it may be to know the motives mankind has really acted upon thus far, for the knowledge-seeker perhaps still more essential is the *belief* in this or that motive, i.e. the motives mankind has imputed to itself and imagined to be the real mainspring of its actions thus far. Men's inner happiness and misery are apportioned according to their belief in this or that motive – *not* by the actual motive! The latter is of but secondary interest.

45
Epicurus

Yes, I am proud to feel differently about the character of Epicurus than perhaps anyone else, and to enjoy in all that I read and hear of him the afternoon of antiquity and its happiness – I see his eye gazing out on a wide, white sea, past the cliffs on which the sun shines, while in this light creatures great and small are playing, as quiet and confident as the light and as that eye itself. Such happiness could only have been contrived by one who had suffered constantly, the happiness of an eye before which the sea of existence has become calm, and which now never tires of the view of its surface, of this many-hued, delicate, trembling skin of the sea; never before was there such modesty in voluptuousness.

46
Our Astonishment

It is deeply and thoroughly fortunate that scientific discoveries *withstand scrutiny*, and consistently furnish the basis for further discoveries – things could well have been otherwise! Indeed, so convinced are we of the uncertain and fanciful quality of our judgements, and of the ever-transitory nature of all human laws and concepts, that it is truly astonishing *how well* the results of science hold up! Formerly nothing was known of this transitoriness of everything human; obedience to the traditional ethos perpetuated the belief that the whole inner life of man yields to iron necessity, bound by eternal fetters; at that time, perhaps when people listened to fables and fairy tales, they felt an astonished delight akin to ours. Those who occasionally wearied of the time-honoured and the timeless must have enjoyed quite a respite from them in the miraculous. Not to stand on firm ground for once! To hang in air! To stray! To go mad! Once upon a time, it was paradise to luxuriate in the miraculous; whereas our supreme happiness resembles that of the castaway who, having climbed ashore, stands with both feet on the old, solid earth – astonished that it does not rise and fall.

47
Of the Suppression of the Passions

When the expression of the passions is consistently prohibited as something 'common', and consigned to coarser natures, both bourgeois and peasant – that is, when what is wanted is not the suppression of the passions as such, but only passionate language and gesticulation, nevertheless the *result* is precisely what is not wanted: the passions themselves become suppressed, or at least weakened and altered – witness the court of Louis XIV and all that depended upon it as the most instructive example of this. Men of the *subsequent* generation, having been brought up not to express them, came to lack the passions themselves, which were supplanted by a superficial, charming and playful disposition – and thereby became incapable of rudeness to such a degree that they received and responded even to insults with nothing but obliging words. Perhaps our own time furnishes the most remarkable counterpart to theirs: wherever I look, in life, in the theatre, and last but not least in literature, people are comfortable with all the *coarser* kinds of passionate outbursts and gesticulations; a certain conventional display of passion is now even expected – but not the passion itself! Even so, in this way we will eventually achieve it, and those who come after us will not just be savage and unruly in form, but *truly savage*.

48
Knowledge of Hardship

Perhaps nothing separates men and eras from one another quite so much as the extent of their knowledge of hardship, mental as well as physical. With respect to the latter, it may be that our contemporaries are all amateurs who, lacking sufficient first-hand experience, must rely on conjecture, their frailties and infirmities notwithstanding. By contrast, those who lived in the age of fear – the longest of all ages – had to protect themselves from violence, and to that end had to be violent themselves. In those days, a man received a long schooling in bodily pain and privation, in the knowledge that even a certain cruelty towards himself, a willingness to suffer, was necessary for his preserva-tion; in those days, a person gave his companions an education in enduring pain, inflicting it quite readily, and when he saw the most terrible things of this kind happen to others, he felt noth-ing but his own safety. Where mental hardship is concerned, I now look at every man to see if he knows it by experience or by description; if he still considers it necessary to feign this know-ledge, as a mark of refinement, say; or if deep down in his heart he does not believe in mental sufferings at all, and is the same at the mention of them as at the mention of great physical ordeals, which bring to mind his toothaches and stomachaches. So it seems to me with most people these days. The fact that so few have experienced pain of either kind, and that the sight of suffering has become comparatively rare, has important conse-quences: pain is considered more hateful and arouses more indignation than ever before; indeed, the mere *thought* of pain is considered almost unbearable, a source of moral anxiety and a reproach to the whole of existence. The emergence of pessim-istic philosophies is by no means a sign of some great and terrible distress; rather, these question marks regarding the worth of life arise when the human condition has been so improved and ameliorated that the inevitable mosquito bites of body and soul are found to be altogether too gruesome and gory, and in the poverty of their experience of actual pain, people will even take *being troubled by ideas* to be suffering of the highest order.

There is already a remedy for pessimistic philosophies and the squeamishness which seems to me our real hardship, the real 'crying need of the hour' – but perhaps this remedy sounds too cruel, and would itself be reckoned among the signs on the basis of which one now proclaims: 'existence is evil'. Well then! The remedy for this 'hardship' is: *hardship.*

49
Magnanimity and Related Matters

When a sentimental person suddenly becomes cold, or a melancholic person amused, and above all when, *out of magnanimity*, an envious or vengeful person suddenly renounces the gratification of such desires – these paradoxical phenomena occur in men in whom there is a powerful inner momentum, in men of sudden satiety and revulsion. Their desires are so quickly and intensely gratified that aversion and disgust soon follow, and then their taste runs to the opposite extreme, provoking a spasm of emotion: in one person sudden coldness, in another laughter, and in a third tears and self-sacrifice. It seems to me that magnanimous people – at least those who have always made the greatest impression – are men with the most extreme thirst for vengeance, to whom the prospect of gratification presents itself, and who drink so deeply of it and so thoroughly drain it to the last drop *in their imaginations* that a tremendous and rapid revulsion follows this rash intemperance – such a man now rises 'above himself', as we say, and forgives his enemies, even blessing and honouring them. With this self-violation, with this outrage against a still-powerful vengefulness, he merely indulges in a new impulse which has now become powerful in him (revulsion) and does so as impatiently and intemperately as he had a short time before *anticipated* the joy of revenge and

exhausted it in fantasy. There is as much egoism in magnanimity as there is in revenge, but of a qualitatively different kind.

50
The Argument of Isolation

The reproach of conscience, even in the most conscientious, is
weak when set against the feeling: 'This and that are contrary
to the wholesome traditions of *your* society.' A cold look or
lips curled in scorn by those with whom and for whom one
was brought up strikes *fear* even in the strongest. What are we
afraid of? Isolation! As the argument which rebuts even the
best arguments for a person or cause!

So speaks the gregarious instinct in us.

51
Sense of Truth

I commend any form of scepticism to which I might reply: 'Let
us put it to the test!' But I should like to hear nothing more of
things and questions which do not admit of experiment. That
is the limit of my 'sense of truth'; beyond that bravado has lost
its rights.

52
What Others Know of Us

What we know of ourselves, what we have in our memory, is
not as important to our happiness as people think. One day
what others know (or think they know) about us is forcefully
brought home to us – and then we have to admit that it is the
more powerful. A bad conscience is more easily borne than a
bad reputation.

53
Where Goodness Begins

Where the evil impulse has become so subtle as to be invisible, man imagines a realm of goodness, and the feeling of having entered it at the same time arouses feelings of safety, comfort, benevolence and the like, which before had been deterred and inhibited by the presence of evil impulses. So: the duller the vision, the greater the extent of the good! Hence the perpetual cheerfulness of ordinary people and children! Hence the heartache, the remorseful despair of the great thinkers!

54
The Consciousness of Appearances

Knowing what I know, how wonderful and new, and yet how disturbing and ironic my situation is with respect to the whole of existence! I have *discovered first-hand* that human and animal nature, indeed the whole history and prehistory of feeling within me, continues to love, hate, concoct and conclude – I have suddenly awakened in the middle of this dream, but only to the consciousness of dreaming, and that I *must* continue to dream lest I perish, just as the sleepwalker must continue to dream lest he slip and fall. What is 'appearance' to me now! Surely not what is in opposition to some essence – what can I attribute to any essence other than the predicates of its appearance! Surely not a dead mask that conceals the face of some unknown variable, and which might well be torn off it! To me, appearance itself is alive and effective, and it goes so far in its self-mockery as to give the impression that it is appearance and will-o'-the-wisp and dance of spirits and nothing more – and that I too among all these dreamers, I the 'knowledge-seeker', also dance my dance, that the knowledge-seeker is a means of prolonging this worldly dance, and is to that extent one of the stewards of life's festival, and that the sublime consistency and consilience of all that we know is perhaps the best means of *preserving* the community of reverie, *preserving* the perfect intelligibility of all the dreamers to one another, and in so doing *preserving the continuity of the dream.*

55
The Ultimate Sense of Nobility

What then makes a person 'noble'? Certainly not that he makes sacrifices; even the desperate libertine makes sacrifices. Certainly not that he follows his passions; there are despicable passions. Certainly not that he acts for others, without selfishness; perhaps the consistency of selfishness is at its greatest precisely in the noble.

Rather, the passion that agitates the noble man is, unbeknownst to him, a thing apart: the use of a rare and singular standard, bordering on folly; warming to things that feel cold to all others; divining the worth of things for which scales have not yet been invented; sacrificing on altars consecrated to an unknown god; a bravery that forgoes honour; an abundant self-sufficiency which bestows upon men and things. Hitherto it has been what is rare in man, and blindness to this rarity, that made men noble. Here, however, let us consider that everything customary, parochial and indispensable – in short, what has most preserved the species and what, generally speaking, has been in the course of mankind the *rule* thus far – has been unfairly judged and on the whole maligned, in favour of the exceptions. To become the advocate of the rule – that may be perhaps the ultimate refinement, the ultimate form in which the sense of nobility will reveal itself on earth.

56
The Desire for Suffering

When I think of the desire to do something, how it constantly arouses and incites millions of young Europeans who can endure neither their boredom nor themselves, then I realize that they must harbour a desire to suffer, and to draw from their suffering a plausible reason for action, for deeds. Absence of hardship is the real hardship![27] Hence the political demagoguery, hence the many false, imaginary, exaggerated 'crises' of every possible variety, and the blind willingness to believe in them. The world of youth demands that unhappiness, not happiness, should come or be visible *from without*; from the very beginning their imaginations are busily making a dragon out of it so that in the end they might slay it. If these youths with their addiction to hardship had the strength to do themselves some good, to draw upon their inner resources, they would also know how to create hardships of their very own. Then what they imagine might be more subtle, and what gratifies them more melodious; whereas now they fill the world with their outrage about hardship, and hence all too often with the *sense of hardship* in the first place! They do not know what to do with themselves – and so they make a mural of others' unhappiness; they always need others! And always other others! Pardon me, my friends, I have ventured to make a mural of my *happiness*.

BOOK II

BOOK II

57
To the Realists

You sober men who consider yourselves armed against passion
and fantasy, and who like to make your emptiness into a matter of pride and an ornament, you call yourselves realists, and
imply that the world actually is the way that it appears to you;
before you alone does reality stand unveiled, and it may well
be that you yourselves are the best part of it – oh, you dear
images of Saïs![1] But when you yourselves are unveiled, are you
not, unlike the cold-blooded fish which see in every water, still
extremely passionate and blind? Are you not still too much like
enamoured artists? And what is 'reality' to an enamoured artist! You still carry about with you judgements which had their
origin in the passions and infatuations of earlier centuries!
Your sobriety still partakes of a hidden and ineradicable
drunkenness! Your love of 'reality', for example – oh, that is an
old and immemorial 'love'! In every perception, in every sensation, there is a bit of this old love; and similarly also some kind
of fantasy, prejudice, folly, ignorance, fear and everything else
that has worked on it and been woven into it. That mountain
there! That cloud there! What in them is 'real'? Subtract for
once the phantasm and every human *addition* from them, you
sober men! As if you could do that! As if you could forget your
origin, your history, your training – all of your humanity and
animality! No, there is no 'reality' for us – but neither is there
for you, you sober men – we are not so different from each

other as you suppose; and perhaps our determination to escape
from drunkenness is every bit as respectable as your conviction
that you are altogether *incapable* of it.

58
Only as Creators!

This has caused me the greatest difficulty, and continues to
cause me the greatest difficulty: to bear in mind that *what
things are called* is unspeakably more important than what
they are. The reputation, the name and appearance, the worth
and weight of a thing – which are originally and for the most
part erroneous and arbitrary, which are thrown over the thing
like a garment and are quite alien to its nature and even to its
skin – have gradually, through belief in them and their continuous growth from generation to generation, grown into it and
become its very body, so to speak; what began as its appearance
almost always ends up as its nature, and becomes *effective* as
such! One would have to be a fool to think it sufficient merely
to indicate this origin, this fog-cover of illusion, in order to destroy what passes for natural, to *destroy* this so-called '*reality*'!
It is only as creators that we can destroy!

But let us not forget this: it is sufficient to create new names
and judgements and verisimilitudes, in order eventually to create new 'things'.

59
We Artists!

When we love a woman we quickly come to have an antipathy
towards nature, when we recall all the disgusting natural functions to which every woman is subject; we would rather avoid
thinking about them altogether, but if for once our soul touches
upon this subject, it stirs impatiently, and, as I said, looks down
on nature with contempt – we are incensed; nature seems to
meddle with our possessions, and with the most profane hands.
We then shut our ears to all physiology, and we secretly decree,
'I will hear nothing of it! Man is nothing but *soul and form*!'

To all lovers, 'the man beneath the skin' is abominable and unthinkable, a blasphemy against God and love.

Well, just as the lover still feels about nature and natural functions, so too did every worshipper of God and His 'holy omnipotence' once feel; everything that was said about nature by astronomers, geologists, physiologists and physicians he regarded as meddling with his most precious possession, and thus as an assault on it – and as an act of impertinence by the assailant to boot! The 'law of nature' sounded to him like a libel of God; in essence, he would have rather regarded the whole of mechanics as attributable to free and voluntary moral action – but because nobody could render him this service, he *concealed* nature and mechanics from himself as best he could, and lived in a dream. Oh, those men of former times knew *the art of dreaming*, and did not even need to go to sleep first! And even we modern men still know it all too well, despite our determination to remain awake! It is enough to love, to hate, to desire, to feel anything at all – and *immediately* the spirit and the power of the dream overcome us, and with eyes wide open and oblivious to all danger, we scramble up the most dangerous paths, to the roofs and towers of fantasy, and without any vertigo, as if we were born to climb – we daytime sleepwalkers! We artists! We concealers of nature! We moonstruck and God-struck men! We deathly silent, tireless wanderers on heights which we do not regard as heights, but as our plains, as our safety!

60
Women and Their Actions at a Distance

Do I still have ears? Am I only ear, and nothing else? Here I stand amid the breaking waves, whose white tongues lick at my feet – from all sides they howl, threaten, shriek and roar at me, while from the deepest depths the old earth-shaker himself[2] sings his aria, dull as a bellowing bull; he stomps with such an earth-shaker's beat that even the hearts of these weathered rock monsters tremble. Then, suddenly, as if from nowhere, there appears beyond the entrance to this hellish

labyrinth, only a few yards away – a great sailing ship, reticent
as a ghost, gliding past. Oh, what ghostly beauty! With what
magic it takes hold of me! What? Has all the peace and silence
in the world embarked on it? Is my happiness itself not to be
found in this silence, my happier self, my second immortalized
self? Not yet dead, but no longer alive? A transitional being,
ghostly, silent, observing, gliding, floating? Resembling the
ship with its white sails which like some tremendous butterfly
passes over the dark sea! Yes! To pass *over* existence! That is
it! That would be the very thing!

It seems that the noise here has made me daydream. All great
noise causes us to place our happiness in silence and distance.
When a man stands in the midst of *his* noise, surrounded by the
breaking waves of his projects and plans, he probably also sees
silent, magical beings gliding past him, for whose happiness
and seclusion he longs – *they are women*. He almost thinks that
his better self dwells among them; with them even the loudest
breaking waves fall deathly silent, and life itself becomes a
dream of life. However! However! My noble enthusiast, even
on the most beautiful yachts there is also much noise and com-
motion, and, alas, much of it petty and pitiful! The magic and
the most powerful effect of women is, to use the language of the
philosophers, an action at a distance,[3] an *actio in distans*; but
this requires, first and foremost – *distance*!

61

In Honour of Friendship

The sentiment of friendship was regarded by antiquity as the
highest sentiment, higher even than the most vaunted pride of
the self-sufficient and wise, a kindred but less sacred sentiment. This is very well expressed by the story of the Macedonian
king who made a gift of a talent to an Athenian philosopher.[4]
The philosopher, who despised the world, returned it to
him. 'What?' said the king. 'Has he no friend?' By which he
meant to say, 'I honour the pride of this wise and independent
man, but I should have honoured his humanity even more, had

the friend in him conquered his pride. The philosopher has lowered himself in my eyes, for he has shown that he does not know one of the two highest sentiments – and the higher one at that!'

62
Love

Love forgives the lover even his lust.

63
Woman in Music

How is it that warm and rainy winds also give rise to a musical mood and an inventive delight in melody? Are these not the same winds that fill the churches and inspire amorous thoughts in women?

64
Sceptics

I am afraid that women who have grown old are more sceptical in the secret recesses of their hearts than any man; they believe in the superficiality of existence as in its essence, and to them all virtue and profundity is merely a veil over this 'truth', a very desirable veil over a *pudendum* – thus a matter of decency and modesty, and nothing more!

65
Devotion

There are noble women with a certain poverty of spirit who, in order to *express* their deepest devotion, and not knowing what else to do, offer up their virtue and modesty: it is the highest thing they have to offer. And often this gift is accepted without committing the recipient to as deep an obligation as the giver supposed – a very melancholy story!

66
The Strength of the Weak

All women are adept at exaggerating their weaknesses, indeed they are inventive in weakness, in order to appear as utterly fragile ornaments to which even a speck of dust does harm; their very existence is supposed to make man acutely aware of his heavy-handedness, and to make him feel guilty about it. Thus do they defend themselves against the strong and the 'law of the jungle'.

67
Pretending to Be Oneself

She loves him now, and ever since she has been gazing ahead with quiet confidence, like a cow; but alas! It was precisely the fact that he found her changeable and incomprehensible that had been the source of his fascination! He had too much steady weather in himself already! Would she not do well to pretend to be her old self? To pretend not to love him? Is it not love itself that advises thus? *Vivat comoedia!*[5]

68
Will and Willingness

Someone brought a youth to a wise man and said, 'Look, this one is being corrupted by women!' The wise man shook his head and smiled. 'It is men', he exclaimed, 'who corrupt women; and everything that women lack should be atoned for and reformed by men – because it is man who creates for himself the image of woman, and woman moulds herself according to this image.' 'You are too sympathetic towards women,' said one of the bystanders, 'you do not know them!' The wise man answered, 'Man's nature is will, woman's is willingness – such is the law of the sexes, truly a hard law for woman! All human beings are innocent of its existence, women, however, are doubly innocent; who could have enough balm and sympathy for them!' 'What balm! What sympathy!' someone else in the crowd exclaimed, 'Women need to be better educated!' 'Men need to be better educated,' said the wise man, and made a sign to the youth to follow him.

The youth, however, did not follow him.

69
Capacity for Revenge

There is no disgrace in being unable and therefore unwilling to defend oneself; but we think little of a person who has neither the capacity nor the inclination for revenge – whether it be man or woman. Would a woman be able to hold us (or, as they say, 'captivate' us) if we did not firmly believe that, under certain circumstances, she was perfectly capable of wielding a dagger (any kind of dagger) *against* us? Or against herself; which in certain cases might be the more exquisite revenge (Chinese revenge).

70
Women Who Master the Masters

A deep and powerful contralto voice of the kind heard from time to time in the theatre can suddenly reveal to us hitherto undreamed-of possibilities; all at once a curtain is lifted and for a moment we believe that somewhere in the world there might be women with high, heroic, royal souls, women willing and able to make grand replies, resolutions and self-sacrifices, women willing and able to rule over men because in them, the best in man (apart from his sex) has become the ideal incarnate. To be sure, these kinds of voices are not specifically intended to convey the idea of such a woman: usually they represent the ideal male lover, a Romeo for example; but judging from my experience, when the theatre uses them to represent the ideal female lover, it frequently miscalculates, as does the composer who expects such effects from such a voice. *These* lovers beggar belief: their voices still contain a tinge of the motherly and housewifely, especially when their tones resound with love.

71
Of Female Chastity

There is something quite astonishing and monstrous in the way
that noble women are educated; there may be nothing more
paradoxical. All the world agrees that they are to be educated
with as much ignorance as possible *in eroticis*, and their souls
filled with a deep sense of shame about such things, indeed,
that they are to respond with the most extreme aversion and
intolerance at the merest mention of them. It is only here that
the 'honour' of women is really at stake; for what else do we not
forgive them! But here they are to remain ignorant in their very
hearts – they are to have neither eyes, nor ears, nor words, nor
thoughts for this, their 'wickedness'; indeed, to possess knowledge of it is already to be wicked. And then! To be thrown
with the terrible suddenness of a thunderbolt into reality and
knowledge, with marriage – and by the very man they love and
cherish the most; to have to experience a contradiction between
love and shame, indeed, to have to feel rapture, vulnerability,
duty, compassion, fear and who knows what else, at the unexpected proximity of God and beast!

    In this way, we tie a psychological knot without equal! Even
the sympathetic curiosity of the wisest observer of men is not
enough to divine how this or that woman is able to find the
solution to this enigma and the enigma in this solution; and
what terrible, wide-reaching suspicions in the meantime must
stir in her poor unhinged soul; and how the ultimate philosophy and scepticism of woman casts anchor at this point!

    Afterwards the same deep silence as before; and often even
an inward silence, as she shuts her eyes to herself.

    Young wives therefore make every effort to seem superficial
and thoughtless; the most subtle of them feign a kind of
impertinence.

    Wives easily regard their husbands' existence as calling into
question their honour, and their children as an apology or atone-
ment for them – they need children, and wish for them in a very
different sense than a husband wishes for children.

    In short, one cannot have enough sympathy for women!

72
Mothers

Animals think differently about females than human beings do; they regard the female as the productive being. For them, there is no such thing as paternal love, but instead something more akin to loving a beloved's children, and becoming accustomed to them. Females satisfy their ambitions through their offspring; they are their property and their occupation, something quite intelligible to them with which they can chatter: this is what maternal love amounts to – it may be compared to the love an artist has for his work. Pregnancy has made females gentler, more patient, more timid, more submissive; and by the same token, spiritual pregnancy engenders a contemplative character, which is akin to the female character; such men are masculine mothers.

Among animals, it is the male sex which is regarded as the beautiful sex.

73
Saintly Cruelty

A man came to a saint holding a newborn child in his hands. 'What should I do with this child,' he asked, 'it is miserable, deformed, and has not even enough life in it to die.' 'Kill it,' exclaimed the saint in a terrible voice, 'kill it, and then hold it in your arms for three days and three nights to seal it in your memory – and in this way, you will never again beget a child when it is not the time for you to beget.' When the man had heard this he went away heartbroken; and many censured the saint because he had advised such cruelty; for he had advised the man to kill the child. 'But,' asked the saint, 'is it not more cruel to let it live?'

74
The Unsuccessful

Those poor women always lack success who become restless
and unsure in the presence of him whom they love, and thus
talk too much; for men are most surely seduced by a certain
quiet and phlegmatic tenderness.

75
The Third Sex

'A little man is a paradox, but still a man – but a little woman
seems to me to be a different sex altogether, as compared with
a tall woman' – said an old dancing master. A little woman is
never beautiful,[6] said old Aristotle.

76
The Greatest Danger

Had there not always been a majority of men who regarded their
intellectual discipline, their 'rationality', as their pride, their obligation, their virtue, and who were offended or ashamed by
delirious and extravagant thinking, as friends of sound 'common
sense' – then mankind would have perished long ago! What has
always hovered and still hovers over mankind as its greatest danger is the eruption of *madness* – that is to say, the eruption of
arbitrariness in feeling, seeing and hearing; the indulgence of an
utter want of intellectual discipline; the delight in uncommon
nonsense. It is not truth and certainty which are the antithesis of
the world of the madman, but the universality and universally
binding character of a faith – in short, non-arbitrariness in judgements. And the greatest labour of human beings hitherto has
been to agree with one another on a great many things, and to
impose upon themselves a *law of agreement* – regardless of
whether these things are true or false. This is the intellectual discipline which has preserved mankind – but the opposing impulses
are still so powerful that one cannot speak of mankind's prospects with much confidence. The image of things is constantly

changing, and perhaps will continue to do so at an ever-hastening pace; it is always the choicest spirits who baulk at anything universally binding – those engaged in the pursuit of *truth* above all! That faith, as a faith shared by all the world, continually inspires disgust and a new lust in subtler intellects; and already the slow tempo which it demands for all intellectual processes, this imitation of the tortoise, which is the acknowledged standard, makes artists and poets into turncoats – it is in these impatient spirits that a downright passion for madness erupts, because madness has such a joyful tempo! It thus requires virtuous intellects – ah! I want to use the least ambiguous word – it requires *virtuous stupidity*, it requires the steady beats of the *slow* spirits, so that the faithful of the great comprehensive faith may keep time with one another and continue to dance their dance; it is a necessity of the first order which here dictates and demands. *We others are the exceptions and the danger* – may we always be defended! Well, there is something to be said in favour of the exceptions, *provided that they never want to become the rule.*

77
The Animal with a Good Conscience

The vulgarity of everything which pleases Southern Europe – whether it be the Italian opera (for example, Rossini's or Bellini's)[7] or the Spanish adventure novel (most readily accessible to us in French garb in *Gil Blas*)[8] – is not unknown to me, but it does not offend me either, any more than does the vulgarity which one encounters in a walk through Pompeii, or for that matter in the reading of essentially every ancient book; why is that? Is it that shame is lacking, and that everything vulgar in music or a novel appears with the same confidence and self-assurance as anything noble, charming or passionate? 'Beasts have their rights no less than man, so let them roam freely; and you, my dear fellow, are still a beast too, in spite of everything!' – that seems to me to be the moral of the thing, and the peculiarity of Southern humanity. Bad taste has its rights no less than good taste, and even takes precedence over it when there is a great need for an assured satisfaction and a universal language, the immediate intelligibility of the broad caricature and gesture, as it were; by contrast, good taste, refined taste, always has something of a laboured and tentative character, and is not altogether confident of being understood – it is not, and has never been popular! What is and remains popular is the *mask*! So let it pass, this exaggerated, mask-like quality in the melodies and cadences, in the leaps and drolleries that mark the rhythms of these operas! And what is still true of Southern Europe is emphatically true of life in antiquity! How little we understand of it if we do not understand its innocent delight in masks, in everything mask-like! Here is the bath, the relaxation, of the ancient spirit – and perhaps this bath was all the more necessary for the rare and sublime natures of the ancient world than it was for the vulgar.

On the other hand, a vulgar turn in Northern works, for example in German music, strikes me as unspeakably offensive. There is an element of *shame* in it; the artist has debased himself, and cannot help but blush at what he has done. We too are ashamed, and what makes it so offensive is the suspicion that he thought it necessary to debase himself for *our* sakes.

78
Things for Which We Should Be Grateful

It is only artists, and especially those of the theatre, who have given to men the means of seeing and hearing with some pleasure the nature, the experiences and the desires of every man. It is only they who have taught us to value the hero hidden within each of these ordinary men, and the art of seeing ourselves from a distance as heroes, simplified and transfigured, as it were – the art of imagining ourselves on the stage and being our own audience – and it is only in this way that we are able to disregard a few petty details in ourselves! Without that art we would be nothing but foreground, and would live entirely under the spell of that perspective which makes the closest and meanest seem to be immensely large and to be reality as such.

Perhaps there was a similar sort of merit in the religion which bade us instead to look at the sinfulness of every individual through a magnifying glass, thereby making a great, immortal criminal out of every sinner. And yet, in depicting him surrounded by endless vistas, it too taught man to see himself from a distance, as something past and whole.

79
The Charm of Imperfection

I see here a poet who, like so many men, exercises a higher charm by his imperfections than by any handiwork of his which is complete and perfectly designed – indeed, he owes his reputation and success more to his ultimate limitations than to his considerable strengths. His work never quite expresses what he would really like to express, what he *would like to have seen*: he seems to have had the foretaste of a vision and never the vision itself – but an enormous lust for this vision has remained in his soul; and from this he derives his equally enormous eloquence of longing and craving. With this he raises those who listen to him above his work and above all 'works', and gives them wings to fly higher than hearers have ever flown before; and so, having been made poets and seers themselves, they pay tribute to the author of their happiness, as if he had led them directly to a vision of his holiest and ultimate experiences, as if he had reached his goal, and had actually *seen* and communicated his vision. It enhances his reputation that he never really arrived at his goal.

80
Art and Nature

The Greeks (or at least the Athenians) enjoyed listening to eloquent speech; indeed, they had an avidity for it, which distinguished them more than anything else from non-Greeks. And so they demanded eloquence even from passion on the stage, and cheerfully endured the unnaturalness of dramatic verse – in nature, passion is so taciturn! So silent and embarrassed! Or, if passion finds words, it is so confused, irrational and ashamed of itself! Now, thanks to the Greeks, we are all accustomed to this unnaturalness on the stage, just as we willingly endure that other unnaturalness, passion which *sings*, thanks to the Italians.

And so for us, it has become a need which reality alone cannot meet: to hear men speak eloquently and at length in the most difficult situations; it delights us when the tragic hero can still find words, reasons, eloquent gestures, and on the whole a clear intellectuality, precisely when life approaches the abyss and real men usually lose their heads, and certainly their fine language. This kind of *deviation from nature* is perhaps the most pleasant repast for man's pride: it is on account of this deviation that man loves art as the expression of high, heroic unnaturalness and convention. We justly reproach the dramatic poet when he does not transform everything into reason and language, but always retains a remnant of *silence* – just as we are dissatisfied with an operatic composer who is unable to find a melody for the highest emotion, but only an emotional, 'natural' stammering and shrieking. It is precisely here that nature is to be contradicted! It is precisely here that the common charm of illusion *should* yield to a higher charm! The Greeks went far in this direction – appallingly far! Just as they made the stage as narrow as possible and forbade themselves the use of deep backgrounds for theatrical effect, made facial expression and ease of movement impossible for the actor, and transformed him into a solemn, stiff, masked scarecrow, so too have they deprived passion itself of its deep background, and prescribed for it a law of fine speech; indeed, they have done everything they could to counteract the elementary effect of images which inspire pity and fear;[9] *they simply did not want pity and fear* – with all due respect to Aristotle – but he certainly did not hit the nail, let alone on the head, when he spoke about the ultimate aim of Greek tragedy! Let us consider the Greek tragic poets with regard to what most stimulated their industry, their invention, their rivalry – certainly it was not the intention of overwhelming their audience with emotion! The Athenian went to the theatre *to hear fine speeches*! And it was – pardon my heresy – fine speeches with which Sophocles concerned himself!

It is very different with *serious opera*: all its masters are careful to prevent us from understanding their characters. The inattentive listener may find that catching an occasional word here or there helps, but on the whole the situation must be self-explanatory – the speeches are nothing! That is what they all think, and so they all make sport with the words. Maybe they merely lacked the courage to express fully their ultimate disregard for words; a little more insolence in Rossini, and he would have let the singers sing 'la-la-la-la' throughout – and it would have been perfectly reasonable for him to do so! The characters in the opera are not supposed to be taken 'at their word', but at their tone! That is the difference, that is the fine *unnaturalness*, for the sake of which we go to the opera! Even the *recitativo secco*[10] is not intended to be heard as words and text: rather, this kind of half-music is at first supposed to give the musical ear a little rest (a rest from the *melody*, which affords the most sublime, and therefore also most strenuous, enjoyment of this art) – but very soon something else occurs, to wit, a growing impatience, a growing aversion, a new longing for *whole* music, for melody.

Viewed in this light, how does the case stand with regard to the art of Richard Wagner? Perhaps this case is different? It has often seemed to me as if the words *and* the music of his creations have to be memorized before the performances, because otherwise – so it seemed to me – neither the words nor the music can even be *heard*.

81
Greek Taste

'What is beautiful in it?' asked a geometer,[11] after a performance of *Iphigénie*, 'Nothing is proved in it!' Were the Greeks so very far from this taste? In Sophocles at least, 'everything is proved'.

82
Esprit Un-Greek

The Greeks were indescribably logical and plain in all their thinking, and they did not tire of it, at least not during the long period of their greatest glory. In this regard they were unlike the French, who often are quite happy to make a little leap into the antithesis, and who in fact only tolerate the spirit of logic at all when it betrays by many such leaps its *sociable* courteousness and self-abnegation. Logic they deem necessary, like bread and water; but, like bread and water, they consider it a kind of prison fare as soon as it is supposed to be enjoyed alone. In polite society, one must never wish to be completely in the right, as all pure logic requires; hence the little dose of irrationality in all French *esprit*.

Sociability in the Greeks was far less developed than in the French both past and present, which is why there is so little *esprit* in their cleverest men, and so little wit, even in their wittiest men – alas! These propositions of mine will already be met with incredulity, and many more remain unexpressed!

Est res magna tacere[12] – says Martial, like all garrulous people.

83
Translations

One can estimate the degree to which an age possesses the historical sense by how it makes *translations* and seeks to annex past periods and literatures. The French of Corneille, and even the French of the Revolution, appropriated Roman antiquity in a manner for which we no longer have the courage – owing to our superior historical sense. And Roman antiquity itself: how violently, and at the same time how naively, did it lay hands on everything good and superior belonging to the more ancient antiquity of Greece! How they translated it all into the Roman present! How they deliberately and recklessly brushed away the dust from that moment, like brushing away the dust from the wings of a butterfly![13] This was how Horace occasionally translated Alcaeus or Archilochus, how Propertius translated Callimachus and Philetas (poets of equal rank with Theocritus,[14] if we may be *allowed* to judge); what was it to them that the actual creator had had certain experiences, and had given indications of them in his poem! As poets, they were averse to the antiquarian, investigative spirit which precedes the historical sense; as poets, they rejected these entirely personal matters

and names, and everything unique about the costume and mask
of a city, a coast or a century, and instead immediately substituted the present and the Roman. They seem to be asking us,
'Should we not remake the old for our own benefit, and put
ourselves into it? Should we not be allowed to breathe our soul
into this lifeless body? For it is lifeless, after all; how ugly are
all things lifeless.' They did not know the pleasures of the historical sense; the past and the foreign made them uncomfortable,
and, being Romans, this was sufficient motive for a Roman
conquest. In fact, they conquered when they translated – not
only in that they omitted the historical: no, they also added
allusions to the present, and above all struck out the name of the
poet and put their own in its place – without any feeling of
being a thief, but with the very best conscience of the *imper-
ium Romanum*.

84
Of the Origin of Poetry

The lovers of the fantastic in man, who at the same time sub-
scribe to the doctrine of instinctive morality, conclude thus:
'Suppose that we had always worshipped utility as the supreme
deity, where in the world would poetry have come from? This
process of making all speech rhythmical thwarts rather than
promotes clarity of statement, and has nevertheless sprung up
all over the world and still does, as if in mockery of any practical considerations! The wild and beautiful irrationality of
poetry refutes you, you utilitarians! It is precisely the desire to
escape from utility for once which has elevated mankind,
which has inspired morality and art!' Well, for once I have to
agree with the utilitarians – they are so seldom right that it is
truly pitiful! In those ancient times which called poetry into
existence, at the time when rhythm was first allowed to penetrate speech, people still had utility in mind, and a very
substantial utility at that – though admittedly a *superstitious
utility*! For it had been observed that rhythm – that power
which rearranges all the elements of the sentence, chooses
what words to say, and gives thought new colours, making it

more obscure, more strange and more inaccessible – enabled men to remember an utterance better than unmetrical speech. It was thought that by virtue of rhythm, a human entreaty would be more deeply impressed upon the minds of the gods. It was also thought that the rhythmical beat could make people be heard at greater distances; rhythmical prayer seemed more likely to reach the ears of the gods. But above all, people wanted to take advantage of the elemental sense of being over-whelmed which man himself experiences when he listens to music; rhythm is a constraint: it produces an irresistible desire to yield, to join in; not only the step of the foot, but even the soul itself follows the measure – so probably, people concluded, the souls of the gods as well! They tried, therefore, to *constrain* the gods through rhythm, and to exercise power over them; they cast poetry upon the gods like a magical snare. And there was a still more quaint idea that has perhaps operated even more powerfully in the origin of poetry. Among the Pythagoreans it appeared as a philosophical doctrine and an educational device; but long before there were philosophers, people acknowledged that music had the power of discharging the emotions, of purg-ing the soul,[15] of soothing the *ferocia animi* – and this precisely through the rhythmic element in music. When the proper ten-sion and harmony of the soul were lost, a person had to *dance* to the measures of the singer – that was the recipe of this heal-ing art. With it Terpander quelled a riot, Empedocles calmed a maniac, Damon[16] purged a lovesick youth; with it one even thought to cure the maddened and vengeful gods. This was achieved by driving their emotions to the highest pitch of frenzy and wantonness, thus making the enraged wild, and the venge-ful drunk with vengeance – all the orgiastic cults want to discharge the *ferocia* of a deity all at once, and to make an orgy of it, so that the deity will feel more free and peaceful afterwards, and leave man in peace.

The derivation of the word *melos* is 'means of appeasement', not because the song itself is peaceful, but because its after-effect is pacifying. And not only in the cultic songs, but also in the secular songs of the most ancient times, the presupposition was that the rhythmic exercises a magical influence; for example, in drawing water, or in rowing, the song is for the enchantment of the imaginary daemons associated with the activity: it makes them submissive, bound and the instruments of man. Thus, whenever a person acts, he has occasion to sing – *every* action is linked with the assistance of spirits; magical songs and incantations appear to be the original form of poetry. When verse also came to be used in oracles – the Greeks said that hexameter was invented at Delphi – here, too, rhythm was supposed to exercise a constraining influence. Prophesying – that originally meant (according to what I consider the probable derivation of the Greek word) to determine something; people thought they could control the future course of events by winning over to their side the god Apollo, who according to the oldest conception was far more than a prescient deity. When the formula is pronounced with literal and rhythmical correctness, it binds the future; the formula, however, is the invention of Apollo, who as the god of rhythm can also bind the goddesses of fate.

Taken all in all, was there ever anything more *useful* to the ancient superstitious type of man than rhythm? One could do everything with it: magically further labour; compel a god to appear, draw nigh and harken; arrange the future according to one's wishes; discharge from one's own soul any kind of excess (of fear, of mania, of pity, of vengefulness), and not only from one's own soul, but from the souls of the most evil daemons – without verse one was nothing, but with verse one was almost a god. Such a fundamental feeling cannot be fully eradicated – and even now, after thousands of years of strenuous efforts to combat such superstitions, the wisest among us occasionally are fooled by rhythm, if only to the extent that they *feel* a thought to be closer to the truth when it has a metrical form and approaches with a divine hop, skip and jump. Do you not find it amusing that the most serious philosophers, however rigorous they may otherwise be with regard to certainty, still invoke *poetical maxims* in order to give their thoughts force and credibility? And yet it is more dangerous to a truth when the poet agrees with it than when he contradicts it! For as Homer says, 'Bards lie about many things.'[17]

85
The Good and the Beautiful

Artists *glorify* continually – they do nothing else – that is to say, all those conditions and things which have a reputation for being able to make man feel good or great, or intoxicated, or cheerful, or well and wise. Those *select* things and conditions whose value for human *happiness* is considered settled and assured are the objects of artists; they are always lying in wait to discover such things, and to draw them into the domain of art. I will say this: they are not themselves the assessors of happiness and of those who are happy, but they always throng around these assessors with the greatest inquisitiveness and enthusiasm, in order to put their assessments immediately to use. They do so because, apart from their impatience, they also have the big lungs of heralds and the feet of runners, and thus are always among the first to glorify the *new* good, and often *seem* to be the first to call it good and assess it as good. This, as I have said, is a mistake; they are merely quicker and louder than the actual assessors.

And who then are these? The rich and the idle.

86
Of the Theatre

Once again, this day has given me strong and elevated sentiments, and if I could have music and art in the evening, I know full well what kind of music and art I would *not* like to have: namely, the kind which intoxicates its listeners and *excites them to a fever pitch* of strong and elevated sentiment – listeners with ordinary souls, who in the evening are not like victors on triumphal chariots, but like tired mules to whom life has too often applied the whip. What would those people ever know of 'elevated moods', if there were no means of intoxication and idealistic strokes of the whip! And thus they have their men to inspire them as they have their wines to intoxicate them. But what is it *to me*, this drink and drunkenness of theirs? Does a man who is truly inspired need wine? Rather, he looks back with a kind of disgust at both the means and the mediator which are supposed to produce an effect here without sufficient reason – an imitation of the high tide of the soul!

What? We give the mole wings and proud conceits – before he goes to sleep, before he crawls back into his hole? We send him into the theatre and put great magnifying glasses in front of his weak and weary eyes? Men for whom life is no 'action' but business sit before the stage and look at strange beings for whom life is more than business? 'That is respectable,' you say, 'that is diverting, that is what culture is!'

All too often, this is the kind of culture in which I am lacking, because all too often I find the sight of this kind of thing disgusting. Anyone who has enough tragedy or comedy within himself already probably prefers to stay away from the theatre; or, on those rare occasions when he goes, the entire proceedings – theatre and public and poet included – are for him the real tragic or comedic spectacle, in comparison to which the performance itself means very little. A man who is something like Faust or Manfred[18] cares nothing for the Fausts or Manfreds of the theatre – though it certainly gives him pause that such figures are ever brought into the theatre in the first place. The *strongest* thoughts and passions are brought before those who are capable of neither thought nor passion – but only of *intoxication*? And *this* as a means to that end? Theatre and music as the European form of the hashish-smoking and betel-chewing?[19] Oh who will recount for us the whole history of narcotics! It is almost the history of 'culture' itself, of so-called higher culture!

87
Of the Vanity of the Artists

I believe artists often do not know what they can do best, because they are too vain, and have set their minds on something grander than those seemingly little plants which are able to grow to true perfection in their soil, as something new, rare and beautiful. They thoughtlessly underestimate the ultimate worth of their own garden and vineyard and their love is not equal to their insight. Here is a musician,[20] who, more than any

musician, has his mastery in finding the tones from the realm of
suffering, oppressed, tortured souls, and who can even make
dumb beasts speak. No one is his equal in the colours of late
autumn, in the indescribably moving happiness of a final, all too
final and all too brief enjoyment; he knows the tones for those
mysterious midnights of the soul when cause and effect seem out
of joint, and at any moment something may emerge 'out of nothing'. He draws most successfully from the dregs of human
happiness, from its drained goblet as it were, where, for better or
worse, the bitterest and most distasteful drops have finally min-
gled with the sweetest. He knows that weary shuffling of the soul
which can no longer leap or fly, indeed, which can no longer even
walk; he has the shy glance of secret pain, of understanding without comfort, of farewells without confessions; indeed, as the
Orpheus of all secret misery, he is greater than anyone; and he has
added much to art which was hitherto inexpressible and which
even seemed unworthy of art, and which words in particular
could only chase away and not grasp – those recesses of the soul
which are quite small, even microscopic; oh yes, he is the master
of the quite small. But he does not *want* to be! His *character* loves
to paint daring frescoes on great walls! It entirely escapes him
that his *spirit* has a different taste and inclination, and prefers to
sit quietly in the corners of collapsed houses – there, concealed,
concealed even from himself, he paints his authentic masterpieces,
all of which are very short, often only one measure long – because
only there does he become wholly good, great and perfect, there
and perhaps there alone.

But he does not know it! He is too vain to know it.

88
Seriousness about the Truth

Seriousness about the truth! What different things men understand by these words! Precisely the same views and types of
examination and evidence which a thinker regards as frivolous
but to which he himself, to his shame, has succumbed at one
time or other – precisely the same views may give an artist who
encounters them and accepts them for a while the impression

that the most profound seriousness about the truth has now taken hold of him, and that it is quite admirable that although he is an artist, he also shows the most serious desire for the opposite of appearances. It is thus possible that someone may, by the very pathos of their seriousness, betray just how superficial and undemanding their intellect has hitherto been when playing in the realm of knowledge.

And does not everything which we take to be *weighty* betray us? For it shows what has weight with us, and what does not.

89
Now and Formerly

Of what use is all the artistry in our works of art, if that higher art, the art of the festival, is lost? Formerly all works of art were erected along the great festival road of mankind, as monuments and memorials to its high and happy moments. Now we want to use works of art to lure the exhausted and sickly away from mankind's great road of suffering for brief moments of respite; we offer them a little intoxication and madness.

90
Light and Shadow

Books and writings are different things for different thinkers. One has gathered together in his book as much of the light from an illuminating experience as he could quickly take hold of and bring home; while another has given us only shadows, the grey and black images of what the day before had arisen in his soul.

91
Caution

Alfieri,[21] as is well known, lied a great deal when he told the story of his life to his astonished contemporaries. He lied out of a despotism towards himself which he also exhibited, for example, in the way in which he created his own language, and tyrannized himself into becoming a poet – he finally found a severe form of dignity into which he forced his life and his memory, and must have suffered in the process.

I would also give no credence to a memoir of Plato's, had he written one, any more than I do to Rousseau's *Confessions*, or to Dante's *Vita Nuova*.

92
Prose and Poetry

It is noteworthy that the great masters of prose have almost always been poets, either openly, or secretly and for their own private enjoyment; and truly, good prose is written only *in light of poetry*! For prose is the result of an uninterrupted, polite war with poetry; all its charm consists in the fact that poetry is constantly avoided and contradicted; every abstraction wishes to be presented as a piece of roguishness against poetry and with mocking voice; all dryness and coolness is supposed to drive the lovely goddess to lovely despair; often there are momentary compromises and reconciliations between the two, and then a sudden rebound into laughter; often the curtain is drawn back and harsh light let in just when the goddess was enjoying her twilights and dull colours; often her words are taken from her mouth and sung to a melody which makes her hold her delicate hands over her delicate ears – and so there are a thousand pleasures to this war, the defeats very much included, of which the unpoetic, the so-called prose writers, know nothing – which is why they write and speak only bad prose! *War is the father of all good things;*[22] war is also the father of all good prose!

In this century, there have been four quite peculiar and truly poetic men who have achieved mastery in prose, something for which this century is not otherwise suited, for lack of poetry, as I have indicated. Setting aside Goethe, who may be fairly claimed by the century which produced him, only Giacomo Leopardi, Prosper Mérimée, Ralph Waldo Emerson and Walter Savage Landor, the author of *Imaginary Conversations*, seem to me worthy of being called masters of prose.[23]

93
But Why, Then, Do You Write?

A: I am not one of those who *think* with pen in hand; and still less one of those who entirely give way to their passions before an open inkwell, sitting on their chair and staring at the paper. I am annoyed and ashamed by all writing; writing is for me a necessity – even to speak of it in parables is repugnant to me. B: But why, then, do you write? A: Well, my friend, let me tell you in confidence: I have yet to find any other means of getting *rid* of my thoughts. B: And why would you want to get rid of them? A: Why would I want to? Want to? I have no choice! B: Enough! Enough!

94
Growth after Death

Those bold little words about moral matters which Fontenelle[24] jotted down in his immortal *Dialogues of the Dead* were regarded in his day as the paradoxical and sportive remarks of a not altogether innocuous wit; even the highest judges of taste and intellect – and perhaps even Fontenelle himself – saw nothing more in them. In the meantime, something incredible has occurred: these thoughts turned out to be true! Science proves them! The game becomes serious! And we receive a different impression from reading those dialogues than Voltaire and Helvétius did; we instinctively elevate their author into another and *much higher* order of intellect than they did. Rightly? Wrongly?

95
Chamfort[25]

That such a connoisseur of men and of the crowd as Chamfort should stand by the crowd, instead of standing apart in philosophical renunciation and disapproval – that I am unable to explain, except as follows: there was an instinct in him stronger than his wisdom which had never been satisfied: a hatred of all

nobility of blood; perhaps it was his mother's old and all too
explicable hatred which was sanctified in him by his love for
her – an instinctive desire for revenge from his boyhood
onwards that waited for the moment to strike. But then the
course of his life, his genius, and alas! most likely, the paternal
blood in his veins seduced him into ranking himself among
precisely this nobility and according himself the same rights as
they had – for many, many years! In the end he could no longer
bear the sight of himself, the sight of an 'old man' under the
old regime; he flew into a violent rage of remorse, and in *this*
state put on the garb of the mob as his very own hair-shirt! His
bad conscience was due to his dereliction of duty, the duty to
avenge his mother.

Had Chamfort remained somewhat more philosophical, the
Revolution would not have gained its tragic wit and its sharp-
est sting; it would have been regarded as a much more stupid
affair, and would not have had such a seductive influence on
men's minds. But Chamfort's hatred and vindictiveness educated an entire generation; and the most illustrious men passed
through his school. Bear in mind that Mirabeau[26] looked up to
Chamfort as to his higher and older self, from whom he
expected and endured impulses, warnings and judgements –
Mirabeau, who as a man belongs to an entirely different order
of greatness than even the foremost among the great statesmen
of yesterday and today.

Strange, that despite having such a friend and advocate – we
have Mirabeau's letters to Chamfort – this wittiest of all moralists has remained a stranger to the French, no less than
Stendhal, who perhaps had the most fertile and perceptive
mind of any other Frenchman of *this* century. Is it that Stendhal had too much of the German and the Englishman in him
for the Parisians to find him tolerable – while Chamfort, a man
whose profound soul contained a wealth of ulterior motives,
grim, suffering, ardent – a thinker who found laughter necessary as the remedy for life, and who almost gave himself up as
lost every day in which he had not laughed – seems more like
an Italian, a kinsman to Dante and Leopardi, than a Frenchman? We know Chamfort's last words: *'Ah! Mon ami,'* he said

to Sieyès, *'je m'en vais enfin de ce monde, où il faut que le cœur se brise ou se bronze'*.[27] These are certainly not the words of a dying Frenchman.

96
Two Speakers

Of these two speakers, the one is able to furnish all of the reasons in support of his case only when he yields to passion; only this pumps enough blood and heat into his brain to compel his superior intellectuality to reveal itself. The other may well try to do the same now and again: to argue his case with the aid of passion sonorously, vehemently and ravishingly – but usually without success. His argument becomes obscure and confused; he exaggerates, makes omissions and arouses suspicion against the reasons in support of his case; indeed, he himself feels this suspicion, which explains the sudden shifts in tone from warm and attractive to cold and repulsive, tones which raise a doubt in the listener as to whether his passion is genuine. With him, passion always submerges his intellect; perhaps because it is stronger than in the other man. But he is at the height of his powers when he resists the impetuous storm of his feelings, as if to ridicule them; it is only then that his intellect fully emerges from its hiding place, a logical, sportive, mocking yet altogether formidable intellect.

97
Of the Loquacity of Authors

There is the loquacity of wrath – often in Luther, also in Schopenhauer. The loquacity of too large a stock of conceptual formulae, as in Kant. The loquacity of delight in ever-new ways of expressing the same thing: we find it in Montaigne. The loquacity of malice: whoever reads contemporary magazines should be able to think of one or two such writers. The loquacity of delight in elegant words and turns of phrase, not unusual in Goethe's prose. The loquacity of a noisy and confused sensibility attaining inward satisfaction, in Carlyle, for example.

98
In Praise of Shakespeare

The most beautiful thing I could say in praise of Shakespeare, in praise of *the man*, is that he believed in Brutus, and cast not a shadow of doubt on this kind of virtue! It is to him that Shakespeare dedicated his best tragedy – it is still called by the wrong name – to him, and to the most formidable epitome of a superior morality. Independence of soul! That is what is at issue here! For this, no sacrifice can be too great; for its sake, we must be willing to sacrifice even our dearest friend, even if he is the most magnificent of men, the ornament of the world, a genius without peer – when we actually love freedom as great souls love freedom, and *this* freedom is put at risk by such a man, this is what we must do – but this must be what Shakespeare himself felt! The height at which he placed Caesar was the finest honour he could possibly bestow on Brutus; it is only in this way that he was able to increase the magnitude of Brutus' inner problem to immense proportions and likewise increase the magnitude of the inner strength required to cut *this knot*!

And was it really political freedom which drove the poet to sympathy with Brutus – and made him into his accomplice? Or was political freedom merely a symbol for something inexpressible? Do we perhaps stand before some obscure and as yet unknown event or adventure within the poet's own soul, of which he preferred to speak in signs? What is all of Hamlet's melancholy compared to the melancholy of Brutus! And perhaps Shakespeare also knew this, as he knew the other, from experience! Perhaps he too had his dark hour and his evil angel, just like Brutus!

But whatever similarities and hidden allusions there may have been, Shakespeare abased himself before the whole figure of the man, finding such virtue inaccessible to him and feeling himself unworthy by contrast – the evidence for this being written into the tragedy itself. Twice he presents a poet, and twice he heaps upon him such impatient and extreme contempt that it sounds like a cry – a cry of self-contempt. Brutus, even Brutus loses his patience when the poet appears, self-important, pathetic and

importune, as poets tend to be – creatures who seem to be full
of possibilities for greatness, even for moral greatness, and yet
whose ethics and conduct rarely rise even to the level of common decency. *'I'll know his humours* when he knows his
time – jigging fool, hence!'[28] shouts Brutus. We should translate
this back into the soul of the poet who wrote it.

99
Schopenhauer's Followers

When barbarians come into contact with civilized peoples,
invariably the more primitive culture will adopt the vices, weaknesses and excesses of the more advanced culture first. From that
point onwards, the former feels the attraction exerted by the
latter, and eventually, by way of the vices and excesses it has
appropriated, allows something of the more valuable powers of
the latter to influence it as well. The opportunity to observe this
sort of thing may also be had without expeditions to the lands of
barbaric peoples, though in a refined, intellectualized and far
less palpable form. Consider *Schopenhauer's* followers in Germany. These were men who, when comparing themselves to him
and his superior culture, must have felt barbaric enough to be
fascinated and seduced by him from the very beginning. What,
then, did they accept from their master first? Was it his tough-
mindedness, his determination to be clear and rational, which
often made him seem so very English, and so little German? Or
was it the strength of his intellectual conscience, which *endured*
a lifelong contradiction between what he was and what he
wished to be and which compelled him constantly to contradict
himself on almost every point, even in his writings? Or was it his
scrupulousness in matters of the Church and of the Christian
God? For here he was scrupulous as no German philosopher had
ever been before; he lived and died 'as a Voltairian'. Or was it his
immortal doctrines of the intellectuality of intuition, the *a priori*
character of the law of causality, the instrumental nature of the
intellect, and the non-existence of free will? No, none of this is
considered fascinating; but Schopenhauer's mystical embarrass-
ments and evasions in those passages where the tough-minded

thinker allowed himself to be seduced and corrupted by the vain impulse to be the unriddler of the world, these were considered fascinating: the unprovable theory of the *one will* ('all causes are only the occasional causes for the appearance of this will at this time, in this place',[29] 'the will to life is present in every being, even the slightest, wholly and undivided, as completely as in all beings that ever were, and will be taken together'[30]); the *denial of the individual* ('all lions are at bottom only one lion',[31] 'the multiplicity of individuals is an illusion',[32] the assertion that *development* too is only an illusion – he calls Lamarck's idea 'an ingenious, absurd error'[33]); the ravings about *genius* ('in aesthetic intuition the individual is no longer an individual; he is a pure, will-less, painless, timeless subject of cognition',[34] 'the subject, being entirely absorbed into the intuited object, becomes this object itself'[35]); the nonsense about *pity*, how it facilitates the breaching of the *principii individuationis* which is the source of all morality;[36] additionally, such assertions as 'dying is certainly to be seen as the true purpose of existence',[37] 'the possibility cannot outright be denied *a priori* that a magical effect might not also come from somebody already dead'[38] – these and similar *excesses* and vices of the philosopher were always accepted first and made articles of faith; for vices and excesses are always the easiest to imitate, and do not require any extensive prior training. But let us speak of the most famous of the living Schopenhauerians, Richard Wagner.

What happened to him had already happened to many an artist: he erred in the interpretation of the characters he had created, and misunderstood the implicit philosophy of his own art. For half of his life, Richard Wagner allowed himself to be misled by Hegel; he did the same thing again when he later interpreted his characters in terms of Schopenhauer's doctrine, and began to speak in terms of 'will', 'genius' and 'pity'. Nevertheless, the truth remains that nothing is more contrary to Schopenhauer's spirit than the genuinely Wagnerian element in Wagner's heroes, by which I mean the innocence of the most supreme selfishness, the belief that great passion is inherently good – in a word, the Siegfried quality in the countenances of his heroes. 'All of this smacks more of Spinoza than of me,' Schopenhauer might have said. Now, however advisable it may have been for Wagner to seek elsewhere than in Schopenhauer for philosophical guidance, the fascination to which he succumbed with regard to this thinker blinded him not only to all other philosophers, but even to science itself; increasingly, he wanted his entire art to be the counterpart and complement of the Schopenhauerian philosophy, while emphatically renouncing the nobler ambition of becoming the counterpart and complement of human knowledge and science. And not only was he tempted to do so by the whole mysterious pomp of this philosophy (which would have also tempted a Cagliostro); the peculiar gestures and emotions of the philosophers had also been seducing him all along! For example, Wagner's sputtering about the corruption of the German language is Schopenhauerian; and while his imitation in this regard is commendable, it cannot be denied that Wagner's own style suffers in no small degree from the very blemishes and turgidities, the sight of which so infuriated Schopenhauer; and that with respect to the Wagnerians writing in German, Wagnerizing is beginning to prove as dangerous as any kind of Hegelizing ever did. Wagner's hatred of the Jews, to whom he cannot do justice even with regard to their greatest achievement – for it is the Jews who are the inventors of Christianity – is Schopenhauerian. Wagner's attempt to regard Christianity as having sprung from a seed of Buddhism carried by the wind, and to prepare the way for a Buddhist era in Europe by a temporary rapprochement with Catholic and Christian formulae and sentiments, are both Schopenhauerian. Wagner's preaching in favour of mercy in our dealing with animals is Schopenhauerian; Schopenhauer's well-known predecessor here was Voltaire, who perhaps even like his successors knew how to disguise his hatred of certain things and people as mercy towards animals. At least Wagner's hatred of science, which is manifest in this preaching, is certainly not inspired by any thoughts of tenderness and kindness – nor, it goes without saying, by anything resembling *thinking* at all.

Ultimately the philosophy an artist espouses is of little consequence, as long as it is only a retrospective philosophy, and does no harm to his art itself. We really should resist the temptation to begrudge an artist the occasional, perhaps very unfortunate and presumptuous masquerade; we mustn't forget that inevitably there is something of the actor in all of our beloved artists, and that they would hardly have lasted very long without acting. Let us stay faithful to Wagner in that which is *true* and original in him – and especially in this, that we, his disciples, remain faithful to ourselves in that which is true and original in us. Let him have his intellectual moods and spasms, let us rather consider in all fairness what peculiar nutriments and excrements an art like his *requires* in order to be able to live and grow at all! It makes no difference that as a thinker he is so often wrong; justice and patience are of no importance to *him*. It is sufficient that his life is justified in his own eyes, and remains so – the life which calls to each of us, 'Be a man, and do not follow me – but yourself, but yourself!'[39] *Our* lives should also be justified in our own eyes! We too should grow and flourish in accordance with our own natures, freely and fearlessly, in innocent selfishness! And so, in contemplation of such a man, these words still ring in my ears now as they did before: 'That passion is better than Stoicism and hypocrisy; that to be honest even in evil is better than to lose oneself in traditional morality; that the free man can be good as well as evil, but that the unfree man is an affront to nature, and has no share in either heavenly or earthly comfort; finally, that *anyone who wishes to be free must become so through their own efforts*, and that freedom does not fall into anyone's lap of its own accord like some kind of miraculous gift' (*Richard Wagner in Bayreuth*,[40] p. 94).

100
Learning to Pay Homage

Men must *learn* to pay homage, just as they must learn to show contempt. Whoever ventures on new paths and has led the way for many others, discovers to his amazement how awkward and deficient people are in expressing their gratitude, and indeed how very rarely they are able to express any gratitude at all. It is as if every time they wish to express their gratitude it sticks in their craw, so that all they can do is a great deal of throat-clearing, after which they fall silent. The way in which a thinker becomes aware of the effects his thoughts have on others, of their unsettling and transformative power, borders on comedy: at times it seems as if those on whom this power has been exercised actually feel offended by it, and only know how to express what they fear is a threat to their independence by all sorts of bad behaviour. It takes generations for people to come up with even just a polite convention for expressing gratitude; and it is only very late in the day that gratitude acquires some wit and geniality. By then there is usually *someone* who becomes a great object of gratitude, if not for the good he himself has done, then for the treasure of what is highest and best that his predecessors have gradually accumulated.

IOI
Voltaire

Wherever there has been a court, it has furnished the standard of appropriate speech, and with this also the standard of style for writers. Courtly language, however, is the language of the courtier *who has no speciality* and who even in discussion of scientific subjects forbids himself all convenient, technical expressions, because they smack of the speciality; for that reason the technical expression, and everything which betrays the specialist, is a *fault of style* in countries with a courtly culture. Now that all courts have become caricatures of themselves, we are astonished to find even Voltaire unspeakably prim and proper in this regard (for example, in his judgements concerning such stylists as Fontenelle and Montesquieu) – now, we are all emancipated from courtly taste, whereas Voltaire *perfected* it!

I02
A Word for the Philologists

There are books so valuable and royal that whole generations of scholars are well employed in keeping the texts of these books accurate and readable; that is the faith of philology, and to strengthen this faith again and again is its reason for being. This faith presupposes that there are rare men (though one may not see them) who actually know how to use such valuable books – no doubt, those who write or could write such books themselves. I mean to say that philology presupposes a noble faith – that for the benefit of a few who are always 'to come', and are not yet here, a very great deal of painstaking, and even exhausting, labour has to be done beforehand; it is all labour *in usum Delphinorum*.[41]

103
Of German Music

German music, more than any other, has now become the music of Europe, because the changes which Europe has undergone during the Revolution have found expression only through it: only German music knows how to express the agitation of the popular masses, that tremendous artificial noise which does not even need to be very loud – while Italian opera, for example, knows only choruses of servants and soldiers, but no 'People'. Furthermore, in all German music one can catch the sound of a profound bourgeois jealousy of the *noblesse*, especially of *esprit* and *élégance*, as the expressions of a society which was courtly, chivalrous, old and sure of itself. It is not the music of Goethe's minstrel at the gate, which was also pleasing 'in the hall', that is to say, to the king; it does not mean: 'The knights looked on boldly, and the fair ladies into their laps.'[42] Even the Graces do not appear in German music without pangs of conscience; it is only with Charm, the rural sister of the Graces, that the German begins to feel entirely moral – and from there he feels increasingly so, until he reaches what is for him the pinnacle of moral sentiment: enthusiastic, learned and often gloomy 'sublimity', Beethovenian sublimity. If we wish to imagine the man for *this* music – well, let us just imagine Beethoven as he appeared next to Goethe at their meeting in Teplitz:[43] as semi-barbarism next to culture; as the People next to the nobility; as the good-natured next to the good-intentioned and far more than 'good-intentioned'; as the visionary next to the artist; as the man in need of comfort next to the man who has been comforted; as the man prone to exaggeration and suspicion next to the man imbued with the spirit of reasonableness; a man filled with sorrow and self-torment, foolishly ecstatic, blissfully unhappy, ingenuous and intemperate, pretentious and inelegant: in short, an 'untamed' man. This was how Goethe felt about him and characterized him, Goethe, the exception among Germans, for whom a corresponding music has yet to be found!

Finally, let us consider whether the growing and rampant contempt for melody and the atrophy of the sense for melody among Germans is to be understood not in terms of democratic bad behaviour, but as one portion of the aftermath of the Revolution? For melody takes such an obvious delight in orderliness, and such an aversion to everything developing, unformed and arbitrary, that it sounds like a note from the *old* European order of things, and as a seduction to it, as a return to it.

104
Of the Tone of the German Language

We know the origin of the German which for the past few centuries has been accepted as the standard literary German. Germans, with their reverence for everything which came from the court, deliberately adopted the style of the chancery as the model for all that they had to *write*, especially their letters, documents, wills, and so on. Writing in the chancery style, which was writing in the style of the court and government – that was something distinguished, as opposed to the language of the town in which one lived. Gradually people came to this conclusion, and spoke even as they wrote – thus they became even more distinguished in their inflections, in their choice of words and phrases, and eventually even in their tone: they affected a courtly tone when they spoke, and this affectation became second nature. It may well be that nothing quite like this has ever happened before – the ascendancy of literary over spoken style, the affectation and ostentation of an entire people becoming the basis of a common language that was no longer a mere multitude of dialects. I believe that the sound of the German language in the Middle Ages, and especially after the Middle Ages, was profoundly rustic and vulgar; it has ennobled itself somewhat in the last few centuries, principally because it became necessary to imitate so many French, Italian and Spanish tones, and particularly so for the German (and Austrian) nobility, who were not altogether satisfied with their mother tongue. But despite this practice, German must have sounded unbearably vulgar to Montaigne, to say nothing of Racine; even now, in the mouths of travellers among Italian rabble, it still sounds very rude, woodsy and guttural, as if it had come from smoke-filled rooms and ill-mannered regions.

I have lately noticed that a similar desire for a distinguished tone is spreading among the former admirers of the chanceries, and that Germans are beginning to yield to an altogether peculiar 'tonal magic', which in the long run could become a real danger to the German language – for one seeks in vain for a more abominable tone in Europe. Something scornful, cold, indifferent and impassive in the voice is what now sounds 'distinguished' to Germans – and I hear the willingness to emulate this tone in the voices of young officials, teachers, women and merchants; indeed, even little girls are emulating this officer's German. For it is the officer, and specifically the Prussian officer, who is the inventor of this tone: this same officer, who as a soldier and a professional possesses that admirable tact and self-effacement which all Germans might do well to imitate (German professors and musicians included!). But as soon as he speaks and moves he is the most intrusive and tasteless figure in old Europe – doubtless without being aware of the fact! These good Germans are similarly unaware in their admiration for him as the man of the best and most distinguished society, and are happy to let him 'set the tone'. And set it he does! In the first instance it is the sergeant-majors and non-commissioned officers who mimic and coarsen his tone. Hear the shouts of command where soldiers drill outside the gate of every German city: what arrogance, what high-handedness, what icy scorn can be heard in all this shouting! Could the Germans really be a musical people?

It is certain that they are now militarizing themselves in the tone of their language; it is probable that, being trained to speak in a military manner, they will eventually come to write in a military manner as well. For habituation to specific tones profoundly affects one's character – people soon have the words and phrases, and eventually even the thoughts which match these tones! Perhaps they already write like officers; perhaps I read too little of what is now written in Germany. But one thing I know for certain: the German public declarations which are also heard abroad are not inspired by German music, but by this new tone of tasteless arrogance. In almost every speech of the pre-eminent German statesman, even when he lets himself be heard through his imperial mouthpiece,[44] there is an accent which foreigners' ears reject with disgust; but the Germans endure it, for the Germans endure – themselves.

105
The Germans as Artists

When for once a German actually works himself into a passion (and not, as is usual, into the mere willingness to be passionate), he then comports himself as he must, and gives no further thought to his comportment. The truth, however, is that he then comports himself rather awkwardly and unattractively, and as if without rhythm or melody; so that spectators are embarrassed or disturbed as a result, and nothing more – *unless* he rises to the sublime and the enraptured state of which many passions are capable. Then even the German becomes *beautiful*! The presentiment *of the height at which* beauty begins to pour its magic even over Germans impels German artists to the heights and beyond, and to excesses of passion: they consequently have a truly profound longing to get beyond, or at least to look beyond this unattractiveness and awkwardness – towards a better, lighter, sunnier, more Southern world. And thus their spasms are often merely indications that they would like to *dance*: these poor bears in whom hidden nymphs and satyrs – and sometimes even higher divinities – live and move and have their being!

106
Music as Advocate

'I am thirsting for a master of composition', said an innovator
to his disciple, 'who would adopt my ideas by following my
example and subsequently express them in his own language:
that way I will be better able to penetrate men's ears and hearts.
With tones, you can seduce people to every error and every
truth: who could refute a tone?' 'So you would like to be considered *irrefutable*?', asked the disciple. The innovator replied,
'I would like the seed to become a tree. In order for a doctrine
to become a tree, it must be believed for a good long while; in
order for it to be believed, it must be considered irrefutable. The
tree needs storms and doubts and worms and wickedness, so
that it will make manifest the nature and strength of its seed; let
it break if it is not strong enough! But a seed is never refuted –
merely destroyed!' When he had said this, his disciple cried out
impetuously, 'But I believe in your cause, and consider it so
strong that I will say everything I can think of against it.'
    The innovator chuckled and wagged his finger at him. He
went on to say, 'This kind of discipleship is best, but it is dangerous, and not every kind of doctrine can withstand it.'

107
Our Ultimate Gratitude towards Art

Had we not countenanced the arts and invented this sort of cult
of the untrue, we could not abide the insight now furnished by
science that everything is untrue and mendacious, that delusion
and error are conditions of cognitive and conscious existence.
Our own sense of *honesty* would have left nothing but disgust
and suicide in its wake. Now, however, our honesty is a coun-
tervailing power which helps us to avoid such consequences –
namely, art as the *willingness* to be deceived. We do not always
prevent our eyes from rounding off and poetically completing
things; and then it is no longer the eternal imperfection that we
carry across the river of becoming – for it is a *goddess* that we
intend to carry, and we are proud and childlike in rendering

this service. As an aesthetic phenomenon existence is still *bearable* to us;[45] and through art, we are given the eye and hand and above all the good conscience to be *able* to make ourselves into such phenomena. We must occasionally take a rest from ourselves by artistically distancing ourselves from ourselves, by gazing at ourselves, or down upon ourselves, by laughing *at* ourselves or weeping *over* ourselves; we must discover the *hero*, and likewise the *fool*, that is within our passion for knowledge; we must now and then rejoice in our folly, that we may continue to rejoice in our wisdom! And precisely because we are, in the final analysis, such weighty and serious men, more weights than men, nothing does us so much good as the *fool's cap and bells*: we especially need them when we are alone with ourselves – we need every kind of exuberant, soaring, dancing, mocking, childish and blessed art, lest we lose our *freedom*, our ability to stand *above* things, which our ideal demands of us. It would be a form of *backsliding* for us, especially given our excitable honesty, were we to lapse back into morality for the sake of the extremely rigorous demands which we here make upon ourselves, becoming virtuous monsters and scarecrows in the process. We should also be *able* to stand *above* morality; and not only stand with the anxious rigidity of the man who fears that at any moment he may slip and fall, but to soar and play above it as well! And to that end, how could we do without art, without the fool? For if you are in any way still *ashamed* of yourselves, you are not one of us!

BOOK III

New Struggles

After the Buddha died, people showed his shadow for centuries afterwards in a cave – a monstrous and unearthly shadow.[1] God is dead;[2] but given the ways of men, perhaps for millennia to come there will be caves in which His shadow will be shown.

And we – we still have to subdue His shadow!

109
Let Us Beware!

Let us beware of thinking that the world is a living being. To where would it spread? With what would it nourish itself? How could it grow and multiply? We have a pretty good idea what the organic is; and we are supposed to reinterpret something unspeakably derivative, late, rare and accidental, something we only perceive on the surface of the earth, into something essential, universal and eternal, as do those who call the universe an organism? That disgusts me. Let us beware of believing that the universe is a machine; it is certainly not constructed for any one purpose; we do it too much honour with the word 'machine'. Let us beware of presupposing that something as perfectly shaped as the cyclical movements of our solar system obtains at all times and places; indeed a glance at the Milky Way raises doubts as to whether there are not much rougher and more contradictory movements there, and even stars with eternally linear paths and the like.[3] The astronomical order in which we live is an exception; this order, and the considerable time which it requires, has again made possible that exception of exceptions, the development of organic life. The overall character of the world, however, is from all eternity chaos; not in the sense of a lack of necessity, but rather in the sense of a lack of order, structure, form, beauty, wisdom and whatever else our aesthetically attractive human qualities are called. The failures are by far the most numerous, the exceptions are not the secret purpose; and the whole music box perpetually repeats what should never be called a melody[4] – and finally the very expression 'failure' is already an anthropomorphism which implies censure. But how could we presume to blame or praise the universe! Let us beware of imputing to it heartlessness and irrationality, or their opposites; it is neither perfect, nor beautiful, nor noble, nor wishes to become any of these things; it by no means strives to emulate man! It is by no means subject to our aesthetic and moral judgements! It also has no instinct for self-preservation, indeed, no instincts whatsoever; it also knows no law. Let us beware of saying that there are laws in nature. There are only necessities: there is no one who commands, no one who obeys, and no one who transgresses. When you know that nothing is intentional, then you also know that nothing is accidental; for it is only where there is a world of intentions that the word 'accident' has any meaning. Let us beware of saying that death is the opposite of life. The living is only a species of the dead, and a very rare one at that.

Let us beware of thinking that the world perpetually creates what is new. There are no perpetually enduring substances; matter is as much an error as the god of the Eleatics.[5] But when shall we have done with our caution and care? When will all these shadows of God no longer darken our understanding? When will we have completely demythologized nature? When may we begin to *naturalize* ourselves by means of the pure, newly discovered, newly redeemed nature?

110
Origin of Knowledge

For immense stretches of time the intellect produced nothing but errors; some of them proved useful and conducive to the preservation of the species: whoever hit upon or inherited them was more successful in the struggle on behalf of himself and his offspring. Those erroneous beliefs were continuously passed on until they almost became the common endowment of human nature. Examples include the belief that there are enduring things; that there are identical things; that there are material bodies; that a thing is what it appears to be; that our will is free; that what is good for me is also intrinsically good. It was only very late that the deniers and doubters of such propositions emerged – it was only very late that the truth emerged as the least powerful form of knowledge. It seemed as if we were unable to live with it, our organism was adapted to the opposite; all its higher functions, sensory perceptions, any kind of experience at all, operated with those primordially embodied, fundamental errors. Moreover, even within cognition itself those propositions became the standards according to which 'true' and 'false' were assessed – all the way up to the most abstruse regions of pure logic. Therefore the *strength* of the cognitions did not depend on the degree of truth they possessed, but on their age, their embodiment, their character as conditions of life. Where they seemed to conflict with these conditions, they were never seriously contested; denial and doubt were regarded here as madness. The exceptional thinkers like the Eleatics, who nevertheless espoused and adhered to the opposites of these natural errors, believed that it was also possible to live by these opposites; it was they who invented the sage as the man of immutable, impersonal and universal intuition who is simultaneously the One and the All, with his own faculty for this inverted knowledge; they believed that their knowledge was at the same time the principle of *life*. However, in order to be able to assert all this, they had to *deceive* themselves about their own condition: they had to ascribe to themselves impersonality and permanence without change,

misunderstanding the nature of the mind, denying the dominant role of the instincts in cognition, and in general apprehending
reason as an entirely free and self-originating activity; they
closed their eyes to the fact that they too had arrived at their
propositions out of opposition to common sense, or from a
desire for tranquillity, exclusive possession or domination.

The subtler development of honesty and scepticism eventually made these men impossible: their lives and their judgements
also proved to be dependent on the primordial instincts and
fundamental errors implicit in all sentient existence. The subtler
honesty and scepticism arose wherever two opposing propositions appeared to be equally *applicable* to life, because both
were compatible with the fundamental errors; under these circumstances, a dispute could arise as to which proposition had
the higher or lower degree of *utility* for life. This subtler honesty and scepticism likewise arose whenever new propositions
were shown to be, if not useful, at least not harmful; they could
then be permitted expression as a form of intellectual playful-
ness, something innocent and delightful, like all games.
Gradually the human brain was filled with such judgements
and convictions; and so there arose from this tangled skein
a ferment, struggle and lust for power. Not only utility and
delight, but all sorts of impulses took part in the struggle over
'truths': intellectual struggle became an occupation, an attraction, a vocation, a duty, an honour – knowledge and the pursuit
of truth eventually became needs in their own right. From that
moment forward, not only belief and conviction, but also the
tendency to examine, deny, distrust and contradict became a
power; all the 'evil' instincts were subordinated to the desire
for knowledge and placed in its service. These instincts then
acquired the prestige of the permitted, the honoured, the useful, and eventually the look and the innocence of the *good*. The
desire for knowledge thus became a part of life itself, and, as
life, it became a continually growing power; until finally the
desire for knowledge and those primordial, fundamental errors
confronted each other, both as life, both as power, both in the
same man. The thinker is now the being in whom the impulse
towards truth and those life-preserving errors struggle for the

first time, now that the impulse towards truth has also been *proven* to be a life-preserving power. The importance of this struggle is paramount; all else is a matter of indifference. I am raising the ultimate question concerning the conditions of life, and making an initial attempt to answer it by experiment. How far does truth admit of embodiment? That is the question, that is the experiment.

I I I
Origin of the Logical

How did logic arise in the human head? Doubtless, out of illogic, a domain which must originally have been immense. Countless beings who inferred differently from the way in which we do now perished; and yet they may have come nearer to the truth! For example, whoever was not able to identify the 'same' often enough with regard to food or predators, whoever subsumed too slowly or cautiously, had less chance of survival than those who responded to similar cases by immediately guessing that they were identical. The prevailing tendency, however, was to treat similar cases as identical – an illogical tendency, since nothing is identical – and it was this which created the initial foundation for logic. In order for the notion of substance to arise (something indispensable to logic, although in the strictest sense nothing real corresponds to it), for the longest time it was likewise necessary for the mutability of things not to be seen, not to have been perceived; those creatures who did not see with exactitude had an advantage over those who saw everything 'in flux'. By itself, a sceptical tendency, the exercise of excessive caution in making inferences, is extremely dangerous. No living creature would have survived unless the opposite tendency – the tendency to affirm rather than to suspend judgement, to err and invent rather than to wait and see, to accept rather than to reject, to jump to conclusions rather than to do justice – had not grown extraordinarily strong.

The course of logical thought and inference in our brain as it is now corresponds to a succession of impulses and a struggle between them, which in themselves and taken individually are all very illogical and unjust; on the whole, we only experience the result of this struggle, so quickly and imperceptibly does this primordial process now take place within us.

112
Cause and Effect

'Explanation' is what we call it; but 'description' is what distinguishes us from earlier stages of knowledge and science. We describe better – we explain just as little as our predecessors. We have discovered a complicated process where the more naive investigators of earlier periods saw only two things, 'cause' and 'effect', as they were called; we have done no more than perfect the image of becoming; we have not really fathomed what lies behind it. With each instance, the series of 'causes' lies before us that much more completely; we infer that such-and-such must first precede in order for something else to follow – but in so doing we have *grasped* nothing. For example, the qualitative aspect of every chemical process seems just as 'miraculous' as motion does; nobody has ever 'explained' impact. How could we explain anything! We operate only with things which do not exist, with lines, surfaces, bodies, atoms, divisible times, divisible spaces – how can we expect to explain anything when we start by making everything into an *image*, into our image! At most, we can regard science as humanizing things as faithfully as possible; we always learn to describe ourselves more accurately by describing things and their successions. Cause and effect: such a duality probably never exists; actually, what we have here is a continuum out of which we have isolated a few pieces; just as we always perceive motion as isolated points, and therefore do not really see it, but infer it. The suddenness with which many effects emerge leads us into error; but it is only sudden for us. There is an infinite multiplicity of processes in that second of suddenness which escape us. An intellect which could see cause and effect as a continuum, and not arbitrarily divided and dismembered as we do, an intellect which could see the flow of events – would reject the notion of cause and effect, and would deny all conditionality.

113
On the Doctrine of Poisons

So many things have to come together for scientific thought to arise; and all of these requisite abilities had to be individually invented, exercised and cultivated! But in isolation, they have very often had a completely different effect from that which they have now, when they are confined to scientific thought and keep each other in check – they have acted as poisons, for example, the doubting impulse, the denying impulse, the wait-and-see impulse, the collecting impulse, the disintegrating impulse. Many hecatombs of men were sacrificed before these impulses learned to acknowledge each other's existence and regard themselves as functions of one organizing power in one man! And how far are we still from a time when the powers of art and the practical wisdom of life join forces with the rigours of scientific thought! Were they to do so, a superior organic system might be formed in relation to which the scholar, the physician, the artist and the legislator as we now know them will seem like relics of a bygone era!

114
The Extent of the Moral

When we see a new image, we immediately interpret it with the aid of all the prior experiences we have ever had, in accordance with the *degree* of our honesty and fair-mindedness. There are no experiences which are not at the same time moral experiences, not even in the realm of sense-perception.

115
The Four Errors

Man has been educated by his errors: first, he always only saw himself partially; second, he ascribed to himself fictitious qualities; third, he felt himself to possess a false superiority over animals and nature; fourth, he devised ever-new tables of goods,[6] and for a time accepted them as eternal and unconditional, so that now this, now that human impulse or condition

was given pride of place and was ennobled as a result of this
assessment. When we subtract the effect of these four errors,
we also subtract humaneness, humanity and 'human dignity'.

116
Gregarious Instinct

Wherever we find a morality we find a value judgement and a
hierarchy of human impulses and activities. These value judgements and hierarchies are always the expression of the needs of a
community or herd; that which is to *its* greatest advantage – and
its second-greatest, and third-greatest – is also the supreme
standard by which the value of every individual is measured.
Morality teaches the individual to become a function of the herd,
and to ascribe value to himself only as a function. Since the conditions for the preservation of one community are quite different
from those of another community, there have been quite different moralities; and with respect to substantial transformations of
herds, communities, states and societies yet to come, we can pre-
dict that there will continue to be quite divergent moralities.
Morality is the gregarious instinct in the individual.

117
The Herd's Pang of Conscience

In the longest and remotest ages of mankind the pang of conscience was quite different from the way it is today. Today we
only feel responsible for what we intend and do, and are proud
of *ourselves*. All our professors of law start with this separate
sense of self and sense of pleasure, as if the source of law had
arisen from this. But for the longest time in mankind's history
there was nothing more terrible to a person than to feel separate. To be alone, to feel separate, neither to obey nor to rule, to
signify individuality – that was not a pleasure but a punishment; one was condemned to 'individuality'. Free-thinking was
regarded as inherently disquieting. While we experience law
and order as constraint and sacrifice, formerly it was egoism
that was considered painful and genuinely distressing. To be

oneself, to judge according to one's own weights and measures –
that was found distasteful. The propensity to do so was considered
madness, for every misery and fear was associated with being
alone. At that time, 'free will' was in close proximity to the bad
conscience: the less independently a man acted, the more the
gregarious instinct expressed itself in his conduct, the less of a
sense of personhood he possessed, the more moral he judged
himself to be. Everything that harmed the herd, whether it was
intended or not, caused in him a pang of conscience – and likewise in his neighbour, and indeed in the whole herd! It is in this
regard that our way of thinking has most changed.

118
Benevolence

Is it virtuous when a cell transforms itself into a function of a
stronger cell? It must. And is it evil when the stronger assimi-
lates the weaker? It also must: it is necessary, for it has to
have ample replenishment and wishes to regenerate itself. We
therefore have to distinguish between two different forms of
benevolence, depending upon whether it is the stronger or the
weaker who shows it; in the former case, it is an expression of
the impulse to appropriate, and in the latter, of the impulse to
submit. In the strong, joy is accompanied by desire; the strong
wish to transform something to a function. In the weak, joy is
accompanied by the wish to be desired; the weak would like to
become a function.

Pity is essentially an instance of the former, an agreeable
excitation of the appropriative impulse at the sight of the weak;
it must be remembered, however, that 'strong' and 'weak' are
relative terms.

119
It's Not Altruism!

I see in many people an excess of energy and enthusiasm in
their desire to be a function; they urge themselves to it, and
have the keenest scent for precisely those positions in which

they can be functions. Among such persons are those women who transform themselves into the function of a man, specifically, the function which is more weakly developed in him, becoming his purse, or his politics, or his sociability. Such beings do best when they attach themselves to a foreign body; if they do not succeed in doing so they become angry, irritable and devour themselves.

120
Health of the Soul

In order for Ariston of Chios'[7] popular medical adage 'Virtue is the health of the soul' to be at all useful, it would have to be amended to read, 'Your virtue is the health of your soul.' For nothing is inherently healthy, and every attempt to define things in this way has failed miserably. The determination of *what* health means even just for your *body* depends upon your aim, your horizon, your strengths, your impulses, your errors, and especially the ideals and fantasies of your soul. Thus there are innumerable kinds of physical health; the more we disregard the dogma of 'human equality' and allow the unique and incomparable to rear its head, the more the very idea of normal health, along with the idea of a normal diet, the normal course of a disease, etc. must be abandoned by our physicians. Only then would it be time to turn our thoughts to the health and disease of the *soul*, and to postulate that the peculiar virtue of each person is their health, bearing in mind all the while that the health of one soul could very well look like the opposite of the health of another. Ultimately, the great question would still remain open as to whether we could *do without* disease for the development of our virtue, and especially whether our thirst for knowledge and self-knowledge would not require a diseased soul as much as a healthy one: in short, whether the exclusive desire for health is not a mere prejudice, a mark of cowardice, and perhaps even the subtlest form of backwardness and barbarism.

121

Life No Argument

We have arranged for ourselves a world in which we can live –
by assuming the existence of bodies, lines, surfaces, causes and
effects, motion and rest, form and content; without these articles of faith nobody could now bear to live. But for all that
they remain unproven. Life is no argument; error might be one
of the conditions of life.

122

Moral Scepticism in Christianity

Even Christianity has made a great contribution to enlightenment: it taught moral scepticism in a very forceful and effective
manner, accusing and deprecating[8] with untiring patience and
subtlety; it annihilated every individual's belief in his own 'virtue'; it wiped off the face of the earth those celebrated prigs of
whom there were so many in antiquity, men who, confident in
their own perfection, strutted about with all the dignity of a
matador. When we now read antiquity's books about morality,
for example those of Seneca or Epictetus, after being trained in
this Christian school of scepticism, we feel an amused sense of
superiority, and are full of hidden insights and overviews; it
seems to us as if a child were speaking to an old man, or a
beautiful young enthusiast to La Rochefoucauld: we know better what virtue is! Eventually, however, we have also applied this
very scepticism to all *religious* states and processes, such as sin,
repentance, grace and holiness, and have allowed the worm to
burrow so deeply that we now have the same sense of subtle
superiority and insight while reading any Christian books: we
also know better what the religious sentiments are! And the
time has come to know them well, to describe them well, for
the pious of the old faith are also dying out – let us save their
likeness and type, if only for the sake of knowledge!

123
Knowledge More Than a Means

Even *without* the passion for knowledge, science would still be
promoted; science has hitherto grown and matured without it.
The belief in science, the prejudice in its favour which now
dominates every state in Europe (just as it had once dominated
the Church), rests, in essence, on the fact that this unconditional inclination and impulse is so rarely present, and that
science is *not* considered a passion, but a condition and an
'ethic'. Indeed, for some, curiosity, the *amour-plaisir* of knowledge, is enough; for others, *amour-vanité* and force of habit,
along with the ulterior motive of honours and bread, are
enough; for many, an abundance of leisure, with nothing better to do than to read, collect, organize, observe and recount,
is enough – their 'scientific impulse' is *boredom*. Once, Pope
Leo X (in his letter to Beroaldus) sang the praises of science: he
described it as the most beautiful ornament and the greatest
glory of human life, a noble occupation in prosperity or adversity.[9] 'Without it,' he says finally, 'all human undertakings
should be deprived of a firm footing – even with it they are
changeable and uncertain enough!' But in the end this somewhat sceptical pope, like all other ecclesiastical apologists for
science, keeps his counsel about it. While we may discern in
his words a willingness to place science even above the arts,
which is remarkable enough in so great a patron of them,[10]
ultimately it is only graciousness which prevents him from mentioning what he places high above even science: the 'revealed
truth' and the 'eternal salvation of the soul' – and what are
ornament, glory, preservation, or life's uncertainties to him,
compared to that? 'Science is something secondary, nothing
ultimate or unconditional; it is no object of passion' – this
remained Leo's judgement: the actual Christian judgement
about science! In antiquity, the appreciation of science and the
sense of its dignity were diminished by the fact that, even
among its most ardent disciples, the pursuit of *virtue* came
first. People believed that they had given knowledge the highest

praise when they celebrated it as the best means to virtue. It is something new in history that knowledge wants to be more than a means.

124
In the Horizon of the Infinite

We have left dry land and put out to sea! We have burned the bridge behind us – what is more, we have burned the land behind us! Well, little ship, look out! Beside you is the ocean. True, it does not always roar, and sometimes it is spread out like silk and gold and a gentle reverie, but there will be hours when you realize that it is infinite, and that there is nothing more terrible than infinity. Oh, poor bird that felt free, and now beats against the bars of this cage! Alas, if homesickness should befall you, as if there had been more *freedom* there – when there is no longer any 'land'!

125
The Madman

Have you not heard of that madman who lit a lantern in the bright morning light, ran to the marketplace and shouted incessantly, 'I seek God! I seek God!'? As there were many people standing together who did not believe in God, he caused much amusement. 'Is He lost?', asked one. 'Did He wander off like a child?', asked another. 'Or is He hiding? Is He afraid of us?' 'Has He gone to sea? Has He emigrated?' And in this manner they shouted and laughed. Then the madman leaped into their midst, and looked at them with piercing eyes and cried, 'Where did God go? I will tell you! *We have killed Him –* you and I! We are all His murderers! But how did we do this? How were we able to drink up the sea? Who gave us the sponge to wipe away the whole horizon? What did we do when we unchained this earth from its sun? Where is it heading? Where are we heading? Away from all suns? Are we not constantly falling? Backwards, sidewards, forwards, in all directions? Is there still an above and below? Are we not straying as through an infinite nothingness? Do we not feel the breath of empty space? Has it not become colder? Is night not falling evermore? Mustn't lanterns be lit in the morning? Do we hear nothing yet of the the the noise of the gravediggers who are burying God? Do we smell nothing yet of the divine putrefaction? For even gods putrefy! God is dead! God remains dead! And we have killed Him! How shall we, the most murderous of all murderers, ever console ourselves? The holiest and mightiest thing that the world has ever known has bled to death under our knives – who will wash this blood clean from our hands? With what water might we be purified? What lustrations, what sacred games shall we have to invent? Is not the greatness of this deed too great for us? Must we not become gods ourselves, if only to appear worthy of it? There has never been a greater deed – and because of it, whoever is born after us belongs to a higher history than all history hitherto!'

Here the madman fell silent and looked again at his listeners; they too were silent and stared at him, baffled. At last he threw his lantern on the ground, so that it broke into pieces and went out. 'I have come too early,' he then said, 'this is not yet the right time. This tremendous event is still on its way and headed towards them – word of it has not yet reached men's ears. Even after they are over and done with, thunder and lightning take time, the light of the stars takes time, and deeds too take time, before they can be seen and heard. This deed is further away from them than the farthest star – *and yet they have done it themselves!*'

It is said that on that very day, the madman made his way into various churches, and there intoned his requiem *aeternam deo*. When led out and called to account, he always replied, 'What are these churches now, if not the tombs and sepulchres of God?'

126
Mystical Explanations

Mystical explanations are considered deep; the truth is that they are not even shallow.

127
After-Effect of the Most Ancient Religiosity

Each thoughtless person believes that the will is uniquely effective, that volition is something simple, absolutely given, underived
and intrinsically intelligible. He is convinced that when he
does anything, for example delivers a blow, it is he who strikes,
and that he struck because he *intended* to strike. He does not
notice a problem here; rather, the experience of *volition* is sufficient not only to persuade him that there is such a thing as
cause and effect, but to instil in him the belief that he *understands* that relationship. Of the mechanism that lies behind
the event, and the hundreds of complex and subtle activities
which must transpire before the strike can take place, and likewise the inability of the will to achieve even the smallest
portion of them by itself – of all this he knows nothing. To
him, the will is a magically effective power: the belief in volition as the cause of effects is the belief in magically effective
powers. Now originally, whenever man saw an event take
place, he believed that a will was the cause, and that persons,
volitional beings, were somewhere in the background, bringing it about – the very idea that a mechanism was involved was
far from his mind. But because for immense periods of time
man only believed in persons (and not in matter, forces, things
and so on), the belief in cause and effect has become his fundamental belief which he applies to everything that happens – even
now he still does so instinctively, acceding to an atavistic belief
of the oldest pedigree. The propositions 'no effect without a
cause' and 'every effect is also a cause' appear to be generalizations of much more circumscribed propositions, to wit, 'where
there are effects, there are acts of volition', 'there can only be
effects on volitional beings', 'where there are effects on volitional beings, these are never just purely and passively suffered
with no further effects ensuing from them, but rather, every
form of suffering at the same time stimulates the will (to activity, defence, revenge or retribution)'. In the early history of
mankind, the more general and the more circumscribed propositions were *identical*, the former were not generalizations of

the latter, but rather the latter were meant to *exemplify* the former.

Schopenhauer, with his assumption that being is will, has enthroned a primitive mythology; he seems never to have attempted an analysis of the will, because like everyone he *believed* in the simplicity and immediacy of all volition – while volition is such a well-coordinated mechanism that it frequently escapes all but the most penetrating of observers. Against him, I offer the following propositions. First, in order for the will to arise, an impression of pleasure and pain is necessary. Second, the fact that a vehement stimulus is perceived as pleasure or pain is a matter of the *interpreting* intellect, which for the most part operates unconsciously; one and the same stimulus may be interpreted as pleasure or pain. Third, it is only in intellectual beings that there is pleasure, pain and will; the vast majority of organisms have nothing of the kind.

128
The Value of Prayer

Prayer was invented for those people who never have any thoughts of their own, and to whom spiritual exaltation is unknown, or at least passes unnoticed; what are these people to do in holy places and in those important situations in life where quiet and dignity of some kind are required? So that they at least do not *disturb* others, the wisdom of all founders of religions great and small has been to commend to them formulae of prayer which involve a protracted mechanical labour of the lips, associated with both an effort of the memory and a regular, fixed posture of hands, feet and eyes! They may then, like the Tibetans, ruminate on their 'Oṃ maṇi padme hūṃ' over and over; or, as in Benares, count on their fingers the name of the god Ram Ram Ram (and so on, with or without grace); or honour Vishnu with the recitation of his thousand names, or Allah with his ninety-nine; or make use of prayer wheels and rosaries – the main thing is that they are in a fixed position for a time while performing this labour, and present a tolerable appearance; their manner of prayer was invented for the benefit of the

pious who have thoughts and exaltations of their own. But even
the latter have their weary hours when it does them good to
have recourse to a series of venerable words and sounds and a
mechanical piety to go with them. But supposing that these rare
men – and in every religion, the religious man is an exception –
know how to help themselves, the poor in spirit do not, and to
forbid them their prayerful prattle would mean to take their religion away from them, a fact which Protestantism makes more
and more obvious all the time. What religion wants from such
people is that they should *keep still* with their eyes, hands, legs
and every other part of their bodies; thus for a time they become
beautiful to behold, and – more nearly human.

129
The Conditions for God

'God Himself cannot do without wise men', said Luther,[11] and
not without reason; but 'Still less can God do without unwise
men' – that is something the good Luther did *not* say!

130
A Dangerous Determination

The Christian determination to find the world ugly and bad
has made the world ugly and bad.

131
Christianity and Suicide

From the very beginning, Christianity has taken advantage of
the tremendous longing for suicide as an instrument of power;
it permitted only two forms of suicide, invested them with the
highest dignity and the highest hopes, and forbade all others in
a dreadful manner. But martyrdom, and the gradual disem-
bodiment of the ascetic, were allowed.

132
Against Christianity

It is no longer our reason which decides us against Christianity, but our taste.

133
Principles

An unavoidable hypothesis of which mankind must avail itself again and again, is in the long run more powerful than the best-believed belief in something untrue (like Christian belief). In the long run: here, that means a hundred thousand years.

134
Pessimists as Victims

When a profound dislike of existence gets the upper hand, what usually comes to light is some long-standing great error in a people's diet, and the after-effects that result from it. The spread of Buddhism (*not* its origin) is thus to a considerable extent dependent on the excessive and almost exclusive consumption of rice by the Indians, and on the general atony that results therefrom. Perhaps modern European discontent should be viewed as the result of the fact that, thanks to the influence of Germanic tendencies, so many people in the Middle Ages were given to drink; the Middle Ages, that is, the intoxication of Europe.

The German dislike of life is essentially a winter malady, which includes the effects of cellar air and furnace fumes in German living quarters.

135
Origin of Sin

Sin, as it is now experienced wherever Christianity prevails or once prevailed, is a Jewish sentiment and a Jewish invention; and with respect to this background, which all Christian morality shares, Christianity was in fact bent on 'Judaizing' the whole world. To what an extent it succeeded at this in Europe is most keenly felt in the degree to which we find Greek antiquity – a world without the sense of sin – strange even now, despite our favourable attitude towards assimilating and incorporating it, something which whole generations and many distinguished individuals have not lacked. 'Only when you *repent* is God gracious to you' – a Greek would have found this laughable or offensive; he would say, 'slaves may harbour such sentiments'. We are to imagine here a mighty, indeed an almighty being, who is nevertheless prone to vengeance; his power is so great that no injury can be inflicted upon him except where a point of honour is involved. Every sin is an affront to his dignity, a *crimen laesae majestatis divinae*[12] – and nothing more! Contrition, degradation, grovelling – this is the one and only condition with which his grace is associated; it leads to the restoration of his divine honour! Whether or not some other injury is done by the sin, whether or not the seeds of some profound and growing calamity are sown by it, which, like a disease, takes hold of one man after another and squeezes the life out of him, this vainglorious Oriental potentate in heaven is blithely indifferent; sin is an offence against him, not against mankind! And when God bestows His grace upon a man, He also bestows upon him this blithe indifference to the natural consequences of sin. God and mankind are regarded here as so separated, as so opposed, that in essence sin against the latter is entirely impossible – every deed should be considered *only with a view to its supernatural consequences*, not its natural ones: that is how Jewish sentiment would have it, for Jewish sentiment regards everything natural as inherently unworthy. The *Greeks*, on the other hand, seemed to think that sacrilege too could have dignity – even theft, as with Prometheus, even the slaughter of cattle as the expression of an insane jealousy, as with Ajax; in their need to impute some dignity to sacrilege, to make dignity at least some part of it, they invented *tragedy* – an art and a pleasure which, despite all their poetic gifts and their tendency towards the sublime, remained profoundly alien to the Jews.

136
The Chosen People

The Jews regard themselves as the chosen people among the nations because they are the moral genius among the nations. This moral genius, however, is ultimately due to the fact that, more than any other people, they regard their own humanity with *profound contempt*. In this respect they resemble the French nobility under Louis XIV, and, indeed, the pleasure they take in their divine and holy sovereign resembles the pleasure the French nobility took in their own king. After allowing themselves to be divested of all their power and prerogatives, these nobles became contemptible in their own eyes. In order not to feel this, in order to be able to forget it, they required a king of splendour, authority and power *without equal*, to whom only they had access. By according themselves this privilege, they placed themselves on the same level as the court, and from up there looked down upon everything as beneath them, as contemptible, thereby transcending their ticklish consciences. And so they deliberately built the edifice of royal power higher and higher into the clouds, using the last bricks of their own power to do so.

137
Spoken in Parable

A Jesus Christ was only possible in a Jewish landscape – I mean a landscape over which the gloomy and sublime thundercloud of Jehovah's wrath continually hung. Here alone would a sudden and unexpected ray of sunshine that penetrates the horribly constant and pervasive daylight darkness be regarded as a miracle of 'love', as the light of the most unmerited 'grace'. Here alone could Christ dream of his rainbow and his celestial ladder on which God descended to man; everywhere else the clear weather and sunshine were considered regular and everyday occurrences.

138
Christ's Error

The founder of Christianity thought that people suffered from nothing so much as from their sins – that was his error, the error of someone who felt himself to be without sin, and who thus lacked experience in this respect! And so his soul was filled with that prodigious, fanciful pity for a particular kind of distress that was rare even among his own people, the very people who invented sin in the first place!

But Christians have always known how to provide their master with a justification after the fact; they hallowed his error by making it become the 'truth'.

139
Colour of the Passions

For men like the Apostle Paul, it is a part of their nature to have an evil eye for the passions; they come to be acquainted with only the filthy, perverted and pathetic aspects of them – their ideal impulse, therefore, strives for the annihilation of the passions; they see the divine as completely dispassionate. The Greeks, in a manner quite different from Paul and the Jews, directed their ideal impulse precisely towards the passions, and loved, elevated, gilded and deified them; apparently, they not only felt happier when passionate, but more pure and more divine than ordinarily.

Well, what about the Christians? Were they not trying to become Jews? Is that not what they became?

140
Too Jewish

If God wanted to become the object of our love, then He ought to have forgone judging and justice first – for a judge, even a merciful one, is no object of love. The founder of Christianity displayed an insufficiently refined sensibility in these matters – being a Jew.

141
Too Oriental

What? A God who loves men provided they believe in Him, and
who casts terrible glances and hurls terrible threats at anyone
who does not believe in this love? What? A qualified love as the
feeling of an almighty God? A love which cannot even master a
sense of honour and a petulant desire for revenge? How terribly
Oriental it all is! 'If I love you, what concern is that of yours?'[13]
is already a sufficient criticism of the whole of Christianity.

142
Incense

Buddha says: 'Do not flatter your benefactor!'[14] Repeat this
saying in a Christian church – and it immediately cleanses the
air of everything Christian.

143
The Greatest Advantage of Polytheism

For the individual to establish his *own* ideal and derive from it
his own laws, his own pleasures and his own rights – in the
past that was probably regarded as the most monstrous of all
human aberrations, and as inherently idolatrous; in fact, the
few who have dared to do so have always needed to apologize
to themselves, usually in the following manner: 'Not I! Not I!
But rather *a god* working through me!' It was in the wonderful
art and ability to create gods – in polytheism – that this impulse
could discharge itself, that it purified, perfected and ennobled
itself; for originally this impulse was rather commonplace and
unattractive, not unlike stubbornness, rebelliousness or envy.
Formerly, hostility towards this desire for an ideal of one's
own was the law of every morality. There was only one type
and standard: 'man' – and every people believed itself to
be this type, to be in *possession* of this standard. But in a
distant heaven above and beyond oneself, one could discern a

multiplicity of standards; to worship a particular god was not to deny or blaspheme against the other gods! It was here that individuals were first permitted, that the rights of individuals were first honoured. The invention of gods, heroes and super-human beings[15] of all kinds, as well as of quasi-human and subhuman beings – dwarfs, fairies, centaurs, satyrs, demons, devils – was an inestimable preliminary exercise in upholding the interests and prerogatives of the individual: the freedom one allowed a god with respect to other gods, one eventually gave to oneself with respect to laws, customs and neighbours. Monotheism, by contrast, is the inexorable consequence of the doctrine that there is only one type of man, and only one standard appropriate to him – and therefore the belief that there can be only one god for him, apart from whom there are only false gods. Such a conception was perhaps the greatest danger confronting mankind so far, because it threatened man with the same stagnation at which most other species of ani-mals have already arrived, in that all of them believe in one type of animal and one ideal for their species, and have con-clusively translated this morality of custom into flesh and blood. In polytheism, man's free-thinking and 'poly-thinking' is prefigured – to wit, his ability to create for himself new eyes, his own eyes, eyes which are ever newer, ever more his own. For this reason, man is the only animal for whom there are no eternal horizons or perspectives.

144
Religious Wars

The thing in which the masses have displayed the greatest degree of progress hitherto is religious war; for it proves that the masses have begun to treat concepts with respect. Religious wars arise only when common reason has been refined by dis-putes between sects over the finer points of doctrine; so that even the rabble begins to quibble and regards trifles as import-ant, even considering it possible that the 'eternal salvation of the soul' may hang on small differences between concepts.

145
Danger of Vegetarians

The enormous prevalence of the consumption of rice has led to the use of opium and narcotics, in the same way that the enormous prevalence of the consumption of potatoes has led to the use of spirits – but it also leads to subtler after-effects with respect to modes of thought and sensibility which have a narcotic effect. This is consistent with the fact that those who promote narcotic modes of thought and sensibility, like those Indian sages, praise a purely vegetarian diet, and would like to make it a law for the masses; in this way they hope to create and increase a need which *they* are then in a position to satisfy.

146
German Hopes

Let us not forget that the names of peoples are usually epithets. The Tartars, for example, are called 'the dogs' – thus were they christened by the Chinese. 'Deutschen' (Germans) originally meant 'the heathen', which is what the Goths after their conversion called the great mass of their unbaptized kinsmen, as indicated by their translation of the Septuagint, in which the heathen are referred to with the word which in Greek means 'the nations': see Ulfilas.[16]

It might still be possible for the Germans to make an honorific out of the old epithet, by becoming the first *non-Christian* nation of Europe; it does them honour that Schopenhauer thought this a task for which they were eminently suited. Were they to do so, then the work of *Luther* would be brought to completion, for he taught them to be un-Roman, and to say: 'Here *I* stand! *I* cannot do otherwise!'[17]

147
Question and Answer

What is the first thing primitive peoples accept from Europeans? Liquor and Christianity, the European narcotics.

And from what do they most quickly perish? The European narcotics.

148
Where Reformations Originate

At a time when the Church was highly corrupt, it was least corrupt in Germany, which is why the Reformation originated there, as an indication that even the beginnings of corruption were felt to be intolerable. Comparatively speaking, no people had ever been more Christian than the Germans of Luther's day; in Germany the bloom of Christian culture was ready to burst forth with hundredfold glory – only one more night was needed, but this one night brought the storm which put an end to everything.

149
The Failure of Reformations

It is a testimony to the superior culture of the Greeks that even in quite early times, several attempts to found new Greek religions failed; it suggests that from the very beginning, there must have been many different kinds of individuals in Greece, whose various kinds of distress could not be remedied by a single prescription of faith and hope. Pythagoras and Plato, perhaps even Empedocles, and, already much earlier, the Orphic rhapsodists, set out to found new religions; and the first two in particular had such natural gifts in this regard, not to mention the temperament and disposition for it, that their failure is nothing short of astonishing: all that they accomplished was to found sects. Every time that the reformation of an entire people fails and only sects rear their heads, we may infer that the people already contained various kinds of men, and had begun to break free from the coarser gregarious instincts and from the morality of custom – a condition fraught with significance, one in which everything remains in a state of suspense, a condition which we are accustomed to disparage as one of moral corruption and decline, but which in fact prefigures the ripening of the egg and the imminent breaking of the eggshell. The fact that Luther's Reformation succeeded in the North is a sign that Northern Europe had lagged behind the South, and as yet was only acquainted with needs of nearly the same kind and colour; and there would have been no conversion to Christianity in Europe at all if the culture of antiquity in the South had not been gradually barbarized by an excessive admixture of Germanic barbarian blood, and thereby forfeited its cultural superiority. The more general and absolute the influence of an individual, or the idea of an individual, the more similar and lowly must be the mass upon which it is exercised; while the opposing efforts betray opposing internal requirements, which also wish to prevail and gratify themselves. Conversely, one may always infer that a culture is actually superior when powerful and ambitious natures produce only a small and sectarian effect; this also applies to the individual arts and the fields of knowledge. Where there is ruling, there are masses, and where there are masses, there is a need for slavery. Where there is slavery, individuals are but few, and have the gregarious instincts and the conscience against them.

150
Criticism of Saints

If we want to have a virtue, is it really necessary to have it in its most brutal form? This is how the Christian saints wanted and needed their virtues. The only thing which rendered their lives endurable was the thought that everyone would be overwhelmed with a sense of self-contempt at the sight of their virtue. A virtue with such an effect I call brutal.

151
Of the Origin of Religion

Metaphysical need is not the origin of religions, as Schopenhauer would have it,[18] but only a *later offshoot* of them. Under the influence of religious ideas we have become accustomed to the conception of 'another world' that lies behind, beneath or beyond our own, and feel an uncomfortable sense of emptiness and privation as a result of the destruction of our religious delusions – and 'another world' springs from this feeling once more, only now it is no longer a religious world, but a metaphysical one. However, that which led to the assumption of 'another world' in primitive times was *not* a drive or a need, but a kind of intellectual confusion, an *error* in the interpretation of certain natural processes.

152
The Greatest Change

The light in which we view things, the colours which we lend to them have all changed. We no longer quite understand how men of old understood the most familiar and commonplace things – for example, daytime and wakefulness; because of their belief in dreams they viewed wakefulness in a different light. And likewise the whole of life, with its reflection of death and death's significance; our 'death' is an altogether different death. All experiences shone differently, because a god shone forth from them; all decisions and glimpses of the distant future as well, because they had oracles, and secret portents, and believed in prophecy. 'Truth' was perceived differently, because formerly a madman could be regarded as its mouthpiece – something which makes *us* shudder or laugh. Every injustice made a different impression, because one feared divine retribution, and not only a civil penalty or a bad reputation. What was joy in an age when one believed in the devil and tempter! What was passion when one saw demons lurking everywhere! What was philosophy itself when doubt was felt to be a transgression of the most dangerous kind, and indeed as a crime against eternal love, as distrust of everything good, lofty, pure and merciful!

We have lent new colours to things, we are constantly painting them anew – but what is our more youthful artistry when compared with the *glorious palette* of those Old Masters! I mean those men of old, ancient mankind.

153
Homo Poeta

'To the extent that it is finished, I have single-handedly made this tragedy of tragedies; I have entangled morality with existence so tightly that only a god could unravel them again – as Horace demands![19] Now in the fourth act I have killed all the gods – in the name of morality! What is to become of the fifth act? Where am I to find a tragic resolution? Should I begin to consider a comic resolution?'[20]

154
Different Degrees to Which Life Is Precarious

You know what you experience; you run through life like a drunken man, and occasionally tumble down some stairs. Thanks to your drunkenness, though, you do not break a limb: your muscles are too limp and your head too confused to find the bricks of these stairs as hard as we others do! For us, life is much more precarious: we are made of glass – woe to us if we're *jostled*! And all is lost if we *fall*!

155
What We Lack

We love greatness in nature and it is we who have discovered it; that is because we have no conception of human greatness. With the Greeks it was the reverse: their sense of nature was different from ours.

156
The Most Influential

When a man resists the whole spirit of his age, stops it at the gate and calls it to account, that *must* exert an influence! Whether that is his intention is of no consequence; the thing is that he *can*.

157
Mentiri

Take care! He reflects: soon he will have a lie ready. Whole nations exist at this stage of civilization. After all, consider what the Romans meant by the word *mentiri*![21]

158
An Inconvenient Quality

To find everything deep is an inconvenient quality: it makes us constantly strain our eyes, and in the end we always find more than we wish.

159
Every Virtue Has Its Time

He who is inflexible nowadays often feels remorse because of his honesty; for inflexibility and honesty are virtues which belong to different ages.

160
In Dealings with Virtues

One can be undignified and fawning even towards a virtue.

161
To the Enthusiasts of the Present Age

The ex-priest and the ex-convict are always making false faces; what they want is a face without a past.

But have you ever seen men who know that their faces are a mirror of the future, and who are so polite to you who are enthusiasts of 'the present age' that they make a false face without a future?

162
Egoism

Egoism is the law of perspective for our sensibilities, according to which things close at hand seem large and important, while at a greater distance everything seems to diminish in size and importance.

163
After a Great Victory

The best thing about a great victory is that it deprives the victor of the fear of defeat. 'Why not be defeated for once?', he says to himself, 'I am now rich enough for that.'

164
Those Who Seek Repose

I recognize the spirits which seek repose by the many *dark* objects with which they surround themselves: those who want to sleep darken their chambers, or crawl into a cave.

A hint for those who do not know what they really seek the most, and would like to know!

165
Of the Happiness of the Renouncers

Those who have thoroughly denied themselves something for a
long time will almost imagine, when they accidentally encounter it again, that they have discovered it – and what happiness
there is in being a discoverer! Let us be wiser than the snakes
that lie too long in the same sun.

166
Always in Our Own Company

Everything in nature and history which is my sort of thing
speaks to me, praises me, urges me on and comforts me – other
things I either do not hear, or immediately forget. We are always
only in our own company.

167
Misanthropy and Love

We speak of having had enough of men only when we can no
longer digest them, although our stomachs are full of them.
Misanthropy is the result of an all too greedy philanthropy
and 'anthropophagy' – but who told you to swallow men like
oysters, my dear Prince Hamlet?

168
Of an Invalid

'He is in a bad way!' What does he lack? 'He suffers from a
hunger for praise, and finds no nourishment for it.' Inconceiv-
able! All the world is celebrating him, and sustaining him in
both word and deed! 'Yes, but he has a bad ear for praise.
When a friend praises him it sounds to him as if the friend is
praising himself; when an enemy praises him, it sounds to him
as if the enemy wished to be praised for it; when someone else
praises him – and he is so famous that few remain! – it offends

him that they wish to be neither his friend nor his enemy. He always says, 'What do I care for someone who is able to do justice to me!'

169
Avowed Enemies

Bravery before the enemy is one thing, and bravery elsewhere is another; one can be bold, clear and decisive in public and still be cowardly, confused and indecisive in private. That was how Napoleon judged the 'bravest man' he knew, Murat[22] – from which it follows that avowed enemies may be indispensable to some men, if they are to rise to the level of *their own* virtue, virility and cheerfulness.

170
With the Crowd

So far he has run with the crowd and is its panegyrist; but one day he will be its opponent! For he follows it in the belief that his laziness would not be disappointed: he has not yet learned that the crowd is not lazy enough for him, that it always presses forward, that it does not allow anyone to stand still! And he is so very fond of standing still!

171
Fame

When the gratitude of many to one casts off all shame, the result is fame.

172
The Corrupter of Taste

A: 'You are a corrupter of taste – everybody says so!' B: 'But of course! I corrupt everyone's taste for his party – and no partisan forgives me for that.'

173
Being Profound and Being Thought Profound

Whoever knows that he is profound strives for clarity; whoever would like the crowd to think he is profound strives for obscurity. The reason for this is that the crowd thinks something is profound whenever it cannot see to the bottom of it; it is afraid of the water and hates to get its feet wet.

174
Aloof

Parliamentarianism, that is, public permission to choose between five basic political opinions, curries favour with the crowd who would like to *seem* independent and individual, and like to fight for their opinions. In the end, it is immaterial whether the herd is required to have one opinion, or permitted to have five.

Whoever deviates from those five public opinions, and holds himself aloof from them, always has the whole herd against him.

175
Of Eloquence

Who has possessed the most convincing eloquence thus far? The drumbeat; and as long as kings have this at their command, they will always be the best orators and popular agitators.

176
Pitiable

Poor reigning princes! Suddenly all their rights are turning into claims, and as soon as they do, they begin to sound like pretensions! And if they say 'we', or 'my people', wicked old Europe smiles. Truly, a master of ceremonies of the modern world would not stand on ceremony with them; perhaps he would decree, '*Les souverains rangent aux parvenus.*'[23]

177
On the 'Educational System'

In Germany, superior men lack a great means of education: the laughter of superior men; these do not laugh in Germany.

178
For Moral Enlightenment

The Germans must be talked out of their Mephistopheles, and their Faust as well. These are two moral prejudices against the value of knowledge.

179
Thoughts

Thoughts are the shadows of our feelings – always darker, emptier and simpler than these.

180
A Good Time for Free Spirits

Free spirits take liberties even with regard to science, and for the time being with impunity – as long as the Church is still standing! To that extent, this is a good time for them.

181
Preceding and Following

A: 'Of the two, one always precedes and the other always follows, wherever destiny may lead them. And yet the latter is superior to the other both in intellect and virtue.' B: 'And yet? And yet? That is said for the others' benefit; not for mine, not for ours! *Fit secundum regulam*.'[24]

182
In Solitude

When you live alone you do not speak too loudly, nor do you write too loudly, for fear of that hollow reverberation: criticism by the nymph Echo.

And all voices sound so differently in solitude!

183
The Music of the Best Future[25]

For me, the foremost musician would be the one who was only acquainted with the sorrow of the most profound joy, and no other sorrow; there has never been such a musician.

184
Justice

Better to let oneself be robbed than to surround oneself with scarecrows – that is my taste. And it is, above all, a matter of taste – nothing more!

185
Poor

Today he is poor, not because everything has been taken away from him, but because he has thrown everything away. What does it matter to him? He is accustomed to finding things.

It is the poor who misunderstand his voluntary poverty.

186
Bad Conscience

Everything he does now is good and proper – and yet he has a bad conscience about it all. For the exceptional is his task.

187
Offensiveness in the Presentation

This artist offends me by the way in which he presents his ideas, his very good ideas: so broadly and emphatically, and with such crude rhetorical tricks, as if he were addressing the mob. After devoting some time to his art we always feel as if we have been in 'bad company'.

188
Work

How close are we now to work and worker, even the most leisurely among us! The royal courtesy in the words 'we are all workers'[26] would have been cynical and indecent under Louis XIV.

189
The Thinker

He is a thinker: that is to say, he knows how to make things simpler than they are.

190
Against Praise

A: 'We are only praised by our equals!' B: 'Yes! And he who praises you is saying, "You are my equal!"'

191
Against Many a Defence

One injures a cause in the most perfidious manner by deliberately defending it with erroneous reasons.

192
The Good-Natured

With regard to the good-natured, people whose countenances beam with benevolence, what is it that distinguishes them from other people? What we observe is that they feel comfortable in the presence of a new person, and are quickly enamoured of him; they are therefore well disposed towards him, and their initial judgement is, 'I like him.' In such people there seems to follow, one after another: the desire to appropriate (they are not too particular about the person's worth), rapid appropriation, pleasure in ownership, and then action for the benefit of their new piece of property.

193
Kant's Joke

Kant wished to prove in a way that affronted 'all the world' that 'all the world' was right – that was his secret joke. He wrote against the scholars on behalf of popular prejudice, but for the scholars and not for the people.

194
The 'Candid'

That man probably always acts from ulterior motives; for he is always telling us what they are, and is even generous in doing so.

195
Laughable!

Look at that! He is running away from people – but they follow him anyway, because he is running in *front* of them – they are such sheep!

196
Our Sense of Hearing and Its Limits

We only hear the questions we are able to answer.

197
So Be Careful!

There is nothing we so gladly share with others than the seal
of secrecy – together with what lies under it.

198
Chagrin of the Proud

A proud man is chagrined even at those who help him along;
he casts an evil eye even at the horses of his own carriage.

199
Generosity

With the rich, generosity is often just a kind of shyness.

200
Laughter

Laughter means: to gloat, but with a good conscience.

201
Applause

In applause there is always some kind of noise; even when we
applaud ourselves.

202
A Spendthrift

He still does not have the poverty of the rich man who has already counted his treasure – he expends his spirit with the foolishness of a natural spendthrift.

203
Hic Niger Est[27]

Usually he has no thoughts at all – but in exceptional circumstances he has vile ones.

204
Beggars and Courtesy

'When there is no doorbell, there is no rudeness in knocking on the door with a stone' – so think all beggars and needy people, but nobody seems to agree with them.

205
Need

Need is regarded as the cause of coming into being; in truth, it is often only the effect of having come into being.

206
During the Rain

It rains, and I think of all the poor people who now crowd together with their many cares, and no means of concealing them, each of them ready and willing to wound the other to give themselves a pathetic sense of well-being, even in bad weather.

This, only this, is the poverty of the poor!

207
The Envier

That is an envier – one hopes that he has no children; he would be envious of them, because he can no longer be a child.

208
A Great Man!

Just because someone is 'a great man', we may not infer that he is a man; he may be just a boy, or a chameleon of indeterminate age, or a bewitched female.

209
One Way of Asking for Reasons

There is a way of asking us for our reasons which not only makes us forget our best reasons and leaves us dumbfounded, but even awakens in us a defiance and antipathy towards reason in general: a favourite trick of tyrannical men!

210
Moderation in Diligence

You must not wish to surpass the diligence of your father – that makes you sick.

211
Secret Enemies

To have a secret enemy – that is a moral luxury which even the most high-minded of us can ill afford.

212
Not Letting Oneself Be Deceived

His intellect has bad manners, is hasty and always stammers with impatience; so that we hardly suspect how deep-breathed and broad-chested the soul is in which it is housed.

213
The Way to Happiness

A sage asked of a fool what the way to happiness was. The fool immediately answered as if he had been asked the way to the next town. 'Admire yourself and live on the street!' 'Wait,' cried the sage, 'that is asking too much. It is enough just to admire yourself!' The fool replied: 'But how can you constantly admire unless you constantly despise?'

214
Faith Makes Blessed

Virtue gives happiness and a kind of blessedness only to those who have faith in their virtue – though not to those subtler souls whose virtue consists in a profound distrust of themselves and in all virtue. Ultimately this too is 'faith' that makes 'blessed' – and *not*, mind you, virtue!

215
The Ideal and the Material

You have a noble ideal before you; but are you also a noble enough stone that such a graven image could be formed out of you? And without that – are all your labours not barbaric sculpturing? A blasphemy of your ideal?

216
Danger in the Voice

Those who have a very loud voice are almost incapable of thinking about subtle things.

217
Cause and Effect

We believe in different causes before we see the effect than we do afterwards.

218
My Antipathy

I have no love for people who have to explode like bombs in order to produce an effect, and in whose vicinity one is always in danger of suddenly losing one's hearing – or worse.

219
The Purpose of Punishment

The idea that the purpose of punishment is the edification of those who mete it out – that is the last refuge of its apologists.

220
Sacrifice

Sacrificial animals' thoughts about self-sacrifice are different from those of the spectators; but one has never let them have their say.

221
Consideration

Fathers and sons have much more consideration for each other than mothers and daughters do.

222
Poet and Liar

The poet sees the liar as his brother by milk[28] whose share of the milk he took for himself; thus his brother remains stunted and does not even have a good conscience.

223
Vicariate of the Senses

'We also have eyes to hear with,' said an old confessor who had become deaf, 'and in the land of the blind, the longest-eared man is king.'

224
Animal Criticism

I fear that the animals regard man as a being not unlike themselves, but who has lost his sound animal understanding in an extremely dangerous way – thinking him the silly animal, the laughing animal, the weeping animal, the unfortunate animal.

225
The Natural

'Evil has always made a great sensation! And nature is evil! Therefore, let us be natural!' – thus do mankind's great sensationalists privately conclude, who are all too often counted among great men.

226
The Distrustful and Their Style

We say the strongest things simply, without emphasis, provided that we are surrounded by people who believe in our strength – such an environment teaches 'simplicity of style'. The distrustful lend emphasis to their words; the distrustful lend emphasis to everything.

227
Bad Inference, Bad Shot

He cannot control himself, from which this woman infers that he will be easy for her to control. She casts her hook and line towards him – the poor creature. Soon she will be his slave.

228
Against Mediators

Anyone who wishes to mediate between two resolute thinkers shows themselves to be mediocre: such a person has no eye for the unique; assimilation and identification are characteristic of weak eyes.

229
Stubbornness and Loyalty

The cause has become transparent to him, but he remains an adherent out of sheer stubbornness. He calls it his 'loyalty'.

230
Lack of Reticence

His whole being fails to *convince* – that is because he leaves no good deed undisclosed.

231
The 'Thorough'

Those who are slow to acquire knowledge tend to be of the opinion that slowness is a part of knowledge.

232
Dreams

We dream either not at all, or interestingly.

   We should learn to be awake in the same way – either not at all, or interestingly.

233
The Most Dangerous Point of View

What I do now or leave undone is as important *for all that is to come* as the greatest event of the past; when the effects of our actions are viewed in this immense perspective, all of them are equally great and small.

234
Consolation Speech of a Musician

'Your life does not ring in people's ears: for them your life is silent, and all fineness of melody, all tender resolutions in leading or following, remain concealed from them. It is true that you do not come along the broad street with regimental music – but for all that, these good people have no right to say that your way of life lacks music. Who has ears to hear, let him hear.'[29]

235
Intellect and Character

Many a man reaches his apex through his character, but his intellect does not rise to that level – and with others, it is *vice versa*.

236
To Move the Crowd

Is it not true that the man who wants to move the crowd has
to become an actor who plays himself? Does he not have to
translate himself first into something grotesquely obvious, to
transform his whole personality and cause into a crude and simple performance?

237
The Polite

'He is so polite!'
  Yes, he always has a biscuit for Cerberus[30] with him, and is
so timid that he takes everybody for Cerberus, even you and
me – that is his 'politeness'.

238
Without Envy

He is entirely without envy, but there is no merit in that; for he
wants to conquer a land which no one has yet possessed and
hardly anyone has even seen.

239
The Joyless

A single joyless person is enough to throw a cloud over an
entire household and make it permanently miserable; and it is
a miracle if there is not at least one such person! Happiness is
not nearly so contagious – why is that?

240
On the Seashore

As it is a part of my happiness not to be a householder, I would
never build myself a house; but were I to do so, I would build

it (as many of the Romans did), right into the sea – I would like
to share some secrets with that beautiful monster.

241
Work and Artist

This artist is ambitious and nothing more; ultimately, his work
is just a magnifying glass, which he offers to everyone who
looks at him.

242
Suum Cuique[31]

However great my avarice for knowledge is, I cannot take out
of things any more than what already belongs to me – the possessions of others still remain in them. How is it possible for a
man to be a thief or a robber?

243
Origin of 'Good' and 'Bad'

An improvement is devised only by someone who is able to
feel: 'this is not good'.

244
Thoughts and Words

Even our thoughts cannot be entirely expressed in words.

245
Praise in the Choice

The artist chooses his subject matter; that is his way of
praising.

246
Mathematics

We want to introduce the refinement and rigour of mathematics into all the sciences, to the fullest extent possible, not in the belief that in this way we shall come to know things as they are, but in order thereby to *determine* our human relation to things. Mathematics is only a means to a general and final knowledge of human nature.

247
Habits

All habits make our hand wittier and our wit unhandier.

248
Books

Of what use is a book that never transports us beyond all books?

249
The Sigh of the Knowledge-Seeker

'Oh, my avarice! There is no disinterestedness in this soul of mine – but rather a voracious self which would like to see through the eyes and grasp with the hands of countless individuals – a self which would retrieve the entire past, if possible, and never let it go! Oh, this flame of my avarice! Oh, to be reborn in a hundred beings!'

He who does not know this sigh from experience does not know the passion of the knowledge-seeker either.

250
Guilt

Although the shrewdest judges of the witches, and even the witches themselves, were convinced that the latter were guilty of witchcraft, they were in fact guilty of nothing. So it is with all guilt.

251
Misunderstood Sufferers

The suffering of great men is very different from the suffering
their admirers imagine; for they do not suffer most severely
from the sacrifices and martyrdoms which their tasks require
of them, but from their own momentary lapses into unworthi-
ness and pettiness: in short, from their own doubts as to their
own greatness. As long as Prometheus has pity for men and
sacrifices himself for them, he is great and happy; but as soon
as he falls into jealousy of Zeus and the homage Zeus receives
from mortals – *then* he suffers!

252
Better in Debt

'Better to remain in debt than to pay in coin which does not
bear our image!' – thus does our sovereignty wish it.

253
Always at Home

One day we reach our goal – and henceforth point with pride
to the long distances we travelled to reach it. In truth, we did
not notice that we were travelling. We went so far because in
every place through which we passed, we imagined that we
were already *at home*.

254
Against Embarrassment

He who is always profoundly preoccupied is beyond all embarrassment.

255
Imitators

A: 'What? You want no imitators?' B: 'I don't want anyone to imitate something of mine; I want everyone to generate something of their own: just as *I* do.' A: 'So –?'

256
Skinnedness

All profound men find bliss in being like flying fish[32] for once, and playing on the highest crests of the waves; what they regard as best in things is the fact that they have a surface: their skinnedness – *sit venia verbo*.[33]

257
From Experience

Many people never know how rich they are until they experience first-hand how even the rich become thieves just to steal from them.

258
The Deniers of Chance

No victor believes in chance.

259
From Paradise

'Good and evil are the prejudices of God' – said the serpent.

260
Multiplication Table

One is always wrong, but with two, truth begins.
   One cannot prove anything; but two are already irrefutable.

261
Originality

What is originality? It is to *see* something that as yet has no name, that cannot be referred to, even though it is hiding in plain sight. Men as they usually are require a name for a thing before it is visible to them at all.

For the most part, those with originality have also been those who gave things their names.

262
Sub Specie Aeterni[34]

A: 'You move away from the living faster and faster; soon they will cross you off their lists!' B: 'It is the only way to participate in the privilege of the dead.' A: 'What privilege?' B: 'To die no more.'

263
Without Vanity

When we love, we want our defects to remain hidden – not out of vanity, but out of the desire to spare our beloved the sight of them. Indeed, we would like to seem a god – and this too not from vanity.

264
What We Do

What we do is never understood, only praised or blamed.

265
Ultimate Scepticism

In the end, what are man's truths? His *irrefutable* errors.

266
Where Cruelty Is Needed

Whoever has greatness is cruel to his virtues and other secondary considerations.

267
When We Have a Great Aim

When we have a great aim, we are superior not only to our deeds and judges, but to justice itself.

268
What Makes You Heroic?

To face at the same time your greatest suffering and your greatest hope.

269
What Do You Believe?

In this: that the weights of all things must be determined anew.

270
What Does Your Conscience Say?

'You shall become who you are.'

271
What Is Your Greatest Danger?

Pity.

272
What Do You Love in Others?

My hopes.

273
Whom Do You Call Bad?

Those who always want to put others to shame.

274
What Is Most Humane?

To spare someone shame.

275
What Is the Seal of Liberation?

To no longer be ashamed of oneself.

BOOK IV
Sanctus Januarius[1]

The flaming spear you thrust in me
Broke up the ice within my soul,
And so it hurtles towards the sea,
Now rushing onwards, filled with hope.
Ever brighter, ever sounder,
Freely loving destiny;
Thus my soul extols your wonders,
Fairest month of January!

Genoa, January 1882

276
For the New Year

I am still alive, I am still thinking; I must remain alive, for I must continue thinking. *Sum, ergo cogito; cogito, ergo sum.*[2] Today everyone is allowed to express their fondest thoughts and wishes; well, I too want to say what it is that I have wished for myself today, what thought first crossed my mind at the beginning of this year – a thought with which I may justify, and to which I shall pledge, the rest of my life, a thought to render my life sweet! I want to come to regard everything necessary as beautiful – so that I will become one of those who makes everything beautiful. *Amor fati:*[3] from now on, let that be my love! I do not want to wage war against the ugly. I do not want to accuse anyone, I do not even want to accuse the accusers. May *averting my eyes* be my only negation! All in all, and on the whole, some day I hope only to be an affirmer!

277
Personal Providence

There is a certain high point in life, and once we have attained it, despite all the freedom we have won for ourselves, and the extent to which we deny that there is any benevolent reason or goodness in this beautiful chaos of an existence, we are once again confronted with the greatest threat to our intellectual freedom, and have to face our hardest test. It is only now that the thought of a personal providence impresses itself upon us

with great force, having the best advocate, first-hand experience, to speak on its behalf, for it is a palpable fact that
everything we encounter repeatedly *turns out for the best*. Every
day and every hour, life seems to be eager for nothing more
than to prove this proposition anew; whatever it may be, bad or
good weather, the loss of a friend, an illness, a slander, a letter
not arriving, a sprained ankle, a glance into a shop window, a
counter-argument, the opening of a book, a dream, a swindle:
it becomes apparent immediately, or shortly thereafter, that it
was something 'indispensable' – something full of profound
significance and advantage precisely *for us*! Is there anything
besides such experiences which could so dangerously tempt us
to dismiss the indifferent and unknowable gods of Epicurus,
and believe instead in some anxious and petty divinity who
personally knows every hair on our heads,[4] and who has no
aversion to rendering the most paltry of services? Well – all this
notwithstanding, we wish to leave the gods in peace (and the
serviceable genii as well), and to content ourselves with the
assumption that our own practical and theoretical aptitude for
the arrangement and explanation of events has now reached its
zenith. We do not want to think too highly of our intellectual
dexterity when the wonderful harmony which results from our
playing on our instrument sometimes surprises even us: a harmony which sounds too good for us to dare to attribute it to
ourselves. In fact, now and then, there is one who plays with
us – our old friend chance; occasionally he leads us by the hand,
and even an omniscient providence could not devise a finer
music than that of which our foolish hand is then capable.

278
The Thought of Death

It fills me with a melancholy happiness to live in the midst of this
confusion of streets, of needs, of voices: how much enjoyment,
impatience and desire, how much thirsty life and drunkenness of
life comes into view here every day! And yet it will soon be so
still for all these noisy people, the living with their thirst for life!
Behold how behind every one of them stands his shadow, his

dark companion! It is always like the final moment before a ship full of emigrants sets sail: people have more to say to one another than ever, the hour is pressing, the ocean and its desolate silence waits impatiently behind all the noise – so avid, so certain of its prey! And everyone, everyone thinks that what has gone before is little or nothing, that the near future is everything; hence all this haste, all this clamour, all this constant attempt to shout down and outwit one another! Everyone wants to be pre-eminent in this future – and yet death and the stillness of death are the only things that are certain and common to all in this future! How strange that this one certainty and commonality has almost no power over men, and that nothing is *further* from their minds than the brotherhood of death! I am glad that men try to avoid the thought of death altogether! I should like to do something to make the thought of life still a hundred times *more memorable.*

279
Planetary Friendship

We were friends, and have become estranged from each other. But this is as it should be, and we have no wish to conceal or obscure this fact as if we were ashamed of it. We are two ships, each of which has its destination and its course; we may well cross paths, and celebrate a feast together as we once did – and then the good ships lay quietly in one harbour and in one clime, so that it might have seemed that they had already reached their destination, and that they had the same destination. But then the irresistible force of our tasks drove us apart again into different seas and climes, and perhaps we shall never see each other again – or perhaps we will see each other, but not recognize each other again, the different seas and climes having altered us! That we have become estranged from each other is the law hanging *over* us: by that very fact we shall also become more venerable to each other! By that very fact the thought of our former friendship will become more holy! There is probably some immense, invisible arc and planetary orbit in which our very different courses and destinations may be *included* as small stretches of it – let us raise ourselves to this thought! But our life is too short and our power of vision too slight for us to be more than friends in the sense of that sublime possibility. And so we will *believe* in our planetary friendship, even if we must be terrestrial enemies to one another.

280
Architecture for Knowledge-Seekers

We must recognize sooner or later that what is most lacking in our great cities are broad and spacious places for quiet reflection, places with long, lofty cloisters for when the weather is bad or all too sunny, where no sound of carriages or of town criers would penetrate, and where a more refined decorum would prohibit even the priest from praying aloud: buildings and facilities which as a whole would express the sublimity of contemplation and seclusion. The time is past when the Church can maintain a monopoly on reflection, when the *vita contemplativa* must first be the *vita religiosa*; but everything the Church has built expresses this thought. I do not know how we can be satisfied with their structures, even if they should be divested of their ecclesiastical purpose; these structures speak a far too declamatory and prejudiced language, as houses of God and gaudy places for supernatural intercourse, for us godless ones to be able to think *our thoughts* in them. We want to translate *ourselves* into stone and greenery, we want to walk *in ourselves* when we walk in these halls and gardens.

281
Knowing How to End

Masters of the first form may be recognized by the fact that they know how to end things in a perfect manner, in matters large and small, be it the end of a melody or of a thought, be it the fifth act of a tragedy or of an affair of state. Even the best of the second tier always become restless towards the end, and do not slope downwards into the sea with such proud and calm composure as, for example, the mountains at Portofino do – where the Gulf of Genoa sings its melody to the end.

282
Gait

There are intellectual manners by which even great minds betray that they come from from the mob, or the half-mob – the gait and pace of their thoughts are what betray them; they cannot *walk*. Even Napoleon, much to his profound chagrin, could not walk in a 'legitimate' or princely manner on those occasions when a person really must possess that ability, as in great coronation processions and the like; there too he was always only the leader of a column – proud and hasty at the same time, and very much aware of it.

There is something laughable about those writers who make the folded drapery of their period rustle around them; they want to hide their *feet*.

283
Preparatory Men

I welcome all the signs that a more masculine and warlike age is approaching, which will, above all, restore honour to courage! For it should pave the way to a still-higher age, and gather the strength which the latter will some day require – that age which will carry heroism into knowledge, and *wage wars* for the sake of ideas and their consequences. To that end many brave preparatory men are now needed, who, however, cannot spring from nothing – any more than from the sand and slime of contemporary civilization and the culture of its great cities; men with the ability to remain silent, solitary, resolute, contented with and persistent in invisible activity; men who have an inner inclination to seek in all things that which is to be *overcome* in them; men to whom cheerfulness, patience, simplicity and contempt for the great vanities belong just as much as do magnanimity in victory and forbearance towards the petty vanities of all who are vanquished; men with an acute and independent judgement regarding all victors, and the part chance plays in all victories and all fame; men with their own festivals, their own work days, and their own periods of mourning, accustomed to command with assurance, and equally prepared to obey if necessary, equally proud in the one as in the other, equally serving their own interests; men who are more endangered, more fruitful, more happy! For believe me – the secret to harvesting the greatest fruitfulness and the greatest enjoyment from existence is to *live dangerously*! Build your cities on the slope of Vesuvius![5] Send your ships into uncharted seas! Live in war with your equals and with yourselves! Be robbers and conquerers, you knowledge-seekers, as long as you cannot be rulers and possessors! The time will soon be past when it will be enough for you to live like shy deer hiding in the woods. Eventually knowledge will stretch out her hand to take what is due to her – for she intends to *rule* and *possess* the things of this world, and you with them!

284
Belief in Oneself

In general, few people believe in themselves – and of those few, some possess this belief as a useful blindness or a partial eclipse of the intellect (what would they behold if they could get *to the bottom* of themselves!), while others must first acquire it; everything good, proficient or great that they do is in the first place an argument against the sceptic who dwells within them: it is a matter of convincing or persuading *him*, and that almost requires genius. Their greatness consists in their self-dissatisfaction.

285
Excelsior![6]

'You will never again pray, never again worship, never again rest in infinite trust – you refuse to stand and unharness your thoughts before an ultimate wisdom, an ultimate virtue, an ultimate power – you have no constant companion and friend for your seven solitudes[7] – you live without a view of a mountain that has snow on its peak and fire in its heart – there is no longer anyone who will reward or punish for you, no longer anyone who will ultimately right wrongs for you – there is no longer any reason for what happens, or any love in what happens to you – there is no longer any resting place for your heart, where there is only finding and no more seeking, you resist any kind of ultimate peace, you desire the eternal recurrence of war and peace[8] – man of renunciation, will you renounce all these things? Who will give you the strength to do so? No one has yet had this strength!'

There is a lake which one day failed to drain, for a dam was erected at the place where it had hitherto drained; since then this lake has been rising higher and higher. Perhaps this very renunciation will also furnish us with the strength with which the renunciation itself can be borne; perhaps from that point onwards man will rise higher and higher, when he no longer *drains* into a god.

286
A Digression

Here are hopes; but what will you see and hear of them, if you have not experienced splendour and glow and dawn in your own souls? I can only evoke – I cannot do more! To move stones, to change animals into men – is this what you want from me? Alas, if you are still stones or animals, you must first seek your Orpheus![9]

287
Delight in Blindness

'My thoughts', said the wanderer to his shadow,[10] 'should show me where I stand, but they should not betray to me *where I am going*. I love ignorance of the future, and do not want to die of impatience and the foretaste of promised things.'

288
Elevated Sentiments

It seems to me that most men do not believe in elevated sentiments at all, unless they last for but a moment, or at most for a quarter of an hour – excepting those few who have themselves experienced a longer duration of elevated feeling. But the man of elevated feeling, the embodiment of a single great sentiment – that has hitherto been only a dream and a delightful possibility: as yet, history has given us no clear examples. Nevertheless it could give birth to such men – when a multitude of favourable conditions have been created and established, conditions which cannot be brought into conjunction today even with the luckiest throw of the dice. Perhaps for these future souls, what we have hitherto experienced as the thrilling exception would simply be their normal condition: a continuous movement between elevation and profundity, between the feeling of elevation and profundity, a constant condition akin both to ascending a staircase and to resting on clouds.

289
All Aboard!

When we consider how a complete philosophical justification of an individual's way of living and thinking affects him – namely, as a warming, blessing and fructifying sun, shining just for him; how it makes him independent of praise and blame, self-sufficient, rich and lavish in happiness and benevolence; how it continually transforms evil into good, brings all his powers to fruition and maturity and prevents the larger or smaller weeds of grief and despondency from springing up – in the end, we exclaim insistently: oh, that many such new suns might yet be created! Even the evil man, the unfortunate man, the exceptional man, should have his philosophy, his rights and his sunshine! They do not need our pity! We must unlearn this arrogant notion, no matter how long mankind has hitherto learned and practised it – no spiritual adviser, confessor or absolver needs to be established for them! Rather, a new *justice* is needed! And a new watchword! And new philosophers! The moral earth is also round![11] The moral earth also has its antipodes! The antipodes also have a right to exist! There is yet another world to discover – and more than one! All aboard, you philosophers!

290
One Thing Is Needful

To 'give style' to one's character – a great and uncommon art! It is practised by the man who surveys all the strengths and weaknesses that his nature affords, and then incorporates them into an artistic plan, until everything appears to be the result of art and reason, and even weaknesses enchant the eye. Here, a great deal of second nature has been added, while there, a piece of first nature has been removed – both times through long practice and daily effort. Here, something ugly which cannot be removed has been hidden; there, it has been reinterpreted as something sublime. Much that is indeterminate and resists shaping has been held in reserve and put to use to create the impression of open vistas – ideally, by suggesting something vast and immeasurable. In the end, when the work has been completed, it reveals itself to be the constraint of the same taste which ruled and fashioned it, as a whole and in detail; whether the taste was good or bad means less than one would suppose – it is enough that it be a singular taste! It is the strong, imperious natures who have the most refined enjoyment and attain perfection when bound and constrained by their own law; the passion of their mighty will is assuaged by the sight of anything natural only once it has been overwhelmed by, and placed in the service of, a style; even when they have palaces to build and gardens to lay out, they are reluctant to give nature her freedom.

Conversely, weak characters who lack self-possession *hate* to be bound to one style; they feel that if this galling constraint were imposed upon them, they would necessarily be demeaned by it; they become slaves as soon as they serve, they hate service. Such people – and they may be of the first rank – are always intent upon interpreting themselves and their surroundings as *free* nature – wild, arbitrary, fantastic, disorderly and surprising; and it is well that they do so, for it is only thus that they do well for themselves! For one thing is needful: that man should *attain* satisfaction with himself – whether it be through this or that poetry, this or that art; only then is man tolerable

to the eye! Whoever is dissatisfied with himself is continually
ready to avenge himself on that account; we others will be his
victims, if for no other reason than that we always have to bear
the sight of him in all its ugliness. For the sight of the ugly
makes one ill-tempered and gloomy.

291
Genoa

For quite some time, I have looked upon this city, surveying the
vast panorama of its hilltops and hillsides with their villas and
gardens, and in the end I must say that what I see when I do so
are the *faces* of past generations – this region is dotted with the
images of bold and autocratic men. They truly *lived* and wanted
to live on – that is what they say to me with their houses, built
and adorned not to indulge a passing fancy, but to stand the test
of time; they were well disposed towards life, however ill-disposed
they may often have been towards themselves. I always imagine
the builder, gazing upon all the buildings near and far which surround him, and likewise upon the city, the sea and the mountain
ranges, exercising control with his gaze like some conqueror;
he intends to incorporate all of them into *his* plan and, by making them a part of it, ultimately to render them his *property*.
The entire region is overgrown with the magnificent, insatiable
selfishness of this desire for property and plunder; and just as
these men recognized no boundaries in the distance, and in their
thirst for new things set a new world[12] beside the old, in the
homeland too they were in competition with each other, inventive in finding ways of expressing their superiority, in finding
ways of placing an infinite personal distance between them. Each
one conquered his homeland all over again by subduing it with
his architectural ideas, and by transforming his house into a
sight for sore eyes, so to speak. In the North, when we consider
the construction of cities, it is law, the universal desire for legality
and obedience, which impresses itself upon us; we may thereby
discern a propensity towards levelling and adaptation to circumstances which must have dominated the souls of all the builders
there. In the South, wherever you turn you find a man who knows

the sea, who knows adventure and the Orient, who entertains an antipathy towards law and his neighbour as if bored by them, who measures that which is already old and established with envious eyes. You find a man who, with an amazing impertinence of imagination, would like (at least in thought) to re-establish these old things, take possession of them and assign his own meaning to them – if for no other reason than this: that on some sunny afternoon, when for once his insatiable and melancholy soul feels satiated, he might for a moment gaze upon nothing but what is his, and upon nothing alien.

292
To the Preachers of Morality

I wish to preach no morality, but to those who do, I would give this advice: if you want to bring the best things and conditions into utter disrepute, continue to speak of them in the same manner as before! Place them at the head of your morality, and prattle on from morning till night about the pleasures of virtue, the repose of the soul, about justice, about inherent rewards and punishments; if you keep carrying on this way, all these good things will finally acquire popularity and a clamour in the streets for themselves; but then all the gold on the outside of them will wear off, and, what is more, all the gold on the *inside* will be transmuted into lead. Truly, you know how to practise alchemy in reverse, the devaluation of what is most valuable! Try just for once another recipe, in order to avoid bringing about opposite results from those you seek: *reject* those good things, deprive them of the applause of the mob and take them out of circulation, make them again the secret embarrassment of solitary souls, and say: *morality is something forbidden*! Perhaps you will thus gain for these things the only kind of men who are of any importance, by which I mean men who are *heroic*. But then there must be something fearsome about morality, and not, as hitherto, something disgusting! Where morality is concerned, might we not want to say today something similar to what was once said by Meister Eckhart: 'I ask God to make me free of God!'[13]

293
Our Air

We know it well: he who only casts a glance in passing at science, in the way that women and unfortunately even many artists do, find the rigour in its service, its inflexibility in matters great and small, the swiftness with which it weighs, judges and condemns, to be something vertiginous and terrifying. It is especially frightening to him that, here, the most difficult is demanded, and the best is done without praise or reward; almost nothing is heard but reproof and sharp admonition – for, as among soldiers, palpable hits are considered the rule, near misses the exception; but the rule, here as everywhere, goes without saying. This 'rigour of science' resembles the forms and courtesies of the very best society: it frightens the uninitiated. But to the man who has grown accustomed to it, nothing is more desirable than to live in this clear, transparent, invigoratingly electrified air, in this *manly* air. Everywhere else it is not pure and lofty enough for him: he suspects that *there*, his best art would be wasted on others, and give little joy to himself; that, through misunderstandings, half of his life would slip through his fingers; that a great deal of caution, secrecy and discretion would always be necessary – what great and useless losses of strength! In *this* rigorous and clear element, however, he has his full strength; here he can fly! Why should he descend again to those murky waters where he has to swim and wade and soil his wings!

No! It is too difficult for us to live there; we cannot help it that we are born for the air, the pure air, we rivals to the rays of light; and that like them we would prefer to ride on particles of aether,[14] not away from, but *towards* the sun! That, however, we cannot do – so let us do what we alone can do: bring light to the earth, be 'the light of the earth'! And to that end we have our wings and our swiftness and our rigour, on whose account we are manly, and even terrible like fire. For they have much to fear from us, those who are unable to receive warmth and light from us!

294
Against the Slanderers of Nature

They are such unpleasant people, these men in whom every natural inclination immediately becomes a disease, something
disfiguring, or even disgraceful – it is *they* who have tempted
us to think that men's inclinations and impulses are evil; *they*
are the source of our great injustice towards our own nature,
towards all nature! There are plenty of people who might yield
to their impulses with grace and nonchalance; but they do not
do so, for fear of that imaginary 'evil essence' in nature! *Hence*
it has come to pass that there is so little nobility to be found
among men; an indication of which will always be to fear nothing from oneself, to expect nothing disgraceful from oneself, to
fly without hesitation wherever we are driven – we freeborn
birds! Wherever we go, there will always be freedom and sunshine all around us.

295
Temporary Habits

I love temporary habits. I consider them an invaluable means of
coming to know *many* things and conditions, and of plumbing
the depths of their sweetness and bitterness. My nature is entirely
suited to such habits, even with regard to my bodily health and
its requirements and, *as far as I can see*, in all other respects as
well, from the lowest to the highest things. I always believe that
this will afford me lasting satisfaction (the temporary habit also
inspires the belief born of passion, the belief that it will last for
ever), and that I am to be envied for having found it and recognized it – and then it nourishes me, morning, noon and night,
and imparts a profound sense of the sufficiency of everything
around me and within me, so that I long for nothing, and lose
all need to compare, disdain or hate. But after a while it has had
its day; the good thing departs from me, not as something
which now inspires disgust – but as something as serenely satisfied with me as I am with it, for which we ought to be grateful
to one another, and so we shake hands and say goodbye. Already

something new is waiting at the door, and likewise my indes-
tructible belief – both foolish and wise – that this new thing
will be right for me, right once and for all. I have the same
experience with cuisines, ideas, people, cities, poems, tastes in
music, doctrines, schedules and ways of life.

On the other hand, I hate *fixed* habits, and feel that a tyrant
is approaching, feel myself *suffocating*, when occasions are
arranged in such a way that fixed habits become seemingly
inevitable: for example, through an official position, through
constant companionship with the same people, through a settled abode or through a singular kind of health. Indeed, I am
inclined to be profoundly grateful for all my misery and sick-
ness, for whatever is imperfect in me, because it leaves me with
a hundred back doors through which I can escape from fixed
habits.

The most intolerable thing for me, indeed, the one truly terrible
thing, would be a life without habits, a life which continually
required improvisation – that would be my exile and my Siberia.

296
A Solid Reputation

A solid reputation was once a matter of the utmost utility; and
wherever society is still governed by the gregarious instinct, it is
only to be expected that every individual will seek to *convey the
impression* that his character and pursuits are invariable – even
when at bottom they are not. 'One can rely on him, he remains
the same' – that is the praise which means the most in every
dangerous social situation. Society takes satisfaction in the
knowledge that it always has a reliable *instrument* in this one's
virtue, in that one's ambition, and in the reflection and passion
of a third – it honours this *instrumental character*, this faithful-
ness, this immutability in opinions, aspirations and even in
vices, with the highest honours. Such an assessment, which
flourishes and comes to fruition along with the morality of custom, forms 'character' and brings all change, second thoughts
and self-transformation *into disrepute*. In any case, however
great the advantage of this way of thinking is in other respects,

for *knowledge* it is the most harmful generalization; for it is precisely the knowledge-seeker's willingness to declare without hesitation that he is opposed to his former opinion, and in general to be suspicious of everything solid about himself, which is here condemned and brought into disrepute. The attitude of the knowledge-seeker, being incompatible with a 'solid reputation', is regarded as something *dishonourable*, while the petrifaction of opinions arrogates all the honour to itself; and we still have to live under the spell of such an influence! How difficult it is to live when one feels the judgement of many thousands of years around one and against one. It is probable that for many thousands of years knowledge was afflicted with a bad conscience, and that a great deal of self-contempt and secret misery must have been concealed in the history of the greatest thinkers.

297
Ability to Oppose

Nowadays, everyone knows that the ability to brook opposition is a good indication of culture. Some even know that the superior man courts and provokes opposition, in order to discover his hitherto unknown biases. But the *ability* to oppose, to *not* have a bad conscience about being hostile towards the familiar, the traditional and the sacrosanct – that is more than both of them, that is the truly great, new and astonishing thing about our culture, and the most important step for the liberated spirit. But who knows that?

298
Sigh

An insight came to me while I was walking, and I tried to capture it in the first words that came to mind so that it would not fly away again. But now it remains caught in these arid and inadequate words, waddling about in them, and has lost all of its original liveliness. When I look upon it now, I cannot imagine how I could have been as happy as I was when I first caught this bird.

299
What One Should Learn from Artists

What means have we for making things beautiful, attractive and desirable when they are not so? And I suppose they never are in themselves! We might learn something here from the physicians, who, for example, dilute what is bitter or put wine and sugar into their mixing bowl; but we have still more to learn from the artists, who are in fact continually engaged in devising such feats and contrivances. To move away from things until much is barely discernible, until much must be imagined *in order that they be seen at all* – or to see things around a corner, as if framed by what obstructs our view – or to position them in such a way that they partially obscure each other, creating an illusion of depth – or to look at them through coloured glasses, or in the red light of evening – or to give them a surface or skin which is not fully transparent: all this we should learn from the artists, while being wiser than they are in other respects. For this acute ability of theirs usually comes to an end where art ceases and life begins; but *we* want to be the poets of our lives, and in the smallest and most commonplace matters first and foremost.

300
Preludes to Science

Do you believe that the sciences would have arisen and grown if wizards, alchemists, astrologers and witches had not preceded them as those who, with their promises and pretences, had to create a thirst, a hunger and a taste for *hidden and forbidden* powers beforehand? Indeed, that infinitely more had to have been *promised* than could ever be fulfilled, if anything in the domain of knowledge were to be fulfilled at all?

Perhaps, just as these things proved to be preludes and preliminaries to science which were *not* practised and experienced as such, so too in some distant age the whole of *religion* may be regarded as an exercise and prelude; perhaps it will prove to have been the unlikely means by which individuals could enjoy the complete self-sufficiency of a god and all of his self-redeeming power. Indeed, one might ask: would man have ever learned to feel hunger and thirst for *himself*, and to derive satisfaction and abundance from *himself*, without that religious schooling and prehistory? Did Prometheus have to first *imagine* that he had *stolen* the light and atoned for that, in order to discover in the end that he had created the light *by coveting the light*, and that not only man, but God too had been the work of his hands and the clay in his hands? That all of it had been mere images in the mind of the imaginative individual, creations in the mind of the creator? And likewise the delusion, the theft, the Caucasus, the vulture and the whole tragic *Prometheia*[15] of all knowledge-seekers?

301
Delusion of the Contemplatives

The superior men are distinguished from the inferior by the fact that they see and hear unspeakably more, and see and hear more thoughtfully – and it is this which distinguishes man from the animals, and the superior animals from the inferior. The world always becomes fuller for him who grows up to the heights of humanity; there are always more interesting fish-hooks dangled before him; he is constantly exposed to more stimuli and is likewise more susceptible to pleasure and pain – the superior man invariably becomes at the same time happier and unhappier. But a *delusion* remains his constant companion: he thinks he is merely a member of the *audience* before which the great drama of life is performed; he calls his nature *contemplative*, and thereby overlooks the fact that he himself is actually the poet and elaborator of his life – that while he admittedly differs a great deal from the *actor* in this drama, the so-called practical man, he differs even more from a mere spectator or patron who takes his seat *before* the stage. To be sure, he possesses the *vis contemplativa* and a retrospective view of his work characteristic of a poet, but at the same time, and more importantly, he has the *vis creativa* which the practical man *lacks*, appearances to the contrary notwithstanding. In point

of fact, it is we thoughtful and perceptive individuals who constantly *make* something which was not there before: the whole
ever-increasing world of value judgements, colours, weights,
perspectives, hierarchies, affirmations and negations. This poetry
of ours is continually learned by rote, rehearsed and translated
into flesh and substance and even into daily life by the so-called
practical man (the actor of our drama, as I said). Whatever has
value in the present world has no intrinsic or natural value –
there is no such thing – but rather the value which has been
given and bestowed upon it, and it was *we* who gave and
bestowed! We alone have created the world *which is of any
concern to man*!

But it is precisely this knowledge which we lack, and if we
catch sight of it one moment, we forget it the next; we misunderstand our greatest strength, we contemplatives, and give
ourselves far too little credit – we are *neither as proud nor as
happy* as we could be.

302
Danger to Those Who Are Happiest

Having refined senses and refined tastes; being accustomed to
the rarest and best food for the intellect as if it were the most
appropriate and convenient fare; having a soul imbued with
strength, boldness and daring; walking through life with a
calm eye and a firm step, prepared for any extremity as much
as for a festival, full of longing for undiscovered worlds and
seas, men and gods; listening to all kinds of cheerful music, as
if, in all likelihood, brave men, soldiers and seafarers had
taken a brief rest and recreation there, and in the most profound moment of enjoyment were overwhelmed with tears and
the whole purple gloom of happy men: who would not want all
this to be *his* property and condition! This was the *happiness
of Homer*! The condition of the man who invented the Greek
gods – nay, who invented *his own* gods! But let us not conceal
the fact that with this Homeric happiness in one's soul, one
is more susceptible to suffering than any other creature under
the sun! And it is only at this price that we purchase the most

precious pearl which the waves of existence have hitherto washed ashore! As its proprietor one always becomes more sensitive to pain and, in the end, too sensitive altogether: for Homer, one small source of annoyance and weariness finally sufficed to ruin life for him. He was unable to solve a foolish little riddle which some young fishermen put to him![16] Yes, it is the little riddles which pose the greatest danger to those who are happiest!

303

Two Who Are Happy

This man, despite his youth, truly knows how to *improvise at life* and astonishes even the most acute observers. That is to say, it seems as if he never errs, even though he constantly plays the most daring of games. One is reminded of those masters of improvisation in the art of music, to whose hands the listeners also would like to ascribe a divine *infallibility*, despite the fact that now and then they too err, just as every mortal does. But they are well practised and inventive, and always ready in a moment to incorporate the most accidental note (wherever their fingering or whim propels them) into the thematic structure and to lend the accident a beautiful sense and soul.

Here is quite a different man; at bottom, all of his plans and intentions go awry. On occasion, those things that his heart was set upon brought him to the edge of the abyss and were almost his downfall; if he managed to escape, it was certainly not with just a 'black eye'. Do you think that he's unhappy about it? He decided long ago not to take his own wishes and plans so seriously. 'If I fail at this,' he says to himself, 'then perhaps I will succeed at that; and on the whole, I do not know if I am not more indebted to my failures than to my successes. Was I made to be stubborn and bull-headed? For *me*, the value of my life, what my life comes to in the end, lies elsewhere; my pride and my misery lie elsewhere. I know more about life, because I was so often on the brink of losing it, and for that reason I *have* more of life than any of you!'

304
In Doing We Leave Undone

At bottom, I find those moral codes distasteful which say: 'Do not do this! Renounce! Overcome yourself!'. On the other hand, I am in favour of those moral codes which urge me to do something again and again, from morning till evening, to dream of it at night, to think of nothing but: do this *well*, do this as only *I* can, and to the best of my ability! The one who lives this way continually finds that one thing after another which is not part of such a life falls by the wayside; without aversion or unwillingness, he notices that now this, now that bids him adieu like the autumn leaves which every restless breeze snatches from the tree; or he does not even notice that they bid him adieu, so firmly has he fixed his eyes upon his goal, always ahead, not sideways, backwards or downwards. 'Our doing should determine what we leave undone; by doing, we leave undone' – so it pleases me, so reads *my placitum*.[17] But I do not wish to strive deliberately for my own impoverishment; I do not like all these negative virtues – virtues whose very essence is negation and self-denial.

305
Self-Mastery

Those moral teachers who first and foremost insist that man exercise self-control thereby subject him to a peculiar affliction – namely, a constant irritability with regard to all natural impulses and inclinations, and, as it were, a kind of itching. Henceforth, whatever may goad, pull, attract or impel him, whether from within or from without – it always seems to this irritable being as if his self-mastery were in danger: he may no longer entrust himself to any of his instincts, to any free beating of his wings, but must constantly adopt a defensive posture, armed against himself, with keen and distrustful eyes, the eternal guardian of the castle into which he has made himself. Yes, he can achieve *greatness* in this way! But how insufferable he has now become to others, how hard to bear even for himself, how impoverished and deprived of the most beautiful contingencies of the soul! Yes, even of all further *instruction*! From time to time we must be able to lose ourselves, if we wish to learn from the things which are not ourselves.

306
Stoic and Epicurean

The Epicurean selects the situations, the persons and even the events which fit with his extremely irritable intellectual constitution; he renounces the rest – that is, the bulk of them – because they would constitute fare too strong and too heavy for him. The Stoic, on the other hand, practises swallowing stones and worms, glass shards and scorpions, without revulsion; his stomach is supposed to become indifferent in the end to everything that the accidents of existence pour into it – he is reminiscent of the members of the Arabic sect the 'Īsāwiyya,[18] with whom we became familiar in Algiers; and like these insensible people, he also enjoys inviting the public to witness the exhibition of his insensibility, the very thing an Epicurean would willingly dispense with – for of course he has his 'garden'! For men subject to the capriciousness of fate, who live in violent times and are dependent on abrupt and changeable men, Stoicism may be quite advisable. But he who *anticipates* that fate will allow him to spin out *a long thread* does well to set himself up as an Epicurean, as all men engaged in intellectual labour have hitherto done! For it would be a great pity for them to forfeit their delicate irritability, and to receive in return the rough and spiny hide of a Stoical hedgehog.

307
In Favour of Criticism

Something now strikes you as an error which you had formerly loved as a truth, or at least as a probability; you shed the opinion and imagine that your reason has thereby gained a victory. But perhaps you were a different person then – at any given moment you are a different person – and at that time the error was necessary for you, just as necessary for you as all your present 'truths' are. It was like a skin, as it were, which covered and concealed from you much that you were not yet allowed to see. Your new life, not your rationality, has killed that opinion for you: *you did not need it any more*, and now it has broken down of its own accord, and its irrationality has crawled out of it like a worm into the light. When we engage in criticism it is nothing voluntary or impersonal – it is, or at least very often it is, proof that there are vital, driving forces in us which are shedding a skin. We negate and must negate because something in us lives and *wants* to affirm itself, perhaps something we are as yet unfamiliar with, perhaps something we are as yet unable to see! This speaks in favour of criticism.

308
The History of Each Day

What comprises the history of each day for you? Look at your habits which comprise it: are they the product of innumerable little acts of cowardice and laziness or of bravery and inventive reason? As different as the two cases are, it is possible that, either way, men would afford you the same praise and you would also bring them the same benefits. But praise and benefits and respectability may suffice for him who only wishes to *have* a good conscience – but not for you, trier of the hearts and reins,[19] who has *knowledge of its inner workings*!

309
Out of the Seventh Solitude[20]

One day the wanderer shut a door behind him, stood still and wept. Then he said: 'Oh, this impulse and inclination towards the true, the real, the non-apparent, the certain! How it vexes me! Why does precisely this dark and passionate taskmaster pursue *me*? I would like to rest, but he does not allow it. How many things tempt me to linger! Everywhere there are gardens of Armida[21] for me, and therefore I must tear myself away and embitter my heart, again and again! I must set out again on my worn and weary feet; and because I must, I often cast fierce glances back at the most beautiful things that could not hold me – *because* they could not hold me!'

310
Will and Wave

How eagerly this wave approaches, as if it were trying to reach something! How it wriggles its way into the innermost crannies of the rocky cliff, as if in such a frightful hurry! It seems that it wants to steal a march on someone; it seems that there is something hidden there, something of value, of great value.

And now it returns, somewhat more slowly, still quite white with excitement – is it disappointed? Did it find what it was looking for? Does it merely pretend to be disappointed?

But already another wave approaches, still more wild and eager than the first, and its soul also seems to be filled with secrets, and a longing for treasure. Thus live the waves – thus live we who will! More I cannot say.

So? Do you distrust me? Are you angry with me, you beautiful monsters? Are you afraid that I will betray your secret? Well! Go ahead and be angry with me, raise your dangerous green bodies as high as you can, make a wall between me and the sun – just as you are doing now! Truly, nothing remains of the world but green twilight and green lightning. Do what you will, you wanton creatures, roar with delight and malice – or dive down again, pouring your emeralds into the depths, casting your endless white tufts of foam and spray over them – it is all the same to me, for it all goes so well for you, and I want it all to go so well for you; how could I betray *you*? For – mark my words – I know you and your secret, I know your kind! Most assuredly, you and I are of the same kind! And most assuredly, you and I share the same secret!

311
Refracted Light

We are not always brave, and when we are weary, then some of us are apt to complain in the following way: 'It is so hard to hurt people – what a pity that it is necessary! What is the use of living in concealment, if we are not willing to keep to ourselves that which gives offence? Would it not be more advisable to live amid the hustle and bustle, and make amends to individuals for the sins we are obliged to commit against everybody? To be foolish with the fools, vain with the vain, enthusiastic with the enthusiastic? Would that not be fair given the inordinate degree to which we diverge on the whole? When I hear of the malice that others bear me – is not my first feeling that of satisfaction? Fair enough! I seem to be saying to them, I am so little in agreement with you, and have so much truth on my side that you might as well make the most of it! Here are my mistakes and shortcomings, here are my delusions, my bad taste, my confusion, my tears, my vanity, my owlish seclusion, my contradictions! Have a good laugh! Laugh and enjoy yourselves! I have no objection to the law and nature of things, which is that our mistakes and shortcomings bring joy to others!

'Of course, once upon a time as soon as someone had a new idea, however moderately new it might be, he could regard himself as so *indispensable* that he ran out into the street with it, exclaiming to everybody: "Behold! The kingdom of heaven is at hand!"[22] I would not miss myself if I were gone. We are none of us indispensable!'

But as I said, we do not think that way when we are brave; we do not think *that way* at all.

312
My Dog

I have given a name to my pain, and call it 'dog' – it is just as faithful, just as importunate and shameless, just as entertaining, just as clever, as any other dog – and I can dominate it and vent my spleen on it, as others do with their dogs, servants and wives.

313
No Images of Martyrs

I will follow the example of Raphael, and never again paint an image of a martyr. There are enough sublime things in the world already for us to have to seek the sublime where it lives as a sister to cruelty. I have a greater ambition, and it is not enough for me to make myself into a sublime torturer.

314
New Domestic Animals

I want to have my lion and my eagle around me, so that I will always have signs and premonitions about how strong or weak I am. When I look down on them today, am I bound to fear them? And will the time come when they look up to me, and in fear?

315
Of the Final Hour

Storms are my danger. Will I have my storm from which I perish, as Oliver Cromwell[23] perished from his? Or will I go out like a candle, not first blown out by the wind, but grown tired and weary of itself – a burnt-out candle? Or finally, will I blow myself out, so as not to burn out?

316
Prophetic Men

You are insensible of the fact that prophetic men suffer terribly; you think only that a beautiful 'gift' has been given to them, and that you would like to have it yourselves – but I will express myself with a simile. How much may the animals suffer from the electricity in the atmosphere and in the clouds! We see that some of them have a prophetic faculty for predicting the weather, for example, monkeys (as is well observed even in Europe, not only in menageries, but also on Gibraltar). But it

never occurs to us that it is by virtue of their *suffering* that
they are prophets! When strong, positive electricity, under the
influence of an as yet invisible approaching cloud, is suddenly
converted into negative electricity, and a change in the weather
is imminent, these animals then behave as if an enemy were
approaching, and prepare to defend themselves or flee; for the
most part, they hide themselves – they do not think of the bad
weather as weather, but as an enemy whose hand they can
already *feel*!

317
In Retrospect

We are seldom aware of the real pathos in any period of our
lives as long as we are still in it, but always think that it is
henceforth the only possible and rational condition for us, that
it is entirely *ethos* and none of it *pathos* – to speak and distinguish like the Greeks. A few notes of music today reminded me
of a winter and a house, and a life of utter solitude, and at the
same time the sentiments which characterized my life then – I
thought I could live this way for ever. But now I understand
that it was altogether pathos and passion, something compar-
able to this sadly encouraging and comforting music – one
must not go on like that for years on end, let alone for aeons;
otherwise one would become too 'unearthly' for this planet.

318
Wisdom in Pain

There is as much wisdom in pain as in pleasure: like pleasure,
pain represents a power for the preservation of the species of
the first order. Were it not so, pain itself would have perished
long ago; that it hurts is no argument against it: it is its very
essence. In pain I hear the commanding call of the ship's cap-
tain: 'Take in the sails!' The bold seafarer known as 'man'
must have learned to set his sails in a thousand different ways,
otherwise he could not have lasted long, for the ocean would
soon have swallowed him up. We must also know how to live

with diminished energies: as soon as pain gives its danger sig-
nal, it is time to diminish them – some great danger, some
storm, is approaching, and we would do well to 'fill the sails'
as little as possible.

It is true that there are men who, on the approach of great
pain, hear the very opposite commanding call, and who never
appear more proud, more warlike or more happy than when
the storm is threatening; indeed, pain itself provides them with
their greatest moments! These are the heroic men, those who
inflict the greatest amount of pain on mankind, those few and
rare men who need just the same apology as pain in general –
and truly, it should not be denied them! They are powers for
the preservation and advancement of the species of the first
order, if for no other reason than that they oppose comfortableness, and do not conceal their disgust at this kind of happiness.

319
As Interpreters of Our Experiences

One form of honesty has always been lacking among founders
of religions and the like – they have never made their experiences a matter of intellectual conscience. 'What did I actually
experience? What took place just then within me and around
me? Was my reason clear enough? Was I sufficiently determined to resist every deception of the senses, and resolute in
repelling anything fantastic?' None of them ever asked these
questions, nor have any of our good religious people yet asked
them. Rather, they have a thirst for things which are *contrary
to reason*, and they do not want it to be too difficult to satisfy
this thirst – so they experience 'miracles' and 'rebirths', and
hear the voices of angels! But we who are different, who are
thirsty for reason, want to look as rigorously at our experiences as if they were scientific experiments, hour after hour,
day after day! We ourselves want to be our experiments and
our experimental animals.

320
Upon Seeing Each Other Again

A: 'Do I fully understand you? You are seeking something? Where, in the midst of the present and actual world, is your nook and star? Where can you lay yourself down in the sun, so that a superabundance of well-being may come to you and justify your existence? Let everybody take care of himself – you seem to say to me – and forget all this talk of the common weal, of concern for others and society!' B: 'I want more; I am no seeker. I want to create my own sun.'

321
New Precaution

Let us no longer think so much about punishment, blame and improvement! We seldom change an individual, and when we do succeed, perhaps something else occurs without our realizing it: he may have succeeded in changing *us*! Rather, let us see to it that our own influence *on all that is to come* offsets and outweighs his influence! Let us refrain from direct conflict – and that includes all blame, punishment and desire for improvement! Instead, let us elevate ourselves that much higher! Let us make ourselves an ever more shining example! Let our light put others in the shade! No! We do not wish to become *darker* ourselves on his account, like all who punish and are dissatisfied! Let us stand aside! Let us look away!

322
A Simile

Those thinkers in whom all the planets move in circular orbits are not the most profound. He who looks into himself, as into an immense space, and carries Milky Ways within himself, also knows how irregular all Milky Ways are: they lead into the chaos and labyrinth of existence.

323
Good Fortune in Destiny

Destiny singles us out for the greatest distinction when it allows us to fight for a while on the side of our enemies. With that, a great victory for us is *foreordained*.

324
In Media Vita[24]

No! Life has not deceived or disappointed me! Every year I find it more genuine, more desirable and more mysterious – ever since the day when the great liberator came to me: the idea that life might be an experiment for the knowledge-seeker – and not a duty, not a tragedy, not a swindle!

For others, knowledge itself may be something else: for example, a day bed, or the way to a day bed, or an entertainment, or a diversion – for me, it is a world of dangers and victories in which even the heroic sentiments have their place, and are free to dance and romp about. '*Life as a means to knowledge*' – with this principle in one's heart one can not only live bravely, but can even *live joyously and laugh joyously*! And who would know how to laugh well and live well, if he did not first know war and victory well?

325
A Part of Greatness

Who can achieve anything great if he does not feel in himself the ability and willingness to *inflict* great pain? The capacity for suffering is but the smallest part of it; weak women and even slaves often attain mastery in that. But not to perish from doubt and distress when inflicting great suffering and hearing the cry of this suffering – that is great, that is a part of greatness.

326

Physicians of the Soul and Pain

All preachers of morality, like all theologians, have a bad habit
in common: all of them try to persuade man that he is in a very
bad way, and that a severe, ultimate, radical cure is necessary.
And because mankind as a whole has too eagerly lent its ears
to these doctrines for centuries, men have come to believe
something of the superstition that things are going quite badly,
so that they are now far too ready to sigh; they no longer find
life worth living and make sad faces at one another as if it were
difficult to *bear*. In truth, they are irrepressibly sanguine about
their lives and in love with them, and unspeakably cunning
and subtle at ridding themselves of anything unpleasant, and
taking the sting out of pain and misfortune. It seems to me that
people always *exaggerate* when it comes to pain and misfortune, as if one were expected to exaggerate here. On the other
hand, people are deliberately silent about the fact that there
are innumerable palliatives for pain: anaesthesia; a feverish
rush of thought; a restful posture; good or bad memories,
intentions and hopes; many kinds of pride and sympathy which
have almost the effect of anaesthetics; and, with the most
extreme pains, falling into a swoon. We know all too well how
to sprinkle a little sweetness over our bitterness, especially
over the bitterness of the soul; we find expedients in our bravery and sublimity, as well as in the nobler deliria of submission
and resignation. A loss is hardly a loss for an hour: somehow a
gift from heaven falls into our lap with it – a new form of
strength, for example – even if it is only a new opportunity to
exercise strength! What fantastical ideas have the preachers of
morality not entertained concerning the inner 'misery' of evil
men! How they have *deceived* us about the misfortunes of passionate men! Yes, deceit is the right word here: they were all
too aware of the superabundant happiness of this kind of man,
but they were as silent as the grave about it, because it refuted
their theory that happiness is the result of the extinction of the
passions and the silencing of the will! And as far as the recipe
of all these physicians of the soul is concerned, and their

touting of a severely radical cure, might we be allowed to ask: is our life really painful and irksome enough for it to be worth-while for us to exchange it for a Stoical way of life, and Stoical petrification? Our lives are *not miserable enough* for us to have to be miserable the way that Stoics are!

327
Taking Things Seriously

For most people, the intellect is a ponderous, murky and creak-ing machine which is difficult to set in motion; they call it 'taking the thing *seriously*' when they work with this machine and try to think well – oh, how burdensome they must find thinking well! That delightful animal, man, seems to lose his good humour whenever he thinks well; he becomes 'serious'! And 'where there is laughing and joyousness, thinking comes to nothing' – so says the prejudice of this serious animal against all 'joyous science'.

Well, then! Let us show that it is prejudice!

328
Doing Stupidity Harm

Without a doubt, the belief, preached with such persistence and devotion, that egoism is reprehensible has done egoism harm on the whole (*to the benefit of the gregarious instinct*, as I shall repeat a hundred times!), especially by depriving it of a good conscience and seeking in it the source of all unhappiness. 'Your selfishness is the bane of your existence' – this sermon sounded for thousands of years; as I say, it did selfishness harm by depriving it of much of its spirit, cheerfulness, ingenuity and beauty; it made selfishness seem stupid, ugly and poisonous!

On the other hand, the philosophers of antiquity taught that there was another principal source of bane: from Socrates onwards, thinkers never wearied of preaching that 'your thought-lessness and stupidity, your way of doing everything in the customary manner, your subordination to the opinion of your neighbour, is the reason why you are so rarely happy – because we are thinkers, we are the happiest'. Let us not decide here whether this preaching against stupidity was any more reasonable than the preaching against selfishness; without a doubt, it deprived stupidity of its good conscience – these philosophers did stupidity *harm*.

329
Leisure and Idleness

There is an Indian savagery, a savagery peculiar to the American Indian blood, in the manner in which Americans strive for gold; and the breathless haste with which they work – the original vice of the New World – has already begun to infect old Europe with its savagery, spreading over it a quite remarkable spiritlessness. We are already ashamed of repose: even long contemplation almost causes a pang of conscience. We think with a pocket watch in hand, just as we take our noonday meal with one eye on the stock exchange gazette; we live like men who are continually afraid of 'missing out' on something. 'Better to do something than nothing' – this principle also is a cord with which any cultivation or superior taste is throttled. And just as visibly, all formality is withering away in this laborious haste, as is the feeling for form itself; the ear and the eye for the melody of movement also wither away. The proof of this is the *clumsy obviousness* which is now everywhere demanded in all situations where someone wishes for once to be honest with another, in dealings with friends, women, relatives, children, teachers, pupils, leaders and princes – no one has any time or energy left for ceremonies, for elaborate courtesies, for any wit in conversation or for any *otium*[25] at all. For life in the pursuit of profit continually compels us to expend our intellectual strength even to the point of exhaustion in constant dissembling, outwitting or anticipating: the real virtue nowadays is to do something faster than somebody else. And so honesty is *allowed* for only a few hours, during which we are tired and would not only like to 'let ourselves go', but to *flop ourselves down* without further ado. The way we write our letters nowadays is also in accordance with this tendency; their style and spirit will always be the real 'sign of the times'. If there is still any enjoyment of society or art, it is the kind of enjoyment that weary and overworked slaves arrange for themselves. Oh how undemanding is the 'joy' of our cultured and uncultured people! Oh how increasingly suspicious we are of all joy! More and more, work is becoming the only activity which has a good conscience; the inclination towards joy already calls itself 'the need to recuperate' and has begun to feel ashamed of itself. 'I owe it to my health' – this is what we say when we are caught at a picnic. Indeed, before too long it may become impossible to yield to an inclination for the *vita contemplativa* (that is to say, to go for a walk with one's thoughts or one's friends) at all without a feeling of self-contempt and a bad conscience.

Well! Formerly it was the other way around: it was work that had a bad conscience. A well-bred man *concealed* his work if necessity compelled him to it. The slave laboured under the apprehension that he was doing something contemptible: 'doing' itself was something contemptible. 'Only in *otium* and *bellum*[26] is there any nobility and honour': so sounded the voice of ancient prejudice.

330
Applause

The thinker needs no applause or hand-clapping, provided that he can be assured of his own hand-clapping; this, however, he cannot do without. Are there men who could also dispense with this, who could do without any kind of applause at all? I doubt it: Tacitus, who was disinclined to slander the wise, said of even the wisest, *quando etiam sapientibus cupido gloriae novissima exuitur*[27] – which to him meant never.

331
Better Deaf Than Deafened

Formerly a person wished to be well spoken of, but that is no longer enough, now that the market has become so large – now, there has to be *shouting*. As a result, even good throats try to outshout each other, and the best wares are offered by hoarse voices; nowadays, without shouting in the marketplace and hoarseness there is no longer any genius.

This is unquestionably an evil age for the thinker: he has to learn to find his silence between two noises, and pretend to be deaf until he actually becomes so. As long as he has not yet learned this, he is unquestionably in danger of perishing from impatience and headaches.

332
The Evil Hour

For every philosopher there has probably been an evil hour when he thought to himself, 'What do I matter, if people do not adopt my weak arguments too?' And just then some wicked little bird flew past him and chirped, 'What do you matter? What do you matter?'

333
What Does It Mean to Know?

Non ridere, non lugere, neque detestari, sed intelligere![28] says Spinoza, so simply and sublimely, as is his wont. However that may be, what is this *intelligere* in the final analysis, but the form in which the other three become palpable to us all at once? Is it not a combination of various and conflicting impulses, that is, the desire to laugh, the desire to mourn, the desire to curse? Before a piece of knowledge is possible, each of these impulses must first present its one-sided view of the thing or occurrence. Afterwards, a struggle emerges between these one-sided views, out of which sometimes arises a compromise, a mutual appease-ment, a recognition of rights on all three sides and a kind of justice and treaty; for by virtue of justice and treaty all these impulses can perpetuate themselves and retain their respective rights with regard to each other. We who are only aware of the final scenes of reconciliation and settling of accounts of these long processes therefore think that *intelligere* is something conciliatory, just and good, something essentially opposed to the impulses; whereas it is in fact only a *certain comportment of these impulses towards one another.* For the longest time, conscious thinking was regarded as the only thinking there is; it is only now that the truth dawns upon us that the greater part of our intellectual activity goes on in us unconsciously and imperceptibly; I believe, however, that the impulses which are here struggling with one another know full well how to make themselves palpable to, and inflict pain on, *one another* – the sudden, immense exhaustion to which all thinkers are subject may have its origin here (it is the exhaustion of the battlefield). Yes, perhaps in our inner struggles there is much concealed *heroism*, but certainly no divinity, no eternal self-repose, whatever Spinoza may have imagined. *Conscious* thinking, and especially that of the philosophers, is the most tenuous and therefore, comparatively speaking, the most mild and tranquil kind of thinking; and so it is precisely the philosopher who is most easily misled concerning the nature of knowledge.

334
We Must Learn to Love

This is our experience of music: we must first *learn to hear*, make out and distinguish a figure and a melody at all, to isolate and demarcate it as a living thing in its own right; then it requires a certain amount of effort and goodwill for us to *tolerate* it despite its strangeness; we need to exercise patience towards its aspect and expression, and generosity of spirit towards what is odd about it – finally there comes a time when we are *accustomed* to it, have come to expect it, and we begin to suspect that we would miss it if it were gone; and now it continues to work its irresistible magic on us more and more, and does not stop until we have become its abject and enraptured lovers, who want nothing more from the world than to experience it again and again.

This is not only the case with music: it is in just this way that we have *learned to love* all the things which we now love. We are always eventually rewarded for our goodwill, our patience, reasonableness and gentleness towards what is strange, by the

strange thing slowly casting off its veil and presenting itself to
us as something new and inexpressibly beautiful – and that is
its *thanks* for our hospitality. Even those who love themselves
will have learned it in this way, for there is no other. Even love
must be learned.

335
Hurrah for Physics!

How many people know how to observe? And of the few who
do – how many observe themselves? 'No one is a neighbour to
himself' – all the triers of the reins know this, much to their
chagrin; and the saying, 'know thyself',[29] in the mouth of a god
and spoken to man, borders on cruelty. But nothing better
demonstrates that matters are desperate with regard to self-
observation than the manner in which *almost everybody*
speaks about the essence of a moral action, this immediate,
unhesitating, convinced, voluble manner, with its characteristic look, smile and agreeable enthusiasm! They seem to want
to say, 'But, my dear chap, that is precisely *my* métier! You
have addressed your question to one who is *particularly well
qualified* to speak upon just the subject, for as luck would have
it, there is nothing about which I am more informed! So, when
a man judges that "*this is right*", accordingly concludes that
"*therefore it must be done*", and then *does* what he has thus
recognized was right and indicated was necessary – then the
essence of his action is *moral*!' 'But, my good man, you are
talking about three actions instead of one: for example, your
judgement that "this is right" is also an action – might we not
judge in a moral or immoral way? *Why* do you consider this in
particular to be right?' 'Because my conscience tells me so;
conscience never speaks immorally, indeed it determines what
is moral in the first place!' But why do you *listen* to the voice
of conscience? And to what extent are you entitled to regard
such a judgement as true and unmistakable? This *faith* of
yours – must it not also be examined conscientiously? Do you
know nothing of the intellectual conscience?[30] A conscience
which comes along after your 'conscience'? Your judgement

'this is right' has a prior history in your impulses, in your inclinations and disinclinations, in what you have experienced and in what you have not experienced; first you must ask: *where* did it come from? And then ask: *what* really impels me to listen to it? You can listen to its command like a brave soldier listening to his commanding officer. Or like a woman in love with the man who commands her. Or like a flatterer and a coward who is afraid of the commander. Or like a numbskull who obeys because no objection has occurred to him. In short, you can listen to your conscience in a hundred different ways. But *the mere fact that* you hear this or that judgement as the voice of conscience, and that consequently you feel a thing to be right, may be due to the fact that you have never given the matter much thought, and have blindly accepted from your childhood whatever you were *told* was right; or it may be due to the fact that, hitherto, the enjoyment of bread and honours has been part and parcel of the thing which you call your duty – it seems 'right' to you, because it seems to be a 'condition of *your* existence' (and the notion that you have a *right* to exist strikes you as indisputable!). The *firmness* of your moral judgement may be nothing more than proof of your personal inadequacy, of your lack of character; your 'moral fortitude' might have its source in your stubbornness – or in your lack of ability to envision new ideals! And, to be brief: if you had thought more carefully, observed more closely and had learned more, you would no longer call this and that your 'duty' and your 'conscience' under any circumstances; insight into *how moral judgements arise at all* would spoil for you these lofty words – just as these other lofty words have already been spoiled for you, words like 'sin', 'salvation' and 'redemption'.

Now, my good man, do not give me any of that nonsense about the categorical imperative![31] That phrase tickles my ear, and I must laugh despite your earnestness in my presence. I am reminded of old Kant, who, as a punishment for having *fraudulently obtained* the 'thing in itself' – also a rather ridiculous notion! – arrived at the notion of the categorical imperative, and with that in his heart, *wandered back* into the notions of God, the soul, freedom and immortality,[32] like a fox who inadvertently wanders back into his own cage – when it was his strength and cunning which had *broken* this cage wide open!

How is that? You admire the categorical imperative within you? This 'firmness' of your so-called moral judgement? This 'unconditionality' of the feeling that 'as I judge, so must every-one judge'?[33] Rather, admire your *selfishness* in feeling that way! And the blind, petty and unassuming nature of your self-ishness! It is selfishness to consider one's *own* judgement a universal law, and a blind, petty and unassuming selfishness besides, for it betrays that you have not yet discovered yourself, that you have not yet created an ideal of your own, entirely your own – such an ideal could never be shared with another, let alone with everyone, everyone! Whoever still judges that 'in this case, everyone must act in this manner' has not yet advanced five steps in self-knowledge; otherwise he would know that there neither are, nor can there be, identical actions. Every action that has ever been done, has been done in an entirely unique and unprecedented manner, and the same will be true of all future actions. Every prescription with regard to our actions (even the most subtle and inward prescriptions of every moral code hitherto) applies only to their rough exterior, and while these prescriptions may convey the impression that there are identical cases, such an impression is *misleading. Every* action, whether viewed prospectively or retrospectively, is and remains impenetrable. Our opinions with regard to 'goodness', 'nobil-ity' or 'greatness' can never be *demonstrated* by our actions, because every action is unknowable, and while our opinions, value judgements and standards of goodness are certainly among the most powerful levers in the machinery of our actions, in any individual instance the law of their mechanism is indeter-minable. Let us *confine* ourselves, therefore, to the purification of our opinions and value judgements, and to the creation of our own original standards of goodness – but let us no longer brood over the 'moral worth of our actions'! Yes, my friends! The time has come for us to turn away in disgust from all this nonsense of some standing in moral judgement over others! The whole thing is in such bad taste! Let us leave this nonsense and this bad taste to those who have nothing better to do than to keep the past alive a little bit longer and who never live in the here and now – let us leave them to the many, to the great majority! We, however, *want to become who we are* – something new, unique, incomparable, self-legislating and self-creating! And to that end, we must become the best students and discoverers of all the laws and necessities in the world. We must be *physicists* in order to be *creators* in that sense – whereas hitherto all value judgements and ideals have been based on an ignorance of physics, or in contradiction with it. And so I say, hurrah for physics! And an even louder hurrah for that which impels us to it – our honesty.

336
Avarice of Nature

Why has nature been so miserly towards men that she does not allow them to shine, this one the more, that one the less, each according to their inner abundance of light? Why are great men not beautifully visible like the rising and the setting of the sun? Would that it were so! Life among men would then be far less ambiguous.

337
Future 'Humanity'

When I look upon this age with the eyes of a distant future age, I find nothing so remarkable about contemporary man than his peculiar virtue and disability known as 'the historical sense'. This is the emergence of something quite new and strange in history; if these seeds were to be cultivated for a few more centuries, we might end up with a wonderful plant, with an equally wonderful odour, due to which our old earth might be more pleasant to inhabit than it has been hitherto. We moderns are just beginning to forge, link by link, the chains of a very powerful sentiment yet to come – and we hardly know what we are doing. It almost seems to us as if it were not a new sentiment, but the waning of all old sentiments – the historical sense is still something so poor and cold, and many are attacked by it as by a frost, and are made poorer and colder by it. For others it appears to be a sign of approaching age, and our planet is regarded by them as a melancholy invalid who, in order to forget his present condition, writes the history of his youth. As a matter of fact, this is one aspect of the new sentiment. Whoever comes to regard the history of mankind in its entirety as *his own history*, in a tremendous generalization feels all the sorrow of the invalid who thinks about health, of the old man who thinks about the dreams of his youth, of the lover who is deprived of his beloved, of the martyr whose ideal is destroyed, of the hero on the evening of the battle which was neither won nor lost but which has brought him wounds and the loss of a friend. But to bear this tremendous amount of sorrow of all kinds, to be able to bear it and yet still be the hero who on the morning of the second day of battle greets the dawn and his prospects, as the man who has a horizon of millennia before and after him, as the heir to all the nobility of the spirits of the past, committed to the preservation of the legacy of the noblest of all the old nobles, while at the same time being the first child of a new nobility the like of which has not yet been seen or even dreamed of: to take all of this upon oneself, to incorporate into one's soul all of the oldest and the newest, the losses, hopes, conquests and victories of mankind and to condense it into one sentiment – this would have to yield a kind of happiness which mankind has not hitherto known, a divine happiness, full of power and love, full of tears and laughter, a happiness which, like the sun in the evening, continually gives away its inexhaustible riches and pours them into the sea, and like the sun, only feels richest when even the poorest fisherman rows with golden oars! This divine sentiment might then be called – humanity!

338
The Willingness to Suffer and the Pitying

Is it beneficial for you to be filled with pity above all else? And is it beneficial to those who suffer for you to be filled with pity? But let us leave the first question unanswered for a moment.

The things from which we suffer most deeply and personally are almost incomprehensible and inaccessible to anybody but ourselves; in this, we are hidden from our neighbour even when we eat from the same pot. But whenever we are *perceived* to be suffering, our suffering is viewed superficially; it is essential to the emotion of pity that it *divest* the suffering of a stranger of its underlying personal character – 'do-gooders' diminish our value and disregard our intentions more than our enemies do. In most of the good deeds which are done for the unfortunate there is something outrageous about the intellectual frivolity with which the pitying person assumes the role of Fortune: he knows nothing of the totality of the inner consequences and interconnections which he calls unhappiness in *my* case or in *yours*! The whole economy of my soul and its tempering by 'unhappiness', the emergence of new sources and needs, the healing of old wounds, the discarding of whole past histories – none of the things which might be associated with unhappiness are of the least concern to our dear friend, the pitying person. He merely wishes to help and does not take into account the fact that we have a personal need for unhappiness; that terror, deprivation, impoverishment, midnights of the soul, adventures, risks and mistakes are as necessary to you and me as their opposites; indeed, that, to speak mystically, the way to one's own heaven always leads through the voluptuousness of one's own hell. No, he knows nothing about that. The 'religion of pity' (or 'the heart') dictates that he help, and he thinks he has helped most when he has helped fastest! If you disciples of this religion actually have the same attitude towards yourselves as you have towards your fellows, if you are not willing to endure your own suffering even for an hour, and are always trying to avoid every unhappy experience you can, if you generally regard pain and sorrow as evil, as detestable, as deserving of destruction, as a blot on existence – well then, besides your religion of pity, you have yet another religion in your heart (which is perhaps the mother of the former): *the religion of comfortableness.* Oh how little you know about human *happiness*, you comfortable and good-natured people – for happiness and unhappiness are sisters and twins which grow tall together, or, in your case, *remain small* together! But now let us return to the first question.

How is it even possible for a man to keep to his *own* path! Things are incessantly clamouring for our attention; we rarely see anything which does not require us to drop everything instantly and rush to somebody's assistance. I know how it is: there are hundreds of respectable and commendable ways of making me *lose my way* and, in truth, all of them highly 'moral' ways! Indeed, the contemporary preachers of this morality of pity even go so far as to say that this alone is moral – to lose *our* way so that we might better rush to our neighbour's assistance. I likewise know for certain that I need only surrender myself to the sight of someone in genuine distress, and I *am* lost! And if a suffering friend said to me, 'Look, soon I am going to die; promise you will die with me', I would promise it, just as the sight of a small mountain tribe fighting for its freedom would make me offer them my hand and my life – to choose bad examples for good reasons. Indeed, there is even a secret temptation in all this arousing of pity, in all these cries for help: our 'own way' is too difficult and demanding, and too far removed from the love and gratitude of others – we are not at all disinclined to run away from it and our own conscience, and to flee into the conscience of others, taking refuge in the lovely temple of the 'religion of pity'. Every time a war breaks out, a desire invariably breaks out at the same time among precisely the noblest people in the nation, though they are naturally loath to disclose it: they enthusiastically throw themselves into this new risk of *death* because they believe that by sacrificing themselves for their country they have finally obtained the permission which they have long sought – the permission to *abandon their aims*; war is for them a detour to suicide, but a detour with a good conscience. And although I prefer to remain silent here about some things, I will not remain silent about my morality, which says to me: live in obscurity so that you are *able* to live for yourself! Live in *ignorance* of that which is most important to your age! Put at least the skin of three centuries between yourself and today! And the clamour of today, the noise of wars and revolutions, shall

be to you but a murmur! You will also want to help, but only
help those whose distress you fully *understand*, because they
share with you one sorrow and one hope – your *friends*; and
only in the same way that you would help yourself – for I want
to make them more courageous, more steadfast, more simple,
more joyous! I want to teach them the importance of something which so few seem to understand these days, and which
the preachers of pity, the preachers of shared sorrow, seem to
understand least of all – the importance of *shared joy*!

339
Vita Femina[34]

To see what is ultimately beautiful in a work, knowledge and
goodwill are not enough: it requires the rarest, most felicitous
of accidents, so that for once the clouds veiling these summits
might be parted and the sun might shine upon them. Not only
must we stand in precisely the right place to see this; our very
soul must draw the veils from its own heights, and must stand
in need of an outward expression and simile to serve as a support in order to retain its composure. However, all these things
so seldom occur at the same time that I am inclined to believe
that the apotheosis of everything good, be it work, deed, man
or nature, has hitherto been for most, and even for the best,
something hidden and shrouded – and if it does reveal itself to
us, *it reveals itself only once*.

Of course, the Greeks prayed: 'May everything beautiful
come twice, or three times!' Oh, they had good reason to call
on the gods, for this ungodly reality gives us scarcely any beauty
at all, or if it does, it does so only once! What I meant to say is
that the world contains a superabundance of beautiful things,
but is nevertheless poor, very poor, in beautiful moments, in
revelations of these things. But perhaps this is life's most powerful magic: it dons a veil interwoven with the golden threads of
beautiful possibility, promising, contrary, coy, mocking, sympathetic, seductive. Yes, life is a woman.

340
The Dying Socrates

I admire the courage and wisdom of Socrates in all that he did, said – and did not say. This mocking and amorous rogue, this Pied Piper of Athens who made even the most wanton youths tremble and sob, was not only the wisest chatterer that ever lived; he was just as great in his silence. I wish that he would also have been silent in the last moment of his life – perhaps then he would have belonged to an even higher order of spirits. Whether it was death, or poison, or piety, or sheer malice – something loosened his tongue at that moment, and he said: 'Oh Crito, we ought to offer a cock to Asclepius.'[35] For those who have ears, these ludicrous and terrible 'last words' mean: 'Oh Crito, *life is a disease*!' Is it possible that a man like him, who had lived cheerfully and to all appearances like a soldier – was a pessimist? He had merely adopted a cheerful demeanour towards life, and all along concealed his ultimate judgement, his innermost sentiment! Socrates, Socrates *suffered from life*! And he still took his revenge on it – with those veiled, horrible, pious and blasphemous words! Did Socrates *have* to avenge himself? Despite the fact that he possessed an abundance of virtue, was he not quite magnanimous enough to resist this temptation?

Oh my friends! We have to surpass even the Greeks!

341
The Greatest Weight

What if one day or night a demon came to you in your most solitary solitude and said to you: 'This life, as you now live it and have lived it, you will have to live again, and innumerable times again, and there will be nothing new in it; but rather every pain and joy, every thought and sigh, and all the unutterably trivial or great things in your life will have to happen to you again, with everything in the same series and sequence – and likewise this spider and this moonlight between the trees, and likewise this moment and I myself. The eternal hourglass of existence will be turned over again and again, and you with it, you speck of dust!'

Would you not throw yourself down and gnash your teeth and curse the demon who spoke to you thus? Or was there one time when you experienced a tremendous moment in which you would answer him: 'You are a god, and I have never heard anything so divine!' If that thought took hold of you as you are, it would transform you and perhaps crush you; the question with regard to each and every thing, 'Do you want this again, innumerable times again?' would weigh upon your actions with the greatest weight! Or how well disposed would you have to become to yourself and to life, that you might *long for nothing more* than this final eternal confirmation and seal?

342
Incipit Tragoedia[36]

When Zarathustra[37] was thirty years old, he left his home and Lake Urmi[38] and went into the mountains. There he enjoyed his spirit and his solitude, and for ten years did not tire of them. But in the end his heart changed, and one morning he arose with the dawn and, facing the sun, spoke to it thus: 'Oh, you great star! What happiness would you enjoy, without those for whom you shine? For ten years you have come up to my cave, and you would have grown weary of your light and of this path, were it not for me, my eagle and my serpent. But we awaited you every morning, received your abundance, and blessed you for it. Behold! I grow weary of my wisdom, like the bee that has gathered too much honey; I need hands outstretched to receive it. I should like to dispense and distribute it until the wise again rejoice in their folly, and the poor in their riches. To that end, I must descend into the depths, as you do in the evening when you go behind the sea and bring light even to the underworld, you superabundant star! Like you I must *go down*, as the people to whom I will descend call it. Bless me then, oh you calm eye, who can behold even an excess of happiness without envy! Bless the cup which wants to run over, so that the water may flow golden out of it, and carry everywhere the reflection of your bliss! Behold! This cup wants to be empty again, and Zarathustra wants to be a man again.'

And with that, Zarathustra began to go down.

BOOK V
We Fearless Ones

Carcasse, tu trembles?
Tu tremblerais bien davantage, si
tu savais, où je te mène.[1]

Turenne

343
What Our Cheerfulness Means

The greatest event of recent times – the fact that 'God is dead', that the belief in the Christian God has become untenable – has already begun to cast its first shadows over Europe. For the few at least whose eyes, whose *suspicious* eyes, are strong enough and subtle enough for this drama, some sun seems to have set, some ancient and profound confidence has turned into doubt; to these eyes our old world must seem to be becoming more vespertine, distrustful, strange and 'old' with every passing day. In the main, however, we may say that the event itself is much too great, too remote, too far beyond most people's capacity to understand, for us to imagine that even the tidings of it could have *reached* their ears, let alone that very many people would already know *what* its actual implications were, or what things would have to collapse, now that this belief had been undermined, because they were built upon it, leaned against it and had become intertwined with it: for example, our entire European morality. With regard to this long and abundant train of consequences which are now imminent, this demolition and destruction, this decline and fall, who nowadays has already divined enough of it to have to play the educator and prognosticator of this tremendous logic of terror, to play the prophet of a gloom and solar eclipse the like of which has probably never before existed on earth?

Even we natural-born speculators who, so to speak, wait on the mountains, posted between today and tomorrow, spanning the contradiction between today and tomorrow, we firstlings and premature births of the coming century for whom the shadows which, incidentally, *should* have arrived by now, the shadows which must soon afterwards envelop Europe – how is it that we ourselves await its advent without properly participating in this gloom, without any concern or fear for *ourselves*? Perhaps we stand too close to the *immediate consequences* of this event – and these immediate consequences, its consequences for *ourselves*, are the reverse of what one might have expected, they are by no means sad and gloomy, but rather like a new and indescribable kind of light, happiness, relief, amusement, encouragement and dawn . . .

In fact, we philosophers and 'free spirits' experience the news that the 'old God is dead' as if illuminated by a new dawn; our hearts are overflowing with gratitude, astonishment, presentiment and expectation – at last the horizon seems free again, even if it is not bright; at last our ships can set sail again, ready to face every danger; every venture of the knowledge-seeker is permitted again; the sea, *our* sea, lies open again before us; perhaps there has never been such an 'open sea'.

344
To What Extent Even We Are Still Pious

It is said with good reason that convictions have no civil rights in science: it is only when they are willing to reduce themselves to the humble status of a hypothesis, of a preliminary experimental standpoint, of a regulative fiction, that they may be allowed to enter the domain of knowledge, and even be accorded a certain value within it – though with the proviso that they must be kept under constant surveillance, under the surveillance of our distrust.

But does that not imply that, strictly speaking, a conviction may gain admission to science only when it *ceases* to be a conviction? Does not the discipline of the scientific spirit only begin when we are no longer allowed any convictions?

Very probably; but it remains to be seen whether there does not have to be some sort of conviction present in the first place

in order for this discipline to begin, a conviction so imperative
and unconditional that it makes us sacrifice all our other convictions. We see that even science rests upon a faith, that there
is no 'presuppositionless' science. The question of whether
truth is necessary must not only be answered in the affirmative
beforehand, it must be answered in the affirmative to such an
extent that the principle, faith or conviction is expressed that
'nothing is more necessary than truth, in comparison to which
everything else is of only secondary importance'.

This unconditional determination to seek the truth: what is
it? Is it the determination *not to be deceived*? Is it the determination *not to deceive*? For the desire for truth could also be
interpreted in this fashion, provided that under the generalization 'I will not deceive' one subsumed the individual case, 'I
will not deceive myself.' But why not deceive? Why not allow
oneself to be deceived?

It should be noted that the reasons for the former are quite
different from the reasons for the latter: we wish not to be
deceived on the assumption that it is harmful, dangerous or disastrous to be deceived – in this sense, science would be a long
exercise of prudence and caution, essentially utilitarian in its
nature, against which we might however reasonably object:
'What? Is wishing-not-to-be-deceived really less harmful, less
dangerous, less disastrous?' What do you know from the outset
about the character of existence that enables you to determine
whether the greater advantage is on the side of unconditional
distrust or unconditional trust? But if both a great deal of trust
and a great deal of distrust should prove necessary, then from
where would science derive its unconditional faith, the conviction on which it rests, that truth is more important than
anything else, more important even than every other conviction? It is precisely this conviction that could not have arisen if
truth *and* untruth had both constantly proved themselves to be
useful, as is the case. Thus the faith in science, which now
undeniably exists, cannot have originated in such a utilitarian
calculation, but rather in spite of the fact that the uselessness
and dangerousness of the 'desire for truth', for 'truth at any
cost', are constantly being demonstrated. 'At any cost': oh, we

understand that well enough, after having offered and slaugh-
tered one faith after another on this altar!

Consequently, 'desire for truth' does not mean 'I do not want
to be deceived', but – there is no other alternative – 'I will not
deceive, not even myself' – *and with that we have reached the
ground of morality.* For we have to ask ourselves searchingly:
'Why not deceive?', especially if it should seem – and it does
seem – as if life aims at appearance, I mean, at error, deception,
dissimulation, delusion, self-delusion; and when, on the other
hand, life in its broad outlines has always shown itself to be
on the side of the most unscrupulous *polytropoi.*[2] It might be
the case that such an intention is, to put it mildly, quixotic, a
piece of enthusiastic madness; but it might also be something
much worse, namely a destructive principle, a principle hostile
to life . . . 'the desire for truth' might well be a concealed desire
for death . . .

Thus the question 'Why have science at all?' leads back to
the moral problem: *why have morality at all* when life, nature
and history are 'immoral'? There is no doubt that the truthful
man in the daring and extreme sense of that word, the man
whose truthfulness is presupposed by science, *thereby affirms
another world,* a world that transcends life, nature and history; and in so far as he affirms this 'other world' – what? Does
he not have to *negate* its counterpart, this world, our world?

But you understand what I am driving at, namely that it is
still a *metaphysical faith* on which our faith in science rests –
and that even we knowledge-seekers of the present day, we
godless anti-metaphysicians, light *our* fire from the flames
enkindled by a faith which goes back thousands of years, that
Christian faith which was also the faith of Plato, that God is
truth, that truth is divine . . .

But what if this faith is becoming ever more incredible; what
if nothing proves to be more divine than error, blindness and
falsehood – what if God Himself should prove to be our most
longest-lasting lie?

345
Morality as a Problem

A personal defect takes its revenge everywhere; an enfeebled, slight, self-effacing and self-denying personality is no longer good for anything – least of all for philosophy. 'Selflessness' has no value in heaven or on earth; great problems all demand *great love* and it is only the frank, strong, self-confident spirits with steady nerves who are at all proficient with them. It makes a considerable difference whether a thinker takes his problems personally, finding in them his destiny, his distress and even his greatest happiness; or merely 'impersonally', that is to say, if he can only grasp and comprehend them with little feelers of cold and inquisitive thought. In the latter case nothing comes of it, I can assure you, for the great problems, assuming that they can be grasped at all, *elude the grasp* of toads and weaklings; that has been their taste since time began – a taste, by the way, which they share with all doughty women.

How is it that I have not yet come across anyone, not even in books, whose position regarding morality was that of a person who knew that morality was a problem, and who experienced this problem as *his own* personal distress, torment, voluptuousness and passion? It is evident that hitherto morality has been no problem at all; rather, it was the one thing on which people could agree, despite all distrust, dissension and disagreement, a holy sanctuary where thinkers catch their breath, recuperate and take a rest even from themselves. I see no one who would have dared to *criticize* moral value judgements. I have found such a thing completely lacking; there is not even an attempt at scientific curiosity, or the fastidious, experimental imagination of psychologists and historians, which easily anticipates a problem and catches it in flight, without really knowing what it has caught. I have hardly been able to locate a few rudiments of a *developmental history* of the origin of these sentiments and value judgements (which is something other than a criticism of them, and also something other than a history of ethical systems); in an individual case[3] I have done all I could to encourage the inclination and aptitude for this kind of history – in vain, as it now appears. Little can be done with these historians of morality (especially the English); usually they themselves are still unwittingly under the direction of a particular morality, and without realizing it serve as its standard-bearers and hangers-on: for example, that popular superstition of Christian Europe which is still faithfully parroted everywhere that the characteristic of moral action consists in selflessness, self-denial, self-sacrifice, or in sympathy and pity. Their usual mistaken assumption is the claim that some kind of consensus exists among peoples, or at least civilized peoples, regarding certain propositions of morality, and that therefore these propositions are unconditionally binding even upon you and me; or, after the truth has been revealed to them that moral value judgements *necessarily* differ among different peoples, they conversely come to the conclusion that *no* morality is binding – which are both equally childish. The error of the more discerning among them is to discover and criticize the possibly foolish opinions of a people about its own morality, or of mankind about human morality in general – that is, about its origin, its religious sanctions, the superstition of free will and the like – and think that precisely by doing so they have criticized the morality itself. But the value of the prescription 'thou shalt' is fundamentally different from and independent of such opinions about it, and from the weeds of error with which it might be overgrown; just as the value of a medicine to a patient is completely independent of whether the patient thinks scientifically about medicine or fills his head with old wives' tales. A morality could even be the outgrowth of an error; but with this insight the problem of its value is not even touched upon.

So far, no one has examined the *value* of that most famous of all medicines called morality, to which end one must first *call it into question.* Well, that is precisely our work.

346
Our Question Mark

But you do not understand that? As a matter of fact, there is no small difficulty in understanding us. We are endeavouring to find the words in which to express ourselves; perhaps we are also endeavouring to find the ears with which others might hear them. Who are we, though? If we wanted simply to refer to ourselves by the older expressions, atheists, unbelievers or even immoralists, we would still be far from believing that those words adequately described us; we are all of those things in such an advanced condition that no one fully grasps our state of mind, indeed, no one is even *able* to grasp it, not even *you*, my inquisitive friends. No, we no longer suffer from the bitterness and passion of the man who has just broken free, and who has to create for himself a faith, a goal and a martyr- dom even, out of his unbelief! We know full well (and have become cold and severe in the realization) that the world is not at all divine, indeed, that it is not even humanly rational, mer- ciful or just; we know that the world in which we live is ungodly, immoral and 'inhuman' – for far too long we have interpreted it falsely and dishonestly, in accordance with our wish and intention to revere it, that is to say, according to a *need*. After all, man is a reverent animal! But he is also a dis- trustful one; and in the end, the fact that the world is *not* as valuable as we had believed is about the surest thing that our distrust has got hold of. And the more distrust, the more phil- osophy! However, we must be careful not to say that the world is any *less* valuable than it should be; it now seems ludicrous to us whenever man claims that he has devised values which are supposed to *surpass* the value of the real world – it is precisely from that idea that we have retreated as from an extravagant aberration, a piece of human vanity and irrationality which for a long time has not been recognized as such. It had its most recent expression in modern pessimism, and an older and stronger one in the teachings of the Buddha; but Christianity also con- tains it, more uncertainly of course, and more ambiguously, but no less seductively on that account. The whole posture of 'man *against* the world', man as 'world-denying' principle, man as the value standard for everything, a judge of the world who ultimately places existence itself on the scales and finds it wanting – we have become aware of the tremendous vulgar- ity of this posture and it disgusts us; we now laugh when we find 'man *and* world' juxtaposed, separated by the sublime

presumption of that little word 'and'! How is that? Have we
not by laughing taken our contempt for mankind one step further? And therefore also our pessimism, our contempt for any
existence which is recognizable by *us*? Have we not in just this
way become smitten with the suspicion that there is an antithesis between the familiar world of our reverences – reverences
which may have rendered life *bearable* – and another world
which we ourselves are: an implacable and profound suspicion about ourselves which is only getting worse and worse,
and by which we Europeans in particular are increasingly
swayed, the deepest suspicion which might easily confront the
coming generation with a terrible alternative: either eliminate
your reverences or – eliminate yourselves! The latter would be
nihilism – but would not the former also be nihilism? This is
our question mark.

347
Believers and Their Need of Belief

How much *belief* someone needs in order to prosper, how many
'firmly held opinions' he needs which he does not want to have
shaken, because he is *attached* to them – is a measure of his
strength (or, to put it more clearly, of his weakness). It seems to
me that Christianity is still regarded as necessary in old Europe,
and so it still finds believers. For man is such that a theological
dogma might be refuted a thousand times, but if he had need of
it he would always accept it as 'true', according to the famous
'demonstration of power'[4] of which the Bible speaks. Some individuals still have need of metaphysics; but also that vehement
longing for certainty which nowadays discharges itself in the
general populace in a scientific and positivistic manner, the
longing to possess something absolutely firm (a longing which,
because of its fervour, leads to casual and negligent attempts at
substantiating the certainty) – this too is nothing but the longing
for some kind of foothold or support; in short, it is that *instinct
of weakness* which does not actually create religious beliefs,
metaphysical ideas and convictions of all kinds, but rather con-
serves them. In fact, a certain air of pessimistic gloom hangs

over all these positivist systems, a sense of weariness, fatalism, disillusionment and fear of further disillusionment – or else a great show of ire, ill-humour, anarchistic indignation and all the other symptoms whereby the sense of weakness masquerades as something else. Even the vehemence with which our cleverest contemporaries lose themselves in wretched corners and alleyways, for example, in fatherlandery (that is, what in France is called *chauvinisme* and in Germany is called 'German'); or in obscure aesthetic denominations in the manner of Parisian *naturalisme*[5] (which only brings out and lays bare that aspect of nature which excites disgust and at the same time astonishment – nowadays they like to call this aspect *la vérité vraie*[6]); or in nihilism of the St Petersburg variety[7] (that is to say, in the *belief in unbelief*, even to the point of martyrdom for it) – this always shows itself first and foremost in the *need* for a belief, foothold, backbone or buttress . . .

Belief is always most desired, is most urgently necessary, where will is lacking; for the will, as the passion of imperiousness, is the distinguishing characteristic of self-mastery and strength. That is to say, the less someone is able to command, the more urgently he desires someone to command him, and command him strictly – a god, a prince, a caste, a physician, a confessor, a dogma, the conscience of a party. From which we might deduce that what accounts for the origin of the two world religions Buddhism and Christianity, and their sudden spread in particular, was a tremendous *disease of the will*. And so it was: both religions discovered a longing for just such a 'thou shalt', attributable to an absurdly large increase in this disease which had driven people to the brink of despair; both religions taught fanaticism in those periods when atony of the will was prevalent, and thereby offered to innumerable people a foothold, a new opportunity for willing, an enjoyment of the will. For fanaticism is actually the only 'strength of will' of which the weak and irresolute are capable, as a kind of hypnotizing of the entire sensory-intellectual system, an excessive preoccupation with, and hypertrophy of, a particular point of view and a particular sentiment which then comes to dominate them – the Christian calls it his *belief*. When a man arrives at the fundamental conviction that he must be commanded, he becomes a 'believer'; conversely, we could imagine a delight in and capacity for self-determination, a *freedom* of will, by which a spirit bids farewell to every belief, to every wish for certainty, being proficient in hanging on to thin ropes and possibilities, and even in dancing on the brink of the abyss. Such a spirit would be the *free spirit* par excellence.

348
Of the Origin of the Scholars

The scholar in Europe grows out of all sorts of strata and social conditions, like a plant which does not require any specific soil; for this reason he is essentially and involuntarily one of the vehicles for democratic thought. But this origin betrays itself. If we have learned to recognize the intellectual *idiosyncrasy* of the scholar in a scholarly text or a scientific treatise – all of them betray such an idiosyncrasy – and if we catch it in the act, we shall almost always get a glimpse of the 'prehistory' of the scholar and his family, especially with regard to their vocations and occupations. Where the sentiment 'that is now proven, now I am finished with it' finds expression, it is commonly the perspective of an ancestor lurking in the blood and instincts of the scholar who approves of a 'finished work' – belief in the proof is only an indication of what has been looked upon by generations of industrious ancestors as a 'job well done'. Here is an example. There is an inclination which manifests itself in the sons of registrars and bureaucrats of all kinds, people whose main task has always been to arrange a variety of material, file it away and in general to schematize it; once they have become scholars, they regard a problem as almost solved as soon as they have schematized it. There are philosophers who are basically nothing but schematizing heads – for them, the form of the paternal occupation has become its content. The talent for classification, for tables of categories, betrays something; a man cannot enjoy with impunity the fact that he is the child of his parents. The son of a lawyer will also have to be a lawyer as a researcher: his primary consideration is to be taken for right, while actually *being* right is at best secondary. We recognize the sons of Protestant ministers and school teachers in scholars by the naive assurance with which they already assume that they have proven their case, when all they have really done is present it heartily and with fervour; they are thoroughly accustomed to people *believing* them – it was a part of their fathers' 'occupation'! A Jew, by contrast, in accordance with the business circles in which he moves and the past of his people, is least accustomed to people believing him. Observe Jewish scholars in this regard – they all place great emphasis on logic, that is, on *compelling* assent by offering reasons; they know that they must conquer with them, even when the resentments of race and class are against them, even where people are loath to believe them. You see, nothing is more democratic than logic; it is no respecter of persons, and takes even the crooked nose for the straight. (By the way, Europe owes no small debt to the Jews with respect to logical thinking and more *scrupulous* intellectual habits; above all the Germans, a lamentably *déraisonnable* race, who even now always need to have some sense knocked into them. Wherever the Jews have had an influence, they have taught us to analyse further, argue more acutely and write more clearly and accurately; their task has always been to persuade a people to 'listen to reason'.)

349
More on the Origin of the Scholars

Wishing only to preserve oneself is the expression of distress, or of a restriction on the proper, fundamental impulse of life which aims at the *extension of power*, and with this intention often enough calls into question and sacrifices self-preservation. We regard it as symptomatic when an individual philosopher, as, for example, the consumptive Spinoza, sees and has to see the decisive factor precisely in the so-called impulse towards self-preservation[8] – they were merely men in distress. The fact that our modern natural sciences have entangled themselves to such an extent in Spinoza's dogma (most recently and in the crudest manner in Darwinism, with its incredibly one-sided

doctrine of the 'struggle for existence'), is probably due to the
origin of most naturalists: they belong in this respect to the
'people', their ancestors were poor and humble folk who were
intimately acquainted with the difficulty of making ends meet.
The whole of English Darwinism is reminiscent of the stifling
air of English overpopulation, like the vulgar smell of hardship and overcrowding. But as a naturalist, one should emerge
from one's human corner; and in nature distress does not
hold sway, but rather abundance, even an absurd extravagance.
The struggle for existence is but an *exception*, a temporary
restriction on the life-will; the struggle whether great or small
everywhere turns on predominance, on growth and expan-
sion, on power, in accordance with the will to power, which is
precisely the will of life.

350
In Honour of Homines Religiosi

The struggle against the Church is of course among other things –
because it signifies so many things – also the struggle of the more
common, more cheerful, more familiar, more superficial natures
against the reign of more grave, more profound, more contemplative, that is to say more malicious and suspicious men, men
who with a long suspicion brood about the value of existence,
and also brood about their own value – the common instinct of
the people, their sensuality, their 'good heart', rebelled against
them. The whole Roman Catholic Church rests on a Southern
suspicion about the nature of man, something which is always
misunderstood in the North, a suspicion which the European
South inherits from the profound Orient, from ancient, mysterious Asia and its form of contemplation. Protestantism is already
a popular uprising in favour of the respectable, faithful and
superficial people (the North was always more good-natured and
shallow than the South), but it was the French Revolution
which first handed the sceptre fully and solemnly to the 'good
man' (to the sheep, to the ass, to the goose and to all who are
incurably shallow troublemakers ripe for the madhouse of
'modern ideas').

351
In Honour of Priestly Natures

I think that philosophers have always felt themselves to be quite
distant from what the people take for wisdom (and who nowadays isn't one of the 'people'?): the piety and gentleness of
the country vicar, the prudent and calm disposition which
resembles nothing so much as the moderate temperament of a
cow which lies in the meadow and *gazes* at life seriously and
ruminatively – probably because philosophers were not 'people'
enough, not country vicar enough, for that kind of thing. Also,
a philosopher would most likely be the last person to be per-
suaded of the people's *ability* to understand something of his
more distant concerns, let alone grasp something of the *passion*
with which he pursues them. It is the great passion of the
knowledge-seeker who lives, and must continually live, within
a thundercloud of the loftiest problems and the most difficult
responsibilities (and which is therefore something entirely different from merely observing life with a dispassionate gaze,
with detachment, certainty and objectivity). The people revere
a very different kind of man when they form their own ideal of
the 'sage', and they are a thousand times justified in rendering
homage with the highest eulogies and honours to precisely that
kind of man – namely, the gentle, simple-minded seriousness of
the chaste priestly natures and all who are related to them. It is
to them that praise is rendered in the popular reverence for wisdom. And who else is more deserving of the people's gratitude
than a man who is one of them and comes from them, but who
is dedicated to them, chosen to be *sacrificed* for their sake –
who believes that he is sacrificed for God's sake – to whom all
can pour their hearts out with impunity, to whom they can
unburden their minds of their secrets, their anxieties or worse
(for the man who 'communicates himself' casts off a part of
himself, and once he has 'confessed' he forgets). Such men satisfy a great need; for sewers filled with pure and purifying
waters are needed for washing away spiritual as well as bodily
filth, and strong, humble, pure hearts filled with rapid streams
of love are needed which are prepared to sacrifice themselves

for such a service of the non-public hygiene – for it *is* a sacrifice, the priest is and remains a human sacrifice . . .

The people regard such men of 'faith', serious individuals who have become silent and been sacrificed to them, as *wise* – that is, as men who have come to possess knowledge, as men who possess 'certainty' in contrast to their own uncertainty. Who would want to deprive them of their reputation for that and the reverence that goes with it?

But surely it is fair for philosophers to regard the priest as one of the 'people' and *not* as a man of knowledge, especially because they themselves do not believe in the existence of 'men of knowledge', and already detect a whiff of the 'people' in this very belief and superstition. In ancient Greece it was left to the play-actors of the spirit, with their overweening arrogance, to call themselves 'wise'; it was *modesty* which led to the invention of the word 'philosopher' – the modesty of such monsters of pride and high-handedness as Pythagoras, as Plato –

352
To What Extent Is Morality Almost Indispensable?

The naked man is generally a shameful sight – I am talking about European men (and by no means about European women!). Suppose that the people at a delightful dinner party were through some magician's trick suddenly to find themselves exposed and unclothed, I imagine that this would not only dampen spirits and dull the strongest appetite – it seems that we Europeans cannot afford to dispense with the masquerade known as clothes. But are there not equally good reasons for the clothing of 'moral men', the way they disguise themselves with moral formulae and notions of propriety, the whole favourable concealment of our actions with notions of duty, virtue, public-spiritedness, respectability and self-denial? Not that I am suggesting that human malice and perfidy – in short, the wicked wild beast in us – should be disguised: on the contrary, it is precisely the fact that we are *tame animals* which is the shameful sight, and which requires the clothing of morality – the fact that the 'inner man' in Europe is not nearly wicked enough 'to let himself be seen' in his wickedness (to be *beautiful* in his wickedness). The European clothes himself *in morality* because he has become a sick, sickly, crippled animal who has good reasons to be 'tame', because he is almost deformed, something scarce half made up,[9] weak and awkward ...

It is not the formidableness of the beast of prey that renders moral clothing necessary, but the gregarious animal with its profound mediocrity, anxiety and boredom. Admit it! *Morality dresses up the European* in more distinguished, more important, more handsome apparel – in 'divine' apparel –

353
Of the Origin of Religions

The actual inventiveness of founders of religions consists in the following: to establish a particular way of life and its daily customs which is to serve as a *disciplina voluntatis* while doing away with boredom; and then to give to that very way of life an *interpretation* by virtue of which it seems to be a good surrounded by a halo of supreme worthiness; so that in the end people will fight for it, and, under certain circumstances, even die for it. In fact, the second of these inventions is the more essential one; the first, the way of life, was usually there already, along with other ways of life, and unaware of the value which it embodies. The significance and originality of the founder of a religion is usually manifested in the fact that he *observes* this way of life, *chooses* it and *divines* for the first time to what ends it should be employed and how it might be interpreted. For example, Jesus (or Paul) encountered the life of the common people in the Roman province, a modest, virtuous, difficult life; he interpreted it, invested it with the highest significance and value. As a result, he possessed the courage to despise every other way of life, the quiet fanaticism of the Moravian Brethren,[10] and a secret, subterranean self-confidence which grew ever stronger until it was finally ready to 'overcome the world' (that is, Rome and the upper classes throughout the empire). The Buddha also encountered the same kind of people scattered among all the classes and social strata of his nation, people who,

owing to indolence, were good and kind (and above all inoffensive), and who, likewise owing to indolence, lived abstemiously,
almost without a care. He understood that this sort of person,
with all its *vis inertiae*, inevitably drifts into a belief which
promises to *prevent* the recurrence of earthly travail (that is to
say, labour and activity of any kind) – this 'understanding' was
his genius. The founder of a religion possesses an infallible psychological knowledge of a specific, mediocre kind of personality,
even though such people have not yet *recognized* that they
belong together. It is he who brings them together: the founding
of a religion is always one long festival of recognition.

354
Of the 'Genius of the Species'[11]

The problem of consciousness (or more properly: of becoming
self-conscious) comes before us only when we begin to grasp the
extent to which we could get along without it; physiology and
ethology have made a start in this direction (though it has taken
them two centuries to catch up with *Leibniz*'s prescient suspicions in this regard). For we could in fact think, feel, will and
remember, we could likewise 'act' in every sense of the word, and
nevertheless none of this need ever 'enter consciousness' (as we
say figuratively). The whole of life would be possible without it
seeing itself in a mirror, so to speak; just as even now the greater
portion of this life goes on without this mirroring – and indeed
even much of our cognitive, affective and volitional life, however
offensive this may sound to an older philosopher. So why have
consciousness at all, when it is in the main superfluous?

Now it seems to me, if you will listen to my answer and its
perhaps extravagant speculation, that the subtlety and strength
of consciousness are always proportional to a man's (or animal's) *capacity for communication*, this capacity being in turn
proportional to the *need for communication*; by which I do not
mean that the individual who is master at communicating and
making his needs known is necessarily the most dependent
upon others for the satisfaction of these needs. But it seems to
me to be so with respect to whole races and successions of

generations, where need and hardship have long compelled men to communicate with and understand one another quickly and subtly; a surplus of the power and art of communication finally exists, a fortune (so to speak) has been accumulated which waits upon an heir to squander it lavishly (the so-called artists are these heirs, as are orators, preachers and authors: all of them men who come at the end of a long succession, 'epigones' in the best sense of the word and, as I said, *squanderers* by their very nature). If this observation is correct, then I may proceed to the conjecture that *consciousness has developed only under the pressure of the need for communication* – that from the very beginning it has been necessary and useful only between man and man (especially between those commanding and those obeying) and has only developed in proportion to its utility. Consciousness is actually nothing but a network of connections between man and man – only as such did it have to develop: a reclusive or predatory man would not have needed it. The fact that our actions, thoughts, emotions and movements even come into consciousness – at least a part of them – is the consequence of a terrible and prolonged imperative to which man was subject: as the most endangered animal, he *needed* help and protection; he needed his kin, he had to express his hardship, to know how to make himself intelligible – and for all this he needed 'consciousness' first and foremost, thus he had to 'know' for himself what he lacked, how he felt and what he thought. For, to say it again, like every living creature, man thinks all the time, but does not know it; the thinking of which we are conscious is only the smallest part of the whole, and, I might add, the most superficial part, the worst part – for this conscious thinking *takes place in words, that is, in the signs of communication*, and it is in this form that the origin of consciousness is disclosed. In short, the development of language and the development of consciousness (*not* of reason, rather, only of reason become self-conscious) go hand in hand. Let us add that it is not only language which serves as a bridge between man and man, but also the facial expressions, circumstances and gestures. What is more, our consciousness of our sense impressions, our ability to stabilize them and project them outside ourselves, has increased to the same extent as our need for communicating them to others through signs. The man who devises signs is at the same time the man who is always more acutely self-conscious; it is only as a social animal that man has learned to become conscious of himself – he is doing so still, and is doing so more and more.

Obviously, my idea is that consciousness is actually not a part of man's individual existence at all, but rather a part of his communal or gregarious nature; from which it follows that it is only in relation to communal and gregarious utility that it develops with any subtlety; and that consequently each of us, no matter how hard we try to *understand* ourselves as individuals, no matter how hard we try to follow the maxim 'know thyself', will never bring into consciousness any more than what is non-individual in us, our 'ordinariness' – that our thought itself is continuously being *outvoted*, so to speak, by the character of consciousness, by the mandate of the 'genius of the species' it contains, and translated back into the perspective of the herd. Without a doubt, basically all of our actions are incomparably personal, unique and infinitely individual; but as soon as we translate them into consciousness, *they no longer seem to be . . .*

In my opinion, this is the proper understanding of phenomenalism and perspectivism: the nature of *animal consciousness* implies that the world of which we are able to become conscious is only a superficial world, a world of signs, a generalized and vulgarized world – that everything which becomes conscious thereby becomes shallow, thin, relatively stupid, general, a sign, a characteristic of the herd; that all consciousness is associated with a great and fundamental corruption, falsification, superficiality and generalization. Finally, the growth of consciousness is dangerous, and whoever lives among the most conscious Europeans even knows that it is a disease. As one might have guessed, it is not the antithesis of subject and object which concerns me here; I leave that distinction to the epistemologists who have remained entangled in the snares of grammar (the metaphysics of the people). Even less is it the antithesis of the 'thing in itself' and the phenomenon; for we do not 'know' enough to be entitled to make such a *distinction*. We have absolutely no organ for *knowledge*, for 'truth'; we 'know' (or believe, or imagine) exactly as much as may be *useful* to us, exactly as much as promotes the interests of the human herd or species; and even what is called 'useful' here is ultimately only what we *believe* to be useful, what we *imagine* to be useful, but perhaps is precisely the most fatal stupidity which will some day lead to our destruction.

355
The Origin of Our Conception of Knowledge

I take this explanation from the street. I heard someone saying 'he knew me', so I asked myself: for most people, what passes for knowledge? What do they want when they seek 'knowledge'? Nothing more than to reduce something strange to something *familiar*. And we philosophers – do we really regard knowledge as anything *more* than that? The familiar, that is, what we are accustomed to, what no longer surprises us, the commonplace, any kind of rule which we are unable to break, anything and everything in which we feel at home – what? Is our need for knowledge not merely this need for the familiar? The desire to discover in everything strange, unusual or questionable something which no longer troubles us? Might it not be the case that the *instinct of fear* is what enjoins us to seek knowledge? Might it not be the case that the knowledge-seeker's sense of triumph is nothing but a restored sense of security? This philosopher[12] imagined the world was 'known' when he had reduced it to the 'Idea'; alas, was it not because the Idea was so familiar to him? Because he had so much less to fear from the 'Idea'?

Oh, how undemanding our knowledge-seekers are! Just look at their principles, at their solutions to the riddle of the world in this regard! Whenever they rediscover something in things, under things or behind things that is unfortunately very familiar to us, for example, our multiplication table, or our logic, or our willing and desiring, they are immediately pleased! For 'whatever is familiar is known': in this they all agree. Even the most cautious among them thinks that the familiar is at least *more easily known* than the strange; for example, that it is methodologically necessary to start with the 'inner world', with 'the facts of consciousness', because it is the world which is more *familiar to us*! Error of errors! The familiar is merely what we are accustomed to, and what we are accustomed to is the most difficult of all to 'know' – that is to say, to regard as a problem, to regard as strange, distant, 'external' . . .

The great certainty of the natural sciences in comparison with psychology and the critique of the elements of consciousness – *unnatural* sciences, one might almost say – rests precisely on the fact that they take what is *strange* as their object; while it is almost something contradictory and absurd to *want* to take what is not strange as an object . . .

356
The Way in Which Europe Is Becoming Ever More 'Artistic'

In our transitional period, when so many things no longer have the power to compel obedience, the cares of life compel almost all male Europeans to assume a definite *role*, their so-called profession; some are allowed to exercise discretion (a discretion more apparent than real, however) as regards which role, but most have it chosen for them. The result is strange enough: almost all Europeans confound themselves with their role as they grow older; they themselves are the victims of their own 'splendid performance' and have forgotten the extent to which chance, caprice and arbitrariness dictated the choice of 'profession' at the time – and how many other roles they *might* have played; but now it is too late! If we look below the surface, we see that their character is actually a *further development* of their role, their nature a further development of their artifice. There were ages in which people believed with a dull confidence, even with a sense of piety, that they were predestined for just this business, for just this way of earning a living, and refused to acknowledge the element of chance in it, the role played by the utterly arbitrary. With the help of this faith, estates, guilds and the hereditary privileges of tradesmen succeeded in erecting those immense and broad-based edifices of society which characterized the Middle Ages, and which may still boast of at least one thing: durability (and on this earth, duration is a value of the highest order!). But conversely, there are ages, genuinely democratic ages, when this faith is increasingly forgotten and replaced by another particular faith, the bold Athenian faith first observed in the age of Pericles, the contemporary American belief, which is increasingly becoming the European belief as well. These are ages when the individual becomes convinced that he can do almost anything, that he can *play almost any role*; when everyone experiments with himself, improvises, experiments anew, experiments with relish; when all nature ceases and becomes art . . .

The Greeks, having adopted this *faith in roles* – an artist's faith, if you will – progressively underwent a curious and not altogether exemplary transformation: *they became genuine actors*; and as such they enchanted and conquered the whole world, and in the end even conquered the conquerors (for it was the *Graeculus histrio*[13] who conquered Rome, and not, as the innocent usually say, Greek culture). But what I fear, what is patently obvious to all who are willing to observe, is that we modern men are already on the same path; and every time a man begins to discover the way in which he plays a role, and the way in which he can be an actor, that is what he becomes . . .

In this way, new human flora and fauna which cannot flourish in more solid and more circumscribed eras arise – or are consigned to 'the bottom', anathematized and disgraced; after which the most interesting and strange periods of history transpire in which 'actors', *all* kinds of actors, are the real masters. By this means another breed of men is always increasingly placed at a disadvantage and ultimately rendered impossible: above all the great 'master builders'; the power to build begins to flag; the courage to make long-range plans becomes discouraged; the organizing geniuses are nowhere to be found; for who would dare to undertake works whose completion might require millennia? The fundamental faith on the basis of which one could calculate, promise and anticipate the future in one's plan, and offer sacrifices to one's plan, is disappearing: the faith that man has value and significance only in so far as he is *a stone in a great edifice*, and to that end he must first of all be *solid*, must first of all be 'stone' . . . and above all, not – an actor!

Briefly – and I fear that this fact will go without mention for some time to come – from now on, what will no longer be built, what *can* no longer be built, is a society in the accepted sense of the term; in order to build that edifice everything is lacking, above all the material. *None of us are any longer material for a society*: that is a truth whose time has come! It seems to me a matter of indifference that meanwhile the most short-sighted, perhaps the most honest, and at any rate the noisiest kind of men nowadays, our friends the socialists, believe, hope, dream and above all squall and scrawl almost the exact opposite; in fact one already reads their watchword of the future, 'free society', on every table and wall. Free society? Yes, yes, but gentlemen, surely you know out of what material it must be built? Out of ironwood,[14] the celebrated iron of wood! And it need not even be made of wood . . .

357
The Old Problem: 'What Is German?'

Let us review the actual achievements of philosophical thought which we owe to German thinkers; is there any admissible sense in which they should be credited to the race as a whole? May we say that they are simultaneously the work of the 'German soul', or at least a symptom of it in the sense in which we are accustomed to think that Plato's ideomania, for example, his almost religious madness with regard to the Forms, is an event in and a testimony to the 'Greek soul'? Or would the opposite be closer to the truth? Were they precisely so individual, so much *exceptions* to the spirit of the race, as, for example, Goethe's paganism with a good conscience was? Or as Bismarck's Machiavellianism with a good conscience, his so-called '*Realpolitik*', was among Germans? Did our philosophers perhaps even contradict the *needs* of the 'German soul'? In short, were the German philosophers really – philosophical *Germans*?

I can think of three cases. First, *Leibniz*'s incomparable insight, which was proven right in opposition not only to Descartes but to everyone who had philosophized to date – that consciousness is only an *accidens* of representation, and *not* its necessary and essential attribute, so that what we call consciousness is only a state of our mental and psychological world (perhaps a morbid state) and *by no means the thing itself* – is there something German about this thought, the profundity of which is still far from exhausted? Is there any reason to suppose that a Latin could not just as easily have stumbled upon this reversal of appearances? For it is a reversal.

Second, let us consider the immense question mark which *Kant* placed after the notion of 'causality' – not that he doubted its legitimacy altogether, as Hume had; rather, he began by carefully delineating the domain within which this notion had any meaning (and we are not yet finished with this demarcation of limits).

Third, let us take the astonishing discovery of *Hegel*, who violated every logical habit and self-indulgence when he dared to teach that our concepts of species develop *out of one another*, with which proposition European thinkers were prepared for the last great scientific movement, for Darwinism – for without Hegel there would have been no Darwin. Is there something German about this Hegelian innovation which first introduced the decisive concept of 'development' into science?

Yes, without a doubt: in all three cases we feel that something of ourselves has been 'revealed' and surmised, and we are thankful for it and at the same time surprised, for each of these three propositions is a thoughtful piece of German self-knowledge, self-experience, self-apprehension. We feel with Leibniz that 'our inner world is far richer, more extensive, more hidden'; as Germans we doubt with Kant the ultimate validity of natural-scientific knowledge, and in general anything which *allows* itself be known *causaliter*; the knowable already appears to us to be *less* valuable simply by virtue of being knowable. We

Germans would have been Hegelians even if there had never been a Hegel, in as much as we (unlike all Latins) instinctively attribute a deeper significance and higher value to becoming, to development, than to that which 'is' – we hardly believe at all in the legitimacy of the concept of 'being'; also in so far as we are disinclined to regard our human logic as logic in itself, the only kind of logic. (We would sooner persuade ourselves that it is only a special case, and perhaps one of the most most quaint and stupid.)

A fourth question would be whether *Schopenhauer* with his pessimism, that is, the problem of the *value of existence*, had to be a German. I do not think so. The event *after* which this problem was to be expected with certainty, so that an astronomer of the soul could have calculated the day and the hour for it – namely, the decline of faith in the Christian God, the victory of scientific atheism – is an entirely European event for which all races deserve some credit and respect. On the contrary, it was precisely the Germans – those same Germans who were Schopenhauer's contemporaries – who *delayed* the victory of atheism the longest, and endangered it the most. Hegel in particular was its delayer par excellence, by virtue of the grandiose attempt he made to persuade us of the divinity of existence, by appealing in the last resort to our sixth sense, 'the historical sense'. As a philosopher, Schopenhauer was the *first* avowed and unwavering atheist we Germans have had; this was the background to his hostility towards Hegel. The ungodliness of existence he regarded as something given, palpable, indisputable; he invariably lost his philosophical temper and became indignant whenever he saw anyone hesitate or beat about the bush here. It is at this point that his utter integrity appears; unconditional, honest atheism is just the *presupposition* for his posing of the problem, as a final and hard-won victory for the European conscience, as the most consequential act in two thousand years' worth of discipline in truthfulness, which forbids itself the *lie* of a belief in God . . .

We can see *what* actually triumphed over the Christian God – Christian morality itself, an ever stricter conception of truthfulness, the confessional subtlety of the Christian conscience, translated and sublimated to the scientific conscience, to intellectual scrupulousness at all costs. Looking upon nature as if it were a proof of a benevolent and protective deity; interpreting history as a tribute to divine reason, as a constant testimony to the existence of a moral world order and moral teleology; interpreting personal experiences as pious men have long interpreted them, as if everything were a dispensation or intimation of Providence, as if everything had been contrived and ordained for the sake of the salvation of the soul: all that is *over* now, it has the conscience *against* it, it is regarded by all the subtler consciences as indecent and dishonest, as chicanery, femininity, weakness and cowardice – by virtue of this rigour, if by nothing else, we are *good* Europeans, the heirs of Europe's longest and bravest self-conquest. When we thus reject the Christian interpretation and condemn its 'meaning' as counterfeit, we are immediately confronted in a formidable manner with the *Schopenhauerian* question: *does existence have any meaning at all?* This is a question which will take a few centuries to be fully understood in all its profundity. Schopenhauer's own answer to this question was – forgive me – something premature and juvenile, a mere half-measure, a way of remaining stuck in the very same Christian and ascetic perspectives of morality, faith in which had been annulled along with the faith in God . . . But he raised the question – as a good European, as I said, and not as a German.

Or did the Germans at least demonstrate their inner affiliation and kinship with Schopenhauer by the way in which they appropriated his question? Did they seem to be prepared for his problem or feel the *need* to address it? It does not sufficiently establish a close affinity to note that there has been some thought given and some ink spilled even in Germany since Schopenhauer first raised the problem – after all, it took long enough! We could just as easily emphasize the strange *ineptitude* displayed by this post-Schopenhauerian pessimism – Germans obviously feel out of their element here. I am not at all alluding here to Eduard von Hartmann;[15] on the contrary, I have long suspected that he is *too clever by half* for us, and am tempted to add that he was an arrant knave from the very beginning. Not only might he have

been having fun at the expense of German pessimism, but he
might even have 'bequeathed' us the legacy of a full understanding of the extent to which we can be played for fools, even
during the era of financial speculation in the early 1870s.[16] But,
I ask, are we to credit to the Germans that old spinning top
Bahnsen, who all his life spun with the greatest of pleasure
around the fixed point of his real-dialectical misery and 'personal bad luck' – would you call that German? (I recommend
herewith his writings for the purpose for which I have used them
myself, as anti-pessimistic fare, especially for their *elegantiae
psychologicae*, which, it seems to me, could alleviate even the
most constipated body and soul.) Or should we count such dilet-
tantes and spinsters as Mainländer,[17] that mawkish apostle of
virginity, among the proper Germans? After all, he was probably a Jew (and all Jews become mawkish when they moralize).
Neither Bahnsen, nor Mainländer, nor even Eduard von Hartmann give us a good handle on the question of whether the
pessimism of Schopenhauer, with his horrified gaze into an
undeified, stupid, blind, crazy and questionable world, his honest horror . . . was not only an exceptional case among Germans
but a German event; while everything else which stands in the
foreground – such as our plucky politics and our joyous jingoism
(which resolutely regards everything with reference to the rather
slight philosophical principle, '*Deutschland, Deutschland, über
Alles*',[18] thus *sub specie speciei*,[19] namely, the German species) –
with great clarity attests to the contrary. No! The Germans of
today are not pessimists! And Schopenhauer was a pessimist,
again, as a good European and not as a German.

358
The Peasant Revolt of the Spirit

We Europeans behold an immense world of wreckage in which
some things still tower above us, many others stand deserted
and dilapidated, but most things have already fallen to the
ground and become overgrown with large and small weeds. It
all looks picturesque enough (was there ever anything so fine-
looking?), but it is a city in ruins. What am I describing? The

Church. The Church is this city in ruins: we behold the religious society of Christendom shaken to its very foundations – belief in God is overthrown, belief in the ascetic ideal of Christianity is now in its death throes. Such an old and well-constructed edifice as Christianity – it was the last construction of the Romans – could not of course be destroyed all at once; all kinds of earthquakes had to shake it, all kinds of spirits which bore, dig, gnaw and moulder have had to help. However, what is most remarkable is the fact that those who have been the most anxious to conserve and preserve Christianity are the very ones who did most to destroy it – I mean the Germans. Apparently, the Germans do not understand the essence of a church. Are they not spiritual enough? Not suspicious enough? In any event, the edifice of the Church rests upon a *Southern* freedom and liberality of the spirit, and also upon a Southern suspicion of nature, man and spirit – it rests upon a very different understanding of man, a very different experience of man, than one finds in the North. From top to bottom, the Lutheran Reformation was the simple folk's indignation against something 'complicated'. To express myself more circumspectly, it was an honest mistake, a crude misunderstanding in which much should be forgiven – they failed to grasp that what they beheld was the expression of a *victorious* Church and not merely corruption; they misunderstood the noble scepticism, the *luxury* of scepticism and tolerance which every victorious, self-confident power permits itself . . .

Nowadays it is obvious enough that in every cardinal question of power, Luther was dangerously superficial, short-sighted and improvident, above all, as a man who came from the common people, in whom everything one inherits from a ruling caste, any instinctive understanding of how to exercise power was completely absent; so that his work, his determination to restore what the Romans had constructed, involuntarily and unconsciously became nothing but the beginning of a work of destruction. With honest indignation, he unravelled and tore asunder what the old spider had woven for such a long time and with such care. He made the Scriptures available to everyone – with the result that, in the end, they fell into the

hands of the philologists, that is, the annihilators of every faith
based upon books. He destroyed the conception of 'the Church'
by repudiating faith in the inspiration of the Councils;[20] for
only on the presupposition that the inspiring spirit which had
founded the Church yet lives, yet builds, yet continues building
its house, can the conception 'the Church' retain its power. He
gave back to the priest sexual intercourse with women; but
three-quarters of the common people's capacity for reverence
(above all among women) rests on the belief that a man who is
exceptional in this respect will also be exceptional in other
respects – it is precisely here that the popular belief in something superhuman in man, in a miracle, in the redeeming God
in man, has its most subtle and delicate advocate. After Luther
had given the priest a wife, he had to *take* from him the
confessional – that was psychologically appropriate; but in so
doing he practically abolished the Christian priest himself,
whose profound usefulness had always consisted in his being a
sacred ear, a silent well and a grave for secrets. 'Every man his
own priest' – behind such formulae and their peasant cunning
there lay concealed in Luther the deepest hatred of 'superior
men' and of the rule of 'superior men' as the Church had conceived them; Luther shattered an ideal which he was unable to
attain, while seeming to combat and abhor its degeneration.
As a matter of fact, this impossible monk overthrew the *domination* of the *homines religiosi*; he thus brought about precisely
the same thing within the ecclesiastical order which he had so
intolerantly opposed in the bourgeois order – a 'peasant revolt'.

All the things which subsequently emerged from his Reformation, both good and bad, which nowadays can be tallied with
almost mathematical precision – who would be naive enough
simply to praise or blame Luther for these consequences? He
was blameless in all of this; he knew not what he did. There
can be no doubt that Europeans' diminishing sense of hierarchy (or increasing sense of benevolence, if one prefers a
moral expression), especially in the North, took a remarkable
step forwards with the Lutheran Reformation; and likewise
there grew out of it a suppleness and restlessness of the spirit,
a thirst for independence, a belief in the right to freedom, and

a certain 'naturalness'. If we are willing to concede to the Reformation the merit of having fostered and prepared the way for what we nowadays revere as 'modern science', we must of course add that it is also responsible for the degeneration of the modern scholar, with his lack of reverence, shame or profundity; for the entirely naive innocence and petty-bourgeois manner with which one pursues knowledge, in short, for the *plebeianism of the spirit* which is peculiar to the last two centuries, and from which even pessimism has not yet delivered us – even 'modern ideas' are a part of this peasant revolt of the North against the more dispassionate, more ambiguous, more suspicious spirit of the South, which built its greatest monument in the Christian Church. Let us not forget what a church ultimately is, as opposed to every 'state': a church is above all a form of domination which secures for the most *spiritual* men the highest position, and *believes* so much in the power of spirituality as to forbid itself all cruder means of violence – for this reason alone, the Church is under all circumstances a *nobler* institution than the State.

359
Revenge on the Spirit, and Other Ulterior Motives of Morality

Morality – where do you think it has its most dangerous and treacherous advocates?

Here is an ill-constituted man, who does not have enough spirit to rejoice, but just enough culture to know it; bored, weary, filled with self-contempt; unfortunately cheated by some inherited fortune out of the last consolation, the 'blessings of labour', the self-forgetfulness in the 'daily toil'; a man who is thoroughly ashamed of his existence – perhaps he harbours a few small vices – but who cannot help indulging his taste for books he has no business reading or more intellectual companionship than he is able to assimilate, making himself vain and irritable in the process: such a thoroughly poisoned man – because for such ill-constituted men, spirit becomes poison, culture becomes poison, possessions become poison, solitude becomes poison – ultimately finds himself in a habitual condition of vengefulness, determined to avenge himself on everything . . .

What do you suppose he would find absolutely necessary for seeming to himself superior to more spirited and intelligent men, for creating the enjoyment of *accomplished revenge*, at least in his own imagination? It is always *morality* that he requires, you can bet on it; always the big moral words, always this tiresome rumbling about justice, wisdom, holiness, virtue; always the Stoical demeanour (how well Stoicism hides what one does *not* possess!); always the mantle of sagacious silence, of affability, of gentleness, and whatever else the mantle of the idealist is called, in which the incurably self-contemptuous and also the incurably vain walk around. Do not misunderstand me: out of such born *enemies of the spirit* there arises every now and then a rare specimen of humanity who is revered by the people under the name of saint or sage; it is out of such men that there arise those moral monsters who make a noise and make history – St Augustine was one of them. Fear of the spirit, revenge on the spirit – oh how often these motivating vices become the root of virtues! Yes, virtues!

And among ourselves, we might well ask whether even the philosopher's claim to *wisdom*, which has been made from time to time all over the earth, the maddest and most immodest of all claims – in India as in Greece, has it not always been *above all a hiding place*? Occasionally, it may be nothing more than a pedagogical ploy, a teacher's tender regard for growing and developing individuals, for disciples who often have to be protected from themselves by faith in a person (by an error) . . .

In most cases, however, it is a hiding place for a philosopher, in which he escapes from exhaustion, age, ague and sclerosis; as a sense of the approaching end, as the wisdom of the instinct which animals have before their death – they go off and fall quiet, they choose solitude, creep into caves and become *wise* . . .

How is that? Wisdom is a philosopher's hiding place from – the spirit?

360
Two Kinds of Causes Which Are Confounded

It seems to me that one of my most essential steps forwards is that I have learned to distinguish the precipitating cause of an action from the cause of acting in such and such a way, in a particular direction, with a particular aim. The first kind of cause involves a certain amount of accumulated energy, waiting to be consumed in some manner, to some end; the second kind of cause, by contrast, involves an entirely insignificant amount of energy, a trivial accident for the most part, according to which the amount of energy 'discharges' itself in some specific and determinate manner: the match in relation to the barrel of gunpowder. Among those trivial accidents and matches I count all so-called 'aims', and to an even greater extent the so-called 'callings' as well: they are relatively arbitrary, and almost a matter of indifference in comparison with the immense amount of energy which, as I have said, presses to be discharged in some way or other. In general, action is viewed differently: we are accustomed to regard precisely the aim (purpose, calling, etc.) as the impetus, according to an age-old error – but that is merely the *directing* energy. As a result, we end up confounding the steersman with the steam, so to speak. And it is not even a steersman much of the time, this directing energy . . .

Is it not the case that more often than not the 'aim', the 'purpose', is a mere pretext, a retrospective self-deception driven by vanity, which does not wish it to be said that the ship followed the stream in which it happened to find itself? That it 'wishes' to go there – because it must? That it has a direction, but absolutely no steersman? We still need a critique of the notion of purposiveness.

361
Of the Problem of the Actor

The problem of the actor has troubled me the longest; I was uncertain (and occasionally I am still) as to whether we might come to grips with the dangerous notion of the 'artist' – a notion hitherto treated with unpardonable leniency – from this point of view. Duplicity with a good conscience; delight in dissimulation issuing forth as a power, pushing aside, submerging and sometimes extinguishing the so-called 'character'; the inner longing to assume a role, to wear a mask, to adopt an *appearance*; an excess of all kinds of adaptive abilities which are no longer able to satisfy themselves in the service of immediate and narrow self-interest: perhaps all of this is not *only* inherent in the actor?

Such an instinct would have most easily developed in families of the lower orders who, under varying pressures and constraints, were obliged to pass their lives in profound dependence; who must cut their coat according to their cloth, repeatedly adapting themselves to new circumstances by passing themselves off as different people; who gradually become able to turn their coat at a moment's notice, thereby almost becoming coats themselves, as masters of the habitual and inveterate art of eternally playing hide and seek which in animals is called mimicry – until eventually this whole ability, retained from one generation to the next, becomes imperious, irrational and unruly, and as an instinct learns how to command the other instincts, creating the actor, the 'artist' (the buffoon, the teller of tall tales, the harlequin, the fool, initially the clown and even the classical type of the servant, Gil Blas; for in such types we have the precursors of the artist, and often enough even of the 'genius'). Also in higher social conditions a similar kind of man grows under similar pressures; only there is the histrionic instinct held in check by another instinct, as it is for example in the 'diplomat' – incidentally, I should think that a good diplomat would be free to become a good thespian, provided he was 'free' at all. However, as regards the *Jews*, the people of the adaptive arts *par excellence*, this line of thought suggests from the outset that we regard them as a world-historical occasion for the cultivation of actors, an actual breeding ground for actors; and in fact the question is extremely timely: what good actor today is *not* – a Jew? Also, the Jew as a born *littérateur*, as the actual ruler of the European press, exercises this power on the basis of his histrionic ability; for the *littérateur* is essentially an actor – he plays the part of the 'expert', the 'specialist'.

Last but not least, *women*. If we consider the whole history of women, are they not first and foremost *obliged* to become actresses? If we listen to the doctors who have hypnotized women, or if we love them ourselves – let ourselves be 'hypnotized' by them – what is always the result? That they 'surrender themselves' to their part, even when they – surrender themselves to us . . .

Woman is so artistic . . .

362
Our Belief in the Masculinization of Europe

We owe it to Napoleon (and not at all to the French Revolution, which aspired to the 'brotherhood' of the nations, and the general exchange of hearts and flowers) that a few warlike centuries unlike any in history may now follow one another – in short, that we have entered upon the *classical age of war*, war at once both scholarly and popular, war on the grandest scale (with regard to means, talents and discipline), war upon which all coming millennia will look back with envy and awe as a piece of perfection; for the national movement out of which this martial glory grows is only the shock of reaction against Napoleon, and would not exist without him. Thanks to him, therefore, the day may come when the *man* in Europe has gained ascendancy again over the merchant and the Philistine; perhaps even over the 'woman' as well, who has been pampered by Christianity and the enthusiastic spirit of the eighteenth century, and still more by 'modern ideas'. Napoleon, who regarded modern ideas, and by immediate implication civilization itself, as something of a personal enemy, has proved to be one of the greatest successors to the Renaissance: he has unearthed an entire portion of the ancient character, the decisive one perhaps, the portion made of granite. And who knows whether this portion of ancient character will not in the end gain ascendancy again over the national movement, and will thus have to make itself the heir and successor of Napoleon in a *positive* sense – for Napoleon, as we know, wanted one Europe,[21] and this as the *mistress of the earth.*

363
How Each Sex Has Its Own Prejudice About Love

Despite all the concessions which I am willing to make to the prejudice in favour of monogamy, I will never admit that we should speak of *equal* rights in the love of man and woman, for these do not exist. The reason is that man and woman understand love differently – and it is one of the conditions of love in both sexes that the one sex does *not* presuppose the same sentiment, the same conception of love, as the other sex. What woman understands by love is clear enough: not merely a *betrothal* of herself, but a full *bestowal* of herself,[22] body and soul, without calculation or reservation. The very idea that it should be subject to conditions fills her with shame and terror. It is precisely by virtue of this absence of conditions that a woman's love is a *faith*; she has no other.

When a man loves a woman, he *wants* precisely this kind of love from her; consequently, the man himself is furthest removed from the presupposition of feminine love; if we suppose, however, that there are also men who are no stranger to the longing to bestow themselves fully in this way, well, they are simply – not men. A man who loves like a woman becomes a slave; a woman who loves like a woman becomes a *more perfect* woman . . .

The passion of woman in its unconditional renunciation of its own rights has precisely the presupposition that the other side does not suffer from an equal pathos, an equal desire for renunciation; for if both parties renounced themselves out of love, this would result in what, exactly? An empty space?

Woman wants to be regarded as a possession and treated as such; she wishes to be assimilated to the notion of a possession and be 'possessed'; consequently what she wants is someone who *takes*, who does not give himself or give himself away but instead is supposed to become richer in 'himself' – by the increase of power, happiness and faith which the woman gives to him. The woman gives herself away, the man adds her to himself. I do not think that this natural contrast can be overcome by any social contract or the greatest determination to do justice, no matter how desirable it may be that we avert our eyes from the harsh, terrible, enigmatic and immoral aspects of this antagonism. For love, conceived in all its wholeness, greatness and fullness, is nature, and as nature it will for ever be something 'immoral'.

Fidelity is accordingly included in a woman's love, it follows from its definition; for a man fidelity *can* easily emerge in the wake of his love, perhaps as a sense of gratitude or an idiosyncrasy of taste and so-called elective affinity,[23] but it does not belong to the *essence* of his love – indeed it does so to so little an extent that we might almost be entitled to speak of a natural contrariety between love and fidelity in man, whose love is just a desire to possess, and *not* a renunciation and a giving away; the desire to possess, however, always comes to an end when he *possesses* ...

As a matter of fact, it is the more subtle and suspicious thirst for possession in a man (who is not easily convinced of truly 'having') which makes his love continue; in this respect, it is even possible that his love may grow with her bestowal of herself – he does not readily admit that a woman has nothing more to 'bestow' upon him.

364
The Hermit Speaks

The art of socializing rests essentially upon the adroitness (something which presupposes long practice) with which we accept an invitation to dinner while lacking any confidence in the chef. Provided we come to the table hungry as a wolf, everything goes easily (even 'the worst society lets you *feel*'[24] – as Mephistopheles says); but we are not always hungry as a wolf when we need to be! Alas, how difficult our fellow men are to digest! First principle: as in the case of a misfortune, summon your courage, boldly help yourself, admire yourself at the same time, grit your teeth and swallow your disgust. Second principle: 'improve' your fellow man, by praise, for example, until he begins to exude self-satisfaction; or catch hold of one small corner of his good or 'interesting' qualities, and pull at it until you get the whole virtue out and can hide the fellow under its folds. Third principle: self-hypnosis. Fix your gaze upon the object of your association as if he were a pocket watch until you cease to feel any pleasure or pain, begin unobtrusively to nod off, become rigid and acquire composure: a home remedy in marriage and friendship which has proved indispensable, although it has not yet been scientifically formulated. It is known in the vernacular as – patience.

365
The Hermit Speaks Again

We also have dealings with 'men'; we also discreetly don the garb in which (and *as* which) we are known, the costume in which we are respected and sought out; and so we enter society in this manner, that is to say, among people in disguise who do not wish to call it that; we also do as any prudent person at a masquerade would, and politely bar the door against any inquisitiveness which does not concern our 'clothes'. But there are other tricks and artifices for associating with or passing among men: for example, as a ghost – which is highly advisable if one wishes to give them a good scare and get rid of them easily. Here is an example: a person reaches for us and is unable to catch hold of us. That is frightening. Or we arrive through a closed door. Or when the lights are out. Or after we are dead. The latter is the artifice of *posthumous* men par excellence. ('What do you think?', such a man said once, impatiently. 'Do you think that we would be willing to endure this strangeness, coldness and stillness around us, this entire subterranean, hidden, mute, undiscovered solitude which is called life but might just as well be called death, if we did not know what was to *become* of us – and that it is only after death that we shall *come into our own* and finally be alive, very much alive, we posthumous men!')

366
At the Sight of a Scholarly Book

We are not like those people whose thoughts are taken from books or instigated by books – it is our habit to think in the open air, walking, leaping, climbing or dancing, preferably on solitary mountains or close to the sea, where even the paths become thoughtful. Our first question concerning the value of a book, a man or a piece of music is: can it walk? Or better still, can it dance?

We seldom read; we do not read any worse for that – oh how quickly we divine how someone has arrived at his thoughts – if it is by sitting before an inkwell with pinched belly and head bent over the paper, then oh how quickly we are finished with his book! You may rest assured that his constipated bowels betray themselves, just as the stuffiness of his room, the low ceiling and cramped quarters in which he scribbles betray themselves.

These were my sentiments upon closing an honest, scholarly book: grateful, very grateful, but also relieved . . .

In the book of a scholar there is almost always something oppressive and oppressed: the 'specialist' comes to light somewhere, with his fervour, his seriousness, his indignation, his overestimation of the niche in which he sits and spins, his hunched back – every specialist has a hunched back. A scholarly book also always mirrors a contorted soul: every craft contorts. Just look at your friends again with whom you spent your youth after they have taken possession of their scientific discipline; notice how the opposite always occurs! Alas, they themselves are now always preoccupied with and possessed by *it*! Grown into their niche, crumpled into unrecognizability, constrained, deprived of their equilibrium, emaciated and awkward everywhere, and only in one place are they . . . rotund – you are at a loss for words when you find them so. Every craft, even if we suppose that it has a golden floor, also has a leaden ceiling above it which presses and presses on the soul until it becomes bizarre and contorted. There is nothing for it. We doubt very much that it is possible to mitigate this disfigurement by any kind of educational artifice. Every kind of *mastery* is paid for dearly on this earth – and perhaps everything is paid for too dearly; someone becomes an expert in a particular subject at the cost of becoming its victim as well. Now you would have it otherwise – 'less expensive' and, above all, less uncomfortable – isn't that so, my dear contemporaries? Very well! But then you immediately get something else: instead of the master craftsman, you get the belletrist, the versatile, 'many-sided' belletrist, who to be sure lacks the hunched back – not counting the way he stoops before you as the shopkeeper of the spirit and the 'bearer' of culture – the belletrist who *is* actually nothing but 'represents' almost everything, who 'represents' and plays at being the expert, who modestly *manages* to get paid, honoured and celebrated in his stead.

No, my scholarly friends! I even bless you because of your hunched backs! I bless you because, like me, you despise the belletrists and parasites of culture! I bless you because you do not know how to make merchandise out of your own spirit, and have so many opinions on which you cannot put a price! And because you do not represent anything which you *are* not! Because your sole desire is to become masters of your craft; because you revere every kind of mastery and proficiency, and ruthlessly reject everything feigned, half genuine, embellished, virtuosic, demagogic and histrionic in *litteris et artibus*[25] – anything whose unconditional *probity* of discipline and schooling cannot be shown!

Even genius does not compensate for such a defect, however well it may be able to deceive with regard to it; this becomes clear once one has intimately observed our most gifted painters and musicians – all of whom almost without exception know how to artificially appropriate for themselves the *semblance* of that probity after the fact, the *semblance* of that solidity of schooling and culture through an artful inventiveness with regard to style, makeshifts and even principles; without of course deceiving themselves about it, without silencing their bad consciences by doing so. For surely you know that all great modern artists suffer from a bad conscience . . .

367
The First Distinction to Be Made Between Works of Art

Everything that is conceived, versified, painted or composed, indeed, even what is built and sculpted, belongs either to monological art or to art before witnesses. Among the latter we should also include the seemingly monological art which includes the belief in God, the whole lyricism of prayer; because there is no solitude for a pious man; this invention must be attributed to us, the godless ones. I know of no deeper distinction in the overall appearance of an artist than this: whether he looks with the eyes of a witness at his nascent work of art (that is to say, at 'himself'); or whether he has 'forgotten the world', which is the essence of every work of monological art – it rests on *forgetting*, it is the music of forgetting.

368
The Cynic Speaks[26]

My objections to Wagner's music are physiological objections: why should I first disguise them with aesthetic formulae? The 'fact' is that I can no longer breathe freely when this music begins to affect me; my *foot* immediately becomes angry with it and rebels against it – for what it needs is measure, dance and march; from the outset it demands from music the delights which are to be found in *good* walking, striding, leaping and dancing.

But my stomach, my heart, my blood and my bowels: do they not protest as well? Am I not becoming hoarse without realizing it?

And so I ask myself: what does my body really *want* from music in general? I believe it wants *relief*: as if all animal functions were to be quickened by light, bold, boisterous, self-assured rhythms; as if the brazen, leaden life should be gilded by means of golden, good, tender harmonies. My heavy heart wants to rest in the hiding places and abysses of *perfection*; for this I need music. What do I care for the drama! What do I care for its spasms of moral ecstasy in which the 'people' find their satisfaction! What do I care for the whole hocus-pocus of the actor's gesticulation!

You may have surmised that I am essentially anti-theatrical at heart – but Wagner, by contrast, was essentially a man of the stage and an actor, the most enthusiastic mimomaniac that has ever existed, even as a musician!

And incidentally, if Wagner's theory was that 'the drama is the end, the music is always only the means to it', his *practice* from first to last was contrary to it, as if he were to say, 'Striking attitudes is the end, the drama and the music alike are always only the means to *it*.' Music as a means of clarifying, strengthening and internalizing dramatic gestures and the actor's appeal to the senses; and Wagnerian drama only an opportunity for striking a number of dramatic attitudes! Along with all other instincts, Wagner possessed the commanding instincts of a great actor in absolutely everything, and, as I said, also as a musician.

I once took some pains to make this clear to a righteous Wagnerian, and had reason to add, 'Be a little more honest with yourself: we are not in the theatre! In the theatre we are only honest in the mass; as individuals we lie, we even lie to ourselves. We leave ourselves at home when we go to the theatre; we renounce the right to our own tongue and choice, to our taste and even to our courage as we would otherwise possess it and practise it within our own four walls against both God and man. No one brings their most refined sense of taste in art into the theatre with them, not even the artist who works for the theatre: there, one is people, public, herd, woman, Pharisee, voting animal, democrat, neighbour and fellow man; there even the most personal conscience is subject to the levelling allure of the 'greatest number'; there stupidity functions as prurience and contagion; there the neighbour reigns supreme, there everyone *becomes* a neighbour.

(I forgot to mention what my enlightened Wagnerian told me in reply to my physiological objections: 'So you are just not healthy enough for our music?')

369
Disparities Within Us

Must we not admit to ourselves, we artists, that there is within us an incredible disparity between our taste, on the one hand, and our creative power, on the other? That they are in the most remarkable way distinct from one another, each keeping to itself and growing independently? By which I mean that they have entirely different degrees and *tempi* of age, youth, maturity, mellowness and rottenness. So that, for example, a musician could spend his entire life creating things which *contradicted* everything which his ears and heart held in high regard, took pleasure in and preferred, because they were spoiled by his appreciation for the music to which he was accustomed to listening – and he might not even be aware of this contradiction! As an almost painfully frequent experience shows, we can easily outgrow the taste of our powers, even without our powers becoming paralysed or hindered in their productivity as a result. But the reverse can occur as well – and it is precisely to this that I would like to draw the attention of artists. A consistently productive artist, a man who is a 'mother' in the grand sense of the term, who knows or hears of nothing but pregnancies and childbirths of the spirit, who has absolutely no time to contemplate the relationship between himself and his work, who is no longer willing to exercise his taste, but simply forgets it, that is to say, lets it stand, leaves it alone or allows it to fall by the wayside – in the end, perhaps such a man will produce works *which he is no longer in a position to judge*, so that he utters nothing but stupidities about them, and believes them as well. This seems to me to be almost the normal relationship fruitful artists have with their own works – no one knows a child worse than its parents – and it is even true (to take a prodigious example) of the whole world of Greek poetry and art: it had no idea what it had done . . .

370

What Is Romanticism?[27]

It may be remembered at least among my friends that I initially
took aim at the modern world with some gross errors and
exaggerations,[28] but at any rate with *high hopes*. I recognized
(from who knows what personal experiences?) the philosophical pessimism of the nineteenth century as the symptom of a
stronger mode of thought, a more daring courage and a more
triumphant *abundance* of life than had been characteristic of
the eighteenth century, the age of Hume, Kant, Condillac and
the Sensualists;[29] so that tragic knowledge seemed to me the
peculiar *luxury* of our culture, its most precious, noble and
dangerous form of extravagance; but nevertheless, on account
of its superabundance, a *permissible* luxury. In the same way I
interpreted German music as the expression of a Dionysian
power in the German soul: I thought I heard in it the earth-
quake with which a primal force was finally being vented, a
force that had been building up for ages – indifferent as to
whether everything else called culture was made to tremble as
a result. It is obvious that at the time I misunderstood both
philosophical pessimism and German music, and what constitutes their actual character – their *Romanticism*. What is
Romanticism? Every art and every philosophy may be regarded
as a remedy and aid in the service of growing, struggling life:
they always presuppose suffering and sufferers. But there are
two kinds of sufferers: those who suffer from a *superabundance of life* and who want a Dionysian art, and likewise a
tragic conception of and insight into life; and those who suffer
from an *impoverishment of life* who seek peace and quiet,
becalmed seas and deliverance from themselves through art or
knowledge, or else intoxication, convulsion, narcosis, madness. All Romanticism in art and knowledge responds to a
twofold necessity in the *latter* kind of sufferers; to them Schopenhauer as well as Wagner responded (and responds) – to
name the two most celebrated and emphatic Romantics, both
of whom were at the time *misunderstood* by me – and by the
way, you must admit in all fairness to myself, not at all to their

disadvantage. The Dionysian god or man who is richest in superabundant life can afford not only to see the terrible and questionable things, but even to do terrible deeds, with all their attendant luxury of destruction, disintegration and negation; for him evil, absurdity and ugliness seem acceptable, so to speak, in consequence of the plenitude of procreative, fructifying power, which can transform every desert into verdant farmlands. Conversely the greatest sufferer, the impoverished man, would have the greatest need for gentleness, peace and benevolence in thought and deed; he would need, if possible, a God who is actually the God of the sick, a 'Saviour'; similarly, he would have need of logic, the abstract intelligibility of existence, for logic soothes the soul and inspires confidence – in short, he would need a certain warm, reassuring narrowness and enclosure within optimistic horizons. In this way I gradually began to understand Epicurus, the opposite of a Dionysian pessimist,[30] and likewise the 'Christian', who in fact is only a kind of Epicurean, and like him essentially a Romantic – and my vision has always become more acute in tracing that most difficult and delicate of all forms of *retrospective inference*, the one in which most mistakes have been made – the inference from the work to its author, from the deed to its doer, from the ideal to him who *has need of* it, from every mode of thought and evaluation to the imperious *necessity* behind it.

With regard to all aesthetic values I now avail myself of this principal distinction: in every case I ask myself, has want or abundance been creative here? From the outset, another distinction would seem to have more to recommend it – it is far more obvious – namely, attention to whether the desire for the fixed and the immortal, for *being*, on the one hand, or rather the desire for destruction, for change, for novelty, for future, for *becoming*, on the other, has been the principle of creation. But both kinds of desire prove on closer examination to be ambiguous, that is to say, explicable precisely in accordance with the preceding scheme, to which I have (and, it seems to me, rightly) given pride of place. The desire for *destruction*, for change, for becoming can be the expression of a power overflowing and pregnant with hope (my *terminus* for this, as is well known, is

'Dionysian'); but it can also be the hatred of the ill-constituted, deprived and unfortunate man who destroys and *must* destroy, because he is provoked and enraged by what exists, indeed, by existence itself – to understand this emotion we need only observe closely our anarchists. The desire to *immortalize* likewise requires a twofold interpretation. It can be the product of grati- tude and love – works born of such a desire are always a kind of apotheosis, perhaps a dithyrambic one, as in Rubens, or a bliss- fully mocking one, as in Hāfez, or a bright and benevolent one, as in Goethe, works which spread a Homeric nimbus of light over all things. However, this desire can also be the expression of the tyrannical will of someone who undergoes great suffer- ing, struggles and torture, someone who would make what is most personal, individual and intimate, what is actually idio- syncratic about his suffering, into a binding law and constraint and thereby take his revenge upon all things, so to speak, stamp- ing and branding them with his *own* image, the image of his *own* torment. The latter impulse finds its most expressive form in *Romantic pessimism*, whether it be as Schopenhauer's phil- osophy of the will, or as Wagner's music – Romantic pessimism, the last great event in the destiny of our culture. (That there may be quite a different kind of pessimism, a classical pessimism – this presentiment and vision belongs to me, as something inseparable from me, as my *proprium* and *ipsissimum*;[31] except that I dislike the sound of the word 'classical', for it has become far too well worn, too approximate and indecipherable. I call that pessimism of the future – for it is coming! I see it coming! – *Dionysian* pes- simism.)

371
We Incomprehensible Ones

Have we ever once complained about being misunderstood, misjudged, confounded with others, vilified, misheard or ignored? For a long time, precisely that will be our lot (until, say, 1901, if may be so modest): it is also our distinction. We would not have enough self-respect if we were to wish it otherwise. People confound us with others – because we ourselves are growing, constantly changing, shedding old bark, sloughing it off every spring; we are always growing younger, more promisingly, higher, stronger, driving our roots always more powerfully into the depths – into evil – while at the same time embracing the heavens more and more lovingly, more and more broadly, absorbing their light more and more thirstily with all our branches and leaves. We grow like trees – that is difficult to understand, as all life is! – not in one place, but everywhere, not in one direction only, but upwards and outwards, as well as inwards and downwards – at the same time our vigour shoots forth into stems, branches and roots; we are no longer free to do any one thing, or to *be* any one thing . . .

Such is our lot, as I said: we grow into the *heights*; and even should it be our undoing – for we dwell ever closer to the lightning – well, we honour it no less on that account; it remains that which we do not share, which we do not wish to communicate, the undoing of everything that ascends into the heights, *our* undoing . . .

372
Why We Are Not Idealists

Previously philosophers were afraid of the senses; have we been perhaps too forgetful of this fear? Nowadays we are all Sensualists, we contemporary and future philosophers – *not* in theory, but in *praxis*, in practice . . .

On the other hand, there were once those who were afraid that the senses would lure them away from *their* world, the cold realm of 'ideas',[32] to some dangerous Southern island where their philosophical virtues would melt away like snow in the sun. Back then, 'wax in the ears' was almost a condition of philosophizing; a genuine philosopher no longer listened to life, and, in as much as life itself is music, he *renounced* the music of life – it is an old philosopher's superstition that all music is Sirens' music.[33]

Now we should be inclined to come to precisely the opposite conclusion (which for all that might well be false), and to regard *ideas*, because of their cold and anaemic appearance and not despite it, as worse means of temptation than the senses – they have always lived on the 'blood' of the philosopher, consuming his senses, and, believe it or not, even his 'heart'. These ancient philosophers were heartless; philosophizing was always a kind of vampirism. Do you not sense something profoundly enigmatic and uncanny about a figure like Spinoza? Do you not see the drama which transpires here, the constantly increasing *pallor* – the increasingly idealistic loss of sensible concreteness? Do you not begin to suspect that some long-concealed blood-sucker lies in the background, which begins by draining the senses, and in the end leaves nothing behind except bones and rattling? By which I mean categories, formulae and words – and forgive me for saying this, but what *remains* of Spinoza, his *amor intellectualis dei*,[34] is rattling and nothing more! For what is *amor*, what is *deus*, if there is no drop of blood left in them? In sum, all philosophical idealism hitherto has been something like a disease, unless it was, as in the case of Plato, the prudence of a superabundant and dangerous health, the fear of being *overpowered* by the senses, the wisdom of a clever Socrates.

Perhaps we moderns are not healthy enough to find Plato's idealism *necessary*? And we fear the senses not because –

373
Science as Prejudice

It follows from the laws of hierarchy that scholars, in so far as they belong to the intellectual middle class, cannot catch sight of the truly *great* problems and question marks. Besides, their courage, and likewise their vision, does not extend so far – and above all, the need which makes them into researchers, their own anticipation and wish that things will be constituted *in such and such a way*, their hopes and fears, are too speedily abated, and they attain satisfaction too soon. For instance, consider the need which makes the pedantic Englishman Herbert Spencer enthuse in his inimitable manner about the final reconciliation of 'egoism and altruism' of which he dreams – something which almost inspires disgust in people like us – the need which circumscribes his sense of what is desirable and ensures that it does not extend beyond this horizon; a humanity which regarded such a Spencerian perspective with its particular vanishing point as unsurpassable would seem to be worthy of contempt, of destruction even! But the *fact* that he has to regard something as his highest hope which others can and should regard merely as an ugly possibility is a question mark Spencer could not have foreseen . . .

It is just the same with the belief with which so many materialistic naturalists are satisfied nowadays, the belief in a world which is supposed to find its analogue and measure in human thought and human conceptions of value, a 'world of truth' which, with the help of our square little human reason, we might finally be able to master. What? Do we really wish to have existence reduced in this way to a calculation exercise, to homework for mathematicians? Above all, we should not wish to divest existence of its *ambiguous* character: *good* taste forbids it, gentlemen, the taste which demands reverence for everything which lies beyond your horizon! The idea that the only interpretation of the world which is justified is the one which justifies *you*; the interpretation which allows research and labour to proceed scientifically in *your* sense (don't you really mean *mechanistically*?); the interpretation according to which the world is susceptible to counting, calculating, weighing, seeing and grasping and nothing more – such an idea is a piece of clumsiness and naïveté, provided it is not insanity and idiocy. On the contrary, would it not be quite probable that the utter superficial and external aspects of existence – its most apparentness, its skin, its sensualization – should let themselves be grasped first? And perhaps to the exclusion of all else? Thus a 'scientific' interpretation of the world as you understand it could still be one of the *stupidest*, that is, the most devoid of significance, of all possible interpretations of the world; I say this in confidence to my friends the Mechanists, who nowadays like to hobnob with the philosophers, and who are firmly convinced that Mechanics is the doctrine of the most basic and the ultimate laws upon which all existence must be constructed as on a foundation. But an essentially Mechanical world would be an essentially *meaningless* world! Suppose we assessed the *value* of a piece of music by how much it could be counted, calculated or formulated – how absurd such a 'scientific' assessment of music would be! What would one have grasped, understood or known of it! Nothing, virtually nothing of what is actually 'music' in it!

374
Our New 'Limitlessness'

How far the perspectival character of existence extends, or whether it even has any other character; whether an existence without interpretation, without 'sense', does not simply become 'nonsense'; on the other hand, whether all existence is not essentially an *interpretive* existence – these questions, as one would expect, cannot be answered even by the most diligent and scrupulously precise analysis and self-examination of the intellect,[35] because the human intellect cannot help seeing itself in its perspectival forms when it attempts such an analysis, and *only* sees itself in them. We cannot see around our own corner; it is hopeless curiosity to want to know what other forms of intellect and perspective *might* exist: for example, whether any creatures could perceive time backwards, or alternately forwards and backwards (which would involve another way of life and another conception of cause and effect). But I think that nowadays we are at least far from the ludicrous presumption of decreeing from our corner that only perspectives from that corner are *possible*. On the contrary, the world has once more become 'limitless' to us, in so far as we cannot deny the possibility that it *contains limitless interpretations*. Once again we are chilled to the bone – but who would want to deify *this* monster of an unknown world in the old way, and then go on to worship this unknown thing as '*the* unknown one'? Oh, this unknown contains far too many *ungodly* possibilities of interpretation, and there is too much devilry, stupidity and foolishness in them – the interpretation with which we *are* familiar, our own human, all too human one, very much included . . .

375
Why We Seem To Be Epicureans

We modern men are careful to guard against any ultimate convictions; our distrust is ever vigilant for the way in which every
strongly held belief, every unconditional affirmation or negation, enchants and outwits our conscience. How is this to be
explained? Perhaps to a certain extent it is the caution of a
child who is 'once bitten, twice shy', the caution of the disappointed idealist; but then again there may be another and a better
component to it, the gleeful curiosity of a former loiterer, who has
been brought to despair by his little street corner and now lux-
uriates and revels in its opposite, in the limitless, in the 'great
outdoors' as such. In this way an almost Epicurean inclination
for knowledge is formed which does not easily lose sight of the
questionable character of things; likewise an aversion to grand
moral phrases and gestures, a taste which rejects all awkward,
crude contrasts and regards its exercised reserve with pride.
For *this* constitutes our pride, this easy tightening of the reins
in our galloping desire for certainty, this self-mastery of the
rider on his wildest rides, for we still have mad, fiery steeds
under us; and if we hesitate, it is least likely to be danger which
makes us hesitate . . .

376
Our Slow Periods

This is what all artists and men of 'works', the maternal species of
men, feel: they always believe that at every divide in their lives – a
work always divides – they have already attained the goal itself;
they would always patiently accept death with the sentiment
'now we are ripe for it'. This is not an expression of fatigue, but
rather that of a certain autumnal sunniness and mildness, which
the work itself, the ripening of a work, always leaves behind in its
author. Then the *tempo* of life slows down, turning thick and
flowing with honey – into a long *fermata*, into the belief in long
fermatas[36] . . .

377
We Homeless Ones

Among the Europeans of today there are not lacking those who are entitled to call themselves homeless in a distinguished and honourable sense; it is to them that I expressly commend my secret wisdom and *gaya scienza*![37] For they have a hard lot and uncertain hopes; it is no mean trick to devise a consolation for them – and what good does it do? We children of the future, how *could* we feel at home these days? We are offended by our era's idealities, endorsement of which might make us feel at home in this fragile, fragmented, transitional period; and as for its 'realities', we do not think they will *last*. The ice which still supports us has worn quite thin; a thawing wind blows, and we ourselves, we homeless ones, are something which breaks the ice, and other all too thin 'realities' . . .

We are not 'conservatives' about anything, nor do we wish to return to some earlier age; we are by no means 'liberal', we do not strive for 'progress', we do not need to stop up our ears against the sirens of the marketplace who sing of the future – we are not in the least bit tempted by their songs of 'equal rights', 'a free society', 'no more masters or servants'! We consider it utterly undesirable that a kingdom of justice and concord should be established on earth (because under any circumstances it would be a kingdom of the most profound conciliatory mediocrity and Chinesery[38]); we rejoice in all who, like ourselves, love danger, war and adventure, who do not resign themselves to anything, or allow themselves to be captured, conciliated or castrated; we count ourselves among the conquerors; we contemplate the necessity of a new social order, even of a new slavery – for every strengthening and elevation of the type 'man' is also accompanied by a new kind of slavery. Is it not obvious that with all this we must feel ill at ease in an age which is fond of claiming the honour of being the most humane, gentle and just age the world has ever known? It is bad enough that precisely these fine words excite in us the ugliest suspicions! It is bad enough that we see in that only the expression – or the masquerade – of a profound weakening, of exhaustion, age and

declining strength! What difference does it make what kind of
tinsel an invalid uses to dress up his weakness? He may parade
it about as his *virtue*; there can be no doubt that weakness
makes people meek, oh so meek, so upright, so inoffensive, so
'humane'!

The 'religion of pity' to which some would like to persuade
us – yes, we are thoroughly acquainted with the hysterical little
men and women nowadays who need precisely this religion as
veil and finery! We are no humanitarians; we would never dare
to speak of our 'love of mankind'; for that, men like ourselves
are not actors enough! Or Saint-Simonian[39] enough or French
enough. One must already be afflicted with a *Gallic* excess of
erotic irritability and amorous impatience to even so much as
approach mankind in an honourable way with such ardour . . .

Love of mankind! Was there ever a more hideous old woman
than 'mankind' among all the old women (unless it were perhaps 'the truth': a question for philosophers)? No, we do not
love mankind! On the other hand, however, we are not nearly
'German' enough in the sense in which the word 'German' is
used nowadays to advocate nationalism and race-hatred, or
take delight in the nationalistic scabies of the heart and poi-
soning of the blood on account of which the peoples of Europe
are currently being separated and segregated from one another
as if by quarantines. We are too unprejudiced, too wicked, too
fastidious for that; also too well informed, too 'travelled': we
would much prefer to live on mountains, aloof and 'untimely',
in past or future centuries, if for no other reason than to spare
ourselves the silent rage to which we know we would be condemned as witnesses to a policy which makes the German
spirit barren by making it vain, and which is a *petty* policy
besides; so that its own creation does not immediately fall
apart again, is it not necessary to plant it between two deadly
hatreds? Does it not *have* to desire the perpetuation of Europe's
petty-statery?

We homeless ones, as 'modern men' we are too manifold
and mixed in race and descent, and are consequently little
tempted to participate in the mendacious racial self-admiration
and indecency which parades about nowadays in Germany as

a sign of German sensibility, and which for the people of the 'historical sense' seems doubly dishonest and obscene. We are, to coin a phrase – and it should be our badge of honour – *good Europeans*, the heirs of Europe, its rich and lavish heirs, but also the exceedingly obligated heirs of millennia of the European spirit; as such, we have also outgrown Christianity, and are averse to it – and precisely because we sprang from it, because our ancestors were Christians of uncompromising righteousness, Christians who, for the sake of their belief, willingly sacrificed blood and treasure, condition and country. We do the same. For what, then? For our unbelief? For all kinds of unbelief? No, you know better than that, my friends! The hidden affirmation in you is stronger than all the negations and reservations with which you and your age are afflicted; and when you have to set sail, you emigrants – once again, it is a *faith* which compels you to do so!

378
'And Become Clear Again'

We, the generous and rich of spirit, who stand by the streets like open fountains and refuse no one who wants to draw from us – unfortunately we do not know how to defend ourselves as we would like; we are unable to prevent our waters from being made *murky* and dark – to prevent the age in which we live from casting the most ephemeral things into us, the filthy birds their ordure, the boys their odds and ends, and the weary wanderers who stop to rest a while their petty or great miseries. But we do what we have always done: we take whatever is cast into us down into our depths – for we are deep, we do not forget – and become clear again . . .

379
The Fool's Interruption

It is no misanthrope who has written this book; nowadays the hatred of man is too expensive. To hate man as one did previously, Timonically, completely, without qualification, with one's whole heart, from an utter *love* of hatred – to that end one would have to renounce contempt – and how much subtle enjoyment, how much patience, how much amiableness, even, do we owe to our contempt! Moreover, in this we are the 'elect of God': subtle contempt is our taste and our prerogative, our art, our virtue perhaps, we, the most modern of the moderns!

Hatred, on the other hand, equalizes, places on the same level – in the end, hatred shows respect; there is *fear* in hatred, a great deal of fear. However, we fearless ones, we who are the most intellectual men of the age, know our advantage well enough to live without fear as the most intellectual of this age. We are hardly likely to be beheaded, locked up or banished; we are not even likely to have our books banned or burned. The age loves intellect, it loves us and needs us, even when it is given to understand that we are artists of contempt; that all dealings with people make us shudder; that all our mildness, patience, humanitarianism and civility cannot persuade our nose to dismiss its prejudice against the proximity of man; that we love nature all the more when it is least humane, and art *precisely when* it is the artist's flight from man, or his mockery of man, or his mockery of himself . . .

380

'The Wanderer' Speaks[40]

In order to be able to see our European morality from a distance, the better to compare it with other past or future moralities, we must do as the wanderer does when he wants to know how high the towers of a city are: to that end, he has to *leave* the city. If 'thoughts on moral prejudices'[41] are not to be merely prejudices about prejudices, they must presuppose a position *outside* morality, somewhere beyond good and evil, a position to which we must ascend, climb or fly – and in any case, a position beyond *our* good and evil, an emancipation from everything 'European', understood as a sum of the authoritative value judgements which have become transmuted into flesh and blood. The fact that we want to get there is perhaps a piece of madness, a peculiar, unreasonable 'thou shalt' – for even we knowledge-seekers have the idiosyncrasies of our own 'unfree will'; the question is not why we want to get there, but whether we *can*. That may depend upon many different conditions; it is principally a question of how light or heavy we are, the problem of our 'specific gravity'. We have to be *very light* in order to push our pursuit of knowledge so far above and beyond our own time, in order to create for ourselves eyes which can survey the millennia, and a clear sky in these eyes as well! We have to have freed ourselves from many of the things by which modern Europeans are oppressed, hindered, held down and made heavy. The man of such a beyond, who hopes to so much as get a glimpse of the highest standards of value of his time must first of all 'transcend' this time in himself – it is a proof of his strength – and consequently not only his time, but also his previous resistance and opposition *to* his time, the suffering he endured because of his time, his untimeliness,[42] his *Romanticism* . . .

381
On the Question of Intelligibility

We not only want to be understood when we write, but also just as surely *not* to be understood. It is by no means an objection to a book that someone finds it unintelligible: perhaps this was precisely the author's intention – perhaps he did not *want* to be understood by 'just anyone'. Every individual with a distinguished intellect and sense of taste, when he wishes to communicate himself, always selects his listeners; by selecting them, he simultaneously excludes 'the others'. All the subtler laws of style have their origin here; they simultaneously ward off, create distance and forbid 'entrance' (or intelligibility, as I have said) – while allowing the words to be heard by those whose sense of hearing resembles the author's. And between ourselves, may I say that, in my own case, I do not want my ignorance or the vivacity of my temperament to prevent me from being understandable to *you*, my friends; certainly not the vivacity, however much it may compel me to come to grips with a thing quickly, in order to come to grips with it at all. For I regard deep problems in the same light as a cold bath – one

gets in quickly, one gets out quickly. The notion that one cannot descend into the depths in this manner, or descend *deeply*
enough – that is a superstition of those who are afraid of the
water, the enemies of cold water; for they speak without experience. Oh, the great cold makes one quick!

And by the way, is it really the case that a thing cannot be
understood or known when it has only been touched upon in
passing, glanced at with eyes flashing? Is it absolutely necessary to sit upon it first? To brood over it like an egg? *Diu
noctuque incubando*,[43] as Newton said of himself? At least
there are truths of a peculiar shyness and ticklishness which
one can only catch hold of suddenly – one must either *take
them by surprise* or leave them alone . . .

Ultimately, my brevity has yet another value: on the questions
which concern me, I have to say a great deal briefly, so that it
will be heard even more briefly. As an immoralist, I have to take
care lest I corrupt someone's innocence, I mean the asses and old
maids of both sexes, who have nothing in life but their innocence; moreover my writings ought to inspire them, elevate them
and encourage them to be virtuous. I can think of nothing
more amusing than to see inspired old asses and maids aroused
by the sweet sentiments of virtue; and 'this I have seen' – thus
spoke Zarathustra. So much with regard to brevity; matters are
worse with regards to my ignorance, of which I make no secret
even in my own eyes. There are hours when I am ashamed of it;
to be sure there are also hours in which I am ashamed of this
shame. Perhaps we philosophers are all in a difficult position
nowadays with respect to knowledge: science is growing, the
most scholarly of us are on the verge of discovering that we
know too little. But it would be even worse if it were otherwise,
if we knew *too much*; our task is and remains first and foremost
not to confuse ourselves with others. We *are* different from the
scholars; although it cannot be denied that we are also scholarly,
among other things. We have different needs, a different growth,
a different digestion; we need more, we also need less. There is
no formula as to how much a spirit requires for its nourishment;
if his taste is for independence, for rapid coming and going, for
wandering, for adventure perhaps, things for which only the

swiftest are prepared, he prefers to live freely on light fare than to be unfree and stuffed. What a good dancer needs from his nourishment is not fat, but great suppleness and strength – and to my knowledge, there is nothing to which the spirit of a philosopher more aspires than to be a good dancer. For the dance is his ideal, also his art and, finally, also the sole object of his devotion, of his 'service to God' . . .

382
The Great Healthiness

We, the new, the nameless, the poorly understood, we firstlings of an as yet uncertain future – for new ends we require new means, namely a new healthiness, a stronger, shrewder, tougher, bolder and more jocular healthiness than any hitherto possessed. He whose soul longs to experience the whole range of previous values and desiderata, and to circumnavigate all the coasts of this ideal 'Mediterranean Sea', who wants to know from his own experience how it feels to be a conqueror and discoverer of the ideal and likewise how it feels to be an artist, a saint, a legislator, a sage, a scholar, a devotee, a prophet and one who stands divinely aloof in the old style, to that end requires first and foremost *great healthiness* – the kind of healthiness which we not only possess, but must constantly acquire and reacquire, because we must constantly sacrifice for it again and again!

And now, after we have long been under way in this manner, we Argonauts of the ideal, who are perhaps more courageous than prudent, and are often enough shipwrecked and brought to grief, but who are, as I said, healthier than people would like to admit, dangerously healthy, restored to health again and again – it would seem that, as a reward for this healthiness, we have an as yet undiscovered country ahead of us, the boundaries of which no one has ever seen, a world beyond all previous countries and corners of the ideal, a world so lavish in the beautiful, the strange, the questionable, the terrible and the divine that our curiosity about it as well as our craving to possess it has gotten carried away with itself – alas, that nothing will satisfy us any more! After such glimpses and with such a burning hunger in our conscience and our science, how could we still be satisfied *with the man of today*? That is bad enough, but it is inevitable that we can hardly take his fondest hopes seriously, and perhaps no longer even consider them at all. Another ideal runs on ahead of us, a strange, tempting, dangerous ideal, an ideal we have no wish to persuade anyone to strive for, because we do not readily admit anyone's *right to it*: the ideal of a spirit who plays naively (that is, involuntarily and from an overflowing plenitude and power) with everything that has hitherto been called holy, good, inviolable, divine; a spirit for whom the highest things which people have reasonably made their standard of value would already signify danger, decay, abasement, or at least recreation, blindness and temporary self-forgetfulness; the ideal of a human and yet superhuman well-being and well-wishing which will often seem to be *inhuman*, for example when it is placed next to all seriousness on earth hitherto, next to all manner of solemnity in bearing, word, tone, look, morality and task, as their incarnate involuntary parody – and yet despite everything, perhaps it is only now that the *great seriousness* begins, the proper question is posed, the destiny of the soul approaches, the hour-hand moves and the tragedy *begins* . . .

383
Epilogue

But while I slowly, slowly bring the painting of this gloomy question mark to a conclusion, and am still willing to remind my readers of the virtues of proper reading – oh, what forgotten and unfamiliar virtues – it seems to me that I hear the sound of the most mischievous, lively, fairy-like laughter: the spirits of my book themselves are pestering me, pulling my ears and calling me to order. 'We cannot take it any more,' they call to me, 'away, away with this raven-black music. Is it not bright morning all around us? And soft green grass and ground, the kingdom of the dance? Was there ever a better time to be joyful? Who will sing us a song, a morning song so sunny, so light and so fully fledged that it will not drive away the crickets[44] – but instead will invite them to join in, to sing and dance? And better a simple rustic bagpipe than such mysterious sounds, such prophecies of doom, sepulchral voices and cries of alarm, with which you have hitherto regaled us in your wilderness, Herr Hermit and Musician of the Future! No! Not such tones! Rather, let us strike up something more pleasant and more joyful!'

Is that how you like it, my impatient friends? Well! Who could not agree? My bagpipe is waiting, and my voice too – it may sound a little hoarse, but what do you expect? After all, we are in the mountains! But at least what you hear will be new; and if you do not understand it, if you misunderstand the singer, what difference does it make? That has always been 'the singer's curse'.[45] It even allows you to hear the music and the melody more clearly, which will make it easier for you to dance to my piping. Shall we begin?

Appendix
'Songs of the Outlaw Prince'[1]

To Goethe

All that is permanent,
Is but your simile!
The god who ensnares us,
Poetic chicanery . . .

The world-wheel which, rolling,
Touches aim after aim
Is grief, say the grumblers,
The fools call it – game . . .

The imperious world-game
Blends real with illusory;
The timelessly foolish[2]
Blends *us* all in thoroughly!

Poet's Vocation[3]

I sat down, refreshment seeking,
In the shadow of a cedar,
When I heard the faintest ticking,
Quick in tempo, strict in metre.

Frowning at its soft persistence,
I ignored it for a time,
But I soon lost all resistance,
And began to speak in rhyme.

Thus inspired, soon thereafter,
That vexatious old woodpecker
Had me overcome with laughter
For a quarter of an hour.
What am I? Some kind of poet?
Is it that my wit's diseased?
'My dear sir, you are a poet,'
Chirped the little bird to me.

Who was it I hoped to ambush,
Like a thief who lies in wait?
Was it maxim? Was it image?
What was it I hoped to bait,
So my rhymes could pounce upon it,
Pinning it in prosody?
'My dear sir, you are a poet,'
Chirped the little bird to me.

Could it be that rhymes are arrows,
Piercing thought's most tender innards?
See the writhing as they burrow
Through the body of the lizard!
Wretched man! You'll die of rhyming,
Or you'll stagger drunkenly!
'My dear sir, you are a poet,'
Chirped the little bird to me.

Awkward maxims, filled with haste,
Drunken wordlets, how they throng!
Phrases piled upon more phrases,
Strung together in a song.

Rabble who find all this pleasing
Are indulged quite willingly.
'My dear sir, you are a poet,'
Chirped the little bird to me.

Bird, are these just jokes you're making?
Or are my wits truly lost?
Is it that my heart is breaking?
Learn to fear me when I'm cross!
But I found I couldn't help it,
Wrath turned into poetry.
'My dear sir, you are a poet,'
Chirped the little bird to me.

In the South[4]

To this crooked branch I'm clinging,
In my weariness I sway.
With this bird I am sojourning,
In his nest, I linger resting.
Where am I? Oh, far away!

Ocean lies there fast asleep,
A crimson sail glides o'er the sea.
Tower, harbour, rock and tree
Ringing idylls, bleating sheep –
Innocent South, welcome me!

When you're plodding, life's absurd,
You're slowed by German gravity.
But blown by wind, and lifted upwards,
I learned how to soar with birds –
And so flew south across the sea.

Reason! How its use annoys me!
Far too soon we reach our aim!
Flight taught me what had deceived me –
Now my blood is up; I'm ready
For new life and newer game . . .

Thinking on your own's sagacious,
Singing by yourself's absurd!
Come and hear me sing your praises,
Quietly, now take your places,
Gather round me, wicked birds!

Young and false and ever flitting,
You seem to be meant for loving
And for other pretty games!
Loath as I am to disclose it,
In the North I loved a crone:
'Truth' was that old woman's name . . .

Pious Beppa[5]

While my figure still is comely,
Piety remains worthwhile,
For God favours all the ladies,
Whose appearance still beguiles.
If I tempt a wretched friar,
God forgives him certainly,
For like all the other friars,
God enjoys my company.

I don't want a grey Church father!
Blushing youths appeal to me!
Even though they're on the prowl,
Full of jealousy and need.

I don't love the old and grey.
And when we're old, God won't love us.
Wondrous wisdom He displays,
In arranging matters thus!

Churchmen, they know how to live,
Wresting from me secret thoughts,
Always offering to forgive –
But honestly, why would they not?
A whisper passes from my lips,
I curtsy, and now filled with grace,
Find that confession's little sin
Is that by which old sin's effaced.

So let us offer praise to He
Who loves the comely maidens,
And who in His heartache willingly
Forgives His own transgressions.
While my figure still is comely,
Piety remains worthwhile;
When I'm ancient let me be
The object of the devil's wiles!

The Mysterious Boat[6]

Last night, as the world was sleeping,
An evening breeze blew through the streets,
All but silent, vaguely sighing.
And nothing, nothing gave me sleep:
Opiates were unavailing,
Guiltlessness gave no relief.

At length, giving up on sleep,
I took a stroll down on the strand.
There in moonlight I did meet

A man and boat upon the sands,
A drowsy shepherd with his sheep,
He drowsily shoved off from land.

Hours passed quite easily,
Or maybe it was years? And then
I felt my mind and thoughts subside,
replaced with infinite ennui,
And as abysses opened wide,
I came out of my reverie.

In the morning, I saw floating
No one's boat upon the swell . . .
'What has happened?' all were asking,
'Was he tired when he fell?'
Nothing happened! We were sleeping,
Everybody slept so well!

Declaration of Love[7]

(But in Which the Poet Fell into a Ditch)

How can it be that he still flies?
And yet quite still his wings remain,
   Aloft, suspended in the sky.
What is it that he hopes to gain?

   Like stars in all their endlessness,
He lives in realms devoid of life,
   He pities all the envious –
To see him, you must scale the heights!

   Oh bird! Oh mighty albatross!
Eternal instincts drive me too.
   My friend, it was of you I thought
and softly wept – yes, I love you!

Song of a Theocritean Goatherd[8]

Lying here, attacked with colic,
Bedbugs feed upon my juices.
Over yonder, people frolic,
Making quite an awful nuisance . . .

She said she could slip away,
And then we'd meet, she would be mine.
I've waited like a dog all day,
But of her there is not a sign!

She promised when her work was done,
She'd come, and she would be with me.
Or will she follow anyone,
Just like the goats who follow me?

How can she buy that silken dress?
And what about my pride? I should
Assess the cost of her caress.
How many ticks are *on* this wood?

Oh, how morose and poisonous,
We oft become when love's delayed!
In sultry evenings, warm with lust,
The toadstools grow in shadowed glade.

Love gnaws at me both night and day,
Just like the seven evils[9] do.
It took my appetite away,
So say goodbye to onion stew!

The moon has sunk below the waves,
And now the stars have gone to bed.
The grey light of the morning breaks –
I really wish that I were dead.

290   THE JOYOUS SCIENCE

These Uncertain Souls

Wavering, uncertain souls:
They fill me with exasperation.
When chagrined with their own selves,
They torture us with veneration.

Since I will not wear *their* harness,
When I meet them on the street,
I'm met with admiring glances,
Filled with envy, sickly-sweet.

If they could with hearty curse,
But turn their noses up at me,
Then they would no longer search,
For me in vain so helplessly.

The Fool in Despair

The things on the table and wall that I write,
With the hands of a fool, don't they give me the right,
To adorn in accordance with personal taste?
But you say that the hands of a fool just deface,
And that table and wall should be cleaned without haste,
Until every trace of me has been effaced!

Allow me! You'll find I have learned to expunge,
Every kind of graffiti with a brush and a sponge,
When I worked as a critic and skilled washerman.
And when I am done, in *your* elegant hand,
On the table and wall, all the words that are writ
Will be wisdom composed of your very own shit.

Rimus Remedium[10]

Or: How Sick Poets Console Themselves

From your witch's lips,
    Awakening disgust in me
    Hour after hour drips.
    I cry out in futility:
    'Curse, oh curse the depths,
The depths of all eternity!'

Hollow is the world:
    A brazen bull[11] – our cries of torment
    Echo from within, but go unheard.
    Our pain does not relent:
'Heartless is the world,
    It's not a thing you can resent!'

Poppy I will pour,
    And fever – may they poison me!
    You'll test my hand and brow no more,
    And yet you ask, 'What gift for me?'
Curse, oh curse the whore
    And all her whorish mockery!

Please! Come back to me!
    The night is cold, and I hear rain –
    Should I be gentler with my pain?
    – Take this coin; see how it gleams?
Should 'felicity'
    Be what I call my pain by name?

The door's ajar instead!
    Oh hell! The wind blows out the light,
    And blows the rain across my bed!
    – And had I not a hundred *rhymes*,
In very little time,
    I'm certain that I would be dead!

What Luck!

I see the pigeons of San Marco[12] throng;
The square is quiet and the morning mild.
Without a care, I send my idle songs,
Like flocks of pigeons up into the sky –
    And lure them back again,
So that their feathers might have rhymes tied on.
    What luck! What luck!

The edifice, protected by blue light
Which floats above like canopies of silk,
Inspires in me *envy*, love and fright . . .
I drink from it its very soul! But will
    I give it back again? –
We'll speak no more of that, you wondrous sight!
    What luck! What luck!

O Campanile,[13] you rise up from the ground,
Victorious, and effortlessly too!
Your ringing drowns out every other sound –
In French, are you the square's *accent aigu*?
    Were I, like you, constrained,
I would want to know by what I'm bound . . .
    What luck! What luck!

No music! Shadows are not darkening,
And waxing into balmy amber night!
It's far too early in the day to sing,
When gold's not yet aglow with rosy light,
    And much day yet remains,
Much day for verse, and stealth, and whispering.
    What luck! What luck!

Towards New Seas[14]

O'er there! I am *decided*,
Henceforth I trust my grip.
Into the open sea I drive
my Genoese sailing ship.[15]

And so all things are shining,
The noon is fast asleep.
Your monstrous eye stares into mine,
Transfixing me, Infinity!

Sils-Maria[16]

Here I sat patiently waiting for nothing,
Beyond good and evil, and erelong enjoying,

The light and the shadow – 'twas all just a game,
All lake and all noon and all time without aim.

My friend![17] As my solitude silently grew,
Zarathustra walked by, and then one became two.

To the Mistral Wind[18]

A Dancing Song

Mistral wind, you raincloud-reaper,
Sorrow-slayer, heaven-sweeper,
Roaring wind, I love you so!
Of one womb, are we two not
Like first-born twins, and to one lot
Not foreordained for evermore?

On the pathways wet with dew,
I danced my way right out to you,
I danced with you – you piped and sang;
And you, without a boat or rudder,
You, as freedom's freest brother,
O'er unruly waters sprang.

Scarce awake, I heard you crying,
And up rocky steps came flying
Towards the cliffside by the sea.
You'd arrived before me, dazzling
Like a diamond fall cascading
From the heights triumphantly.

On the sky's flat threshing floor
You drove your chariot of war,
While pulled by noble stallions.
I saw your whip-hand thrashing
Like a bolt of lightning flashing
As you lashed your horses on and on –

You leaped down from your chariot,
That you might hasten your descent.
An arrow in unhindered flight,
Into the depths, straight down you crashed –
Transfixing like a golden shaft
The roses of the morning light.

Dance across the open sea,
Its rising crests and treacheries –
All hail to you, who make *new* dances!
Let us dance a thousand ways,
And make *our* art for freedom's sake,
May Joyous Science fill our stanzas!

Let us make a flower wreath,
And decorate it with two leaves,
In celebration of our worth.
Let us dance like troubadours,
Dancing between saints and whores,
Or dancing between God and earth!

Those who cannot dance with winds,
Those bound with bandages and pins,
Decrepit men whose time has passed –
Those whose words were never true,
Those virtuously prating fools,
Now from our Eden must be cast!

Kicking dust up as we go,
We blow that dust right up their noses,
Scaring all this sickly breed!
Let us liberate the coastland
From the breath of feebler men,
Whose eyes are too afraid to see!

Let us chase the sun-obscurers,
World-maligners, raincloud-pushers,
Let us make the heavens bright!
Friend, let us together *roar*,
For you, free spirit's spirit, are
A gale, and so is my delight.

And in its mem'ry, it bequeaths
For evermore this flowered *wreath*,
So take it up to where you are!
Throw it skyward, higher, further,
Charging up on heaven's ladder,
Hang it up – upon a star!

Excerpts from
Idylls from Messina

Several of the poems Nietzsche appended to the second edition of *Joyous Science* as 'Songs of the Outlaw Prince' had been previously published under the title *Idylls from Messina* in the periodical *Internationale Monatschrift* in May 1882. The following two poems are the remainder of the 'Idylls' which were not incorporated into the 'Songs'.

'The Little Brig,[1] Called *The Little Angel*'[2]

Little Angel, so they call me –
Now a ship, but once a girl,
Oh, still very much a girl!
Always out of love for thee,
My helm so elegantly turns.

Little Angel, so they call me –
Decked out with a hundred flags;
And my skipper, helm commanding,
Chest puffed out with vanity,
Is the hundred-and-first flag.

Little Angel, so they call me –
Wherever a little flame
Glows for me, I, like a lamb,
Go on my way so longingly
(Being such a little lamb).

Little Angel, so they call me –
Can I blow out of my mouth
Smoke and fire all about,
Barking like an angry puppy?
Oh, I have the devil's mouth!

Little Angel, so they call me –
Once I said a cruel word,
My dear love could not endure it,
To his grave he fled from me:
I killed him with that very word!

Little Angel, so they call me –
Swiftly from the cliff I bounded,
Throwing myself to the ground,
And then my soul could wriggle free,
Through shattered ribs without a sound.

Little Angel, so they call me –
Towards the sea, my soul it draws,
And like a kitten, without pause,
Leaps on this clipper agilely,
Oh yes, my soul has nimble paws.

Little Angel, so they call me –
Now a ship, but once a girl,
Oh, still very much a girl!
Always out of love for thee,
My helm so elegantly turns.

'Pia, caritatevole, amorosissima'[3]

(On Sacred Ground)

Little girl, with lamb most tame,
Who strokes his soft white fleece,
And from whose eyes a burning flame

Shines outwardly and sees,
You charming creature, whimsical,
Beloved, near or far,
So pious, so considerate,
Amorosissima!

What tore from you your necklace,
So your heart with grief was racked?
Was he who loved you feckless,
And could not love you back?
And were you silent, tears a-thronging,
To your gentle eyes?
And did you, silent, die of longing,
Amorosissima?

Nietzsche's Description of
The Joyous Science in *Ecce Homo*

The Joyous Science
('*la gaya scienza*')

The *Dawn* is a book of affirmation, deep but bright and benign. The same applies again and in the highest degree to the *gaya scienza*: in almost every sentence of that book profundity and mischief go tenderly hand in hand. A verse which expresses gratitude for the most wonderful month of January I have ever experienced – the whole book is its gift – betrays all too well from what depths 'science' has emerged and become *joyous* here:

> The flaming spear you thrust in me,
> Broke up the ice within my soul,
> And so it hurtles towards the sea,
> Now rushing onwards, filled with hope.
> Ever brighter, ever sounder,
> Freely loving destiny;
> Thus my soul extols your wonders,
> Fairest month of January!

Who can have any doubt as to what this 'greatest hope' is when he sees the adamantine beauty of Zarathustra's first words shining forth at the end of the fourth Book? Or when he reads the granite sentences at the end of the third Book, with which a destiny *for all time* is first formulated? The 'Songs of the Outlaw Prince', composed for the most part in Sicily, call to mind quite explicitly the Provençal term *gaya scienza*, that unity of *singer*, *knight* and *free spirit* which distinguishes the wonderful early culture of the Provençal people from all ambiguous cultures; the very last poem especially, 'To the Mistral Wind', an exuberant dance song in which, with all due respect! one dances right over morality, is an even more perfect Provençalism.

Notes

EPIGRAPH TO THE FIRST EDITION

1. *To the poet . . . Emerson*: the quote is from Ralph Waldo Emerson's 'History' (1841). Nietzsche substituted 'and sage' for Emerson's 'to the philosopher, to the saint' and 'experiences' for Emerson's 'events'. *Nature and Selected Essays*, ed. and with an Introduction by Larzer Ziff (London: Penguin Classics, 2003), p. 155.

PREFACE TO THE SECOND EDITION

1. *Joyous Science*: one might be tempted to attribute the title to Emerson's expression 'Joyous Science'. However, the earliest that phrase appears in print in Emerson is 1884, two years after the first edition of *The Joyous Science* was published. The German phrase 'fröhliche Wissenschaft' had been in use before Nietzsche: for example, it appears in the 84th, 85th, 89th and 90th letters of Johann Gottfried von Herder's *Letters for the Advancement of Humanity*. See *Briefe zur Beförderung der Humanität*, 10 vols (Riga: Hartknoch, 1796), vol. 7, pp. 77–8, 82, 84, 148, 160–61). Jean Paul also uses the expression in his *Introduction to Aesthetics* (*Vorschule der Aesthetik*), in *Sämtliche Werke* (ed.), 33 vols (Berlin: Reimer, 1841), vol. 18, p. 82. In both of these cases it refers to the art of poetry, especially the poetry of Provence.

2. *In the end, it is only great pain . . . And for that very reason – artists*: most of §§3–4 was reused by Nietzsche with slight modifications for the epilogue to *Nietzsche contra Wagner*. See *Nietzsche contra Wagner*, in *The Portable Nietzsche*, trans. and ed. Walter Kaufmann (New York: Viking Penguin, 1954), pp. 680–84.

3.   *which reveals the apparently genuine to be counterfeit* etc.: 'der
      aus jedem U ein X macht, ein ächtes rechtes X, das heisst den
      vorletzten Buchstaben vor dem letzten' (literally, 'that turns every
      U into an X, a right and proper X, that is, the letter before the
      last'). This sentence is ultimately untranslatable. The expression
      'to turn a U into an X' means to pass off a five thaler for a ten,
      which in Roman numerals is to pass off a V for an X. Nietzsche
      then transforms the object of suspicion, the 'X' thaler, into the
      algebraic variable 'x', the unknown. The letter referred to in
      the portentous final phrase 'the letter before the last' would in the
      German alphabet be the letter 'y', which in German is called
      'Upsilon', following the Greek. This allusion to upsilon refers to
      the fact that Pythagoras is said to have used the letter upsilon as
      a symbol of virtue and right decision. See *Brewer's Dictionary of
      Phrase and Fable*, rev. and enl. Ivor H. Evans (New York: Harper
      & Bros, 1969), p. 801. Thus, instead of translating Nietzsche's
      phrase literally as 'that turns every U into an X, a right and
      proper X, that is, the letter before the last', I translate it quite
      freely as 'which reveals the apparently genuine to be counterfeit,
      makes a known quantity into an unknown one, and, in solving
      that equation, prepares us for an ultimate decision'.
4.   *Egyptian youths*: an allusion to Schiller's poem 'Veiled Image at
      Saïs' (1795). See in Friedrich Schiller, *The Poems of Schiller*, trans.
      E. P. Arnold-Forster (London: William Heinemann, 1901), p. 218.
5.   *Baubo*: Greek mythological figure associated with the goddess
      Demeter, often represented in figurines personifying or possess-
      ing exposed vulvae.

'JEST, TRICK AND REVENGE'
PRELUDE IN GERMAN RHYMES

1.   *Jest, Trick and Revenge*: 'Scherz, List und Rache', the title of a
      libretto written by Goethe in 1784, adapted by Ludwig Bischoff
      and set to music by Max Bruch in 1858. Nietzsche's friend
      Heinrich Köselitz ('Peter Gast') also set it to music in the 1880s.
2.   *Vademecum – Vadetecum*: Go with me – go with yourself.
      'Vademecum' is also an expression for a book you carry with
      you as you go, to consult as needed, i.e. a handbook.
3.   *Food for snakes*: Nietzsche compares himself to the serpent in
      the Garden of Eden, who was cursed by God to eat 'dust'. See
      Genesis 3:14.

4.   *eat a toad*: 'M. Lassay, a very gentle man but who had a great
     knowledge of society, said we should swallow a toad every
     morning to find nothing more disgusting in the rest of the day,
     when we have to go about in the world.' Sébastien-Roch Nicolas
     de Chamfort, *Pensées, maximes, anecdotes, dialogues*, new
     edn, ed. P.-J. Stahl (Paris: Michel Lévy Frères, 1860), pp. 187–8
     (posthumously published in 1796, translation mine). See also
     notes 25 and 27, Book II.

5.   *Seneca et hoc genus omne*: Seneca and his ilk.

6.   *primum scribere, deinde philosophari*: first write, then philoso-
     phize.

7.   *A and O*: alpha and omega.

8.   *the devil's hoof*: 'the devil's hoof' has a double meaning. First, it is
     said that no matter how well disguised, the devil is obliged to show
     his cloven hoof, thus revealing his speech as temptation to be
     resisted. Second, it is an expression for a clubbed foot, so called
     because it was thought to be a punishment for one's parents' sins.
     In this case, the inferences (there are two: that we should love God
     because He is our creation, and that to deny God's existence merely
     because a secular explanation for our belief is available proves
     nothing since God might exist anyway) are being presented both
     as 'lame', i.e. invalid, and as psychological temptations.

9.   *by the sweat of our brows*: Genesis 3:19.

10. *Minerva's pet*: the owl of Minerva, goddess of wisdom. In 1820
     Hegel said, 'the owl of Minerva begins its flight only with the
     onset of dusk,' that is to say, wisdom is always retrospective.
     G.W.F. Hegel, *Elements of the Philosophy of Right*, ed. Allen W.
     Wood, trans H.B. Nisbet (Cambridge University Press, 1991),
     p. 23.

11. *Ecce Homo*: 'Behold the man', Pontius Pilate's remark about
     Jesus at John 19:5. Nietzsche chose this phrase for the title of his
     autobiography.

BOOK I

1.   *waves of countless laughter*: 'Wellen unzähligen Gelächters' is
     Nietzsche's rendition of 'κυμάτων ανήριθμον γέλασμα', *Pro-
     metheus Bound*, lines 89–90. Cf. Aeschylus, *Prometheus Bound
     and Other Plays*, trans. Philip Vellacott (London: Penguin Clas-
     sics, 1961), p. 23. The attribution of the play to Aeschylus has
     been contested.

2.   *rerum concordia discors*: nature's jarring concord. 'What is the
      meaning and effect of nature's jarring concord?' Horace, Epistle
      I, in *The Satires of Horace and Perseus*, trans. Niall Rudd (Lon-
      don: Penguin Classics, 2005), p. 94.

3.   *not every wall can have a window*: 'man kann nicht durch alle
      Wände sehen [literally 'one cannot see through all walls']'. The
      point of the maxim appears to be that a window is a luxury, and
      that without at least some windowless walls the house won't stand.
      Analogously, it is a luxury to have all one's sentiments be noble;
      without at least some practical sentiments, one's life will collapse.

4.   *What you have there, my good man, is also brain*: Bernard Le
      Bovier de Fontenelle (1657–1757), author of *Nouveaux Dia-
      logues des Morts* (1683), which consists of thirty-six dialogues
      between a variety of historical figures both ancient and modern.
      'It's not a heart that you have there, Mme [Claudine Guérin] de
      Tencin told him one day, putting her hand on his chest: this is
      the brain, as in the head.' A. Laborde-Milaà, *Les Grands Écri-
      vains Français: Fontenelle* (Paris: Librairie Hachette et Cie,
      1905), p. 53 (translation mine).

5.   *displacement of boundary stones*: 'For, having ordered every
      one to draw a line around his own land and to place stones on
      the bounds, [Numa Pompilius, second king of Rome] conse-
      crated these stones to *Jupiter Terminalis* and ordained that all
      should assemble at the place every year on a fixed day and offer
      sacrifices to them; and he made the festival in honour to the gods
      of boundaries among the most dignified of all. This festival the
      Romans call *Terminalia*, from the boundaries, and the bound-
      aries themselves [. . .] they call *termines*. He also enacted that,
      if any person demolished or displaced these boundary stones he
      should be looked upon as devoted to the god, to the end that
      anyone who wished might kill him as a sacrilegious person with
      impunity and without incurring any stain of guilt. [. . .] Memor-
      ials of this custom are observed by the Romans down to our
      times, purely as a religious form. For they look upon these bound-
      ary stones as gods and sacrifice to them yearly, offering up no
      kind of animal (for it is not lawful to stain these stones with
      blood) but cakes made of cereals and other first-fruits of the
      earth.' Dionysius of Halicarnassus, *Roman Antiquities*, vol. 1,
      books 1–2, Loeb Classical Library no. 319, trans. Earnest Cary
      (Cambridge, MA and London: Harvard University Press and
      William Heinemann Ltd, 1968), pp. 531, 533.

6. *Mazzini*: Giuseppe Mazzini (1805–72), Italian politician and proponent of Italian unification.

7. *Cyclopean structures*: according to the Greek historian and philosopher Strabo 63BC–23AD, the acropolis at Tiryns was built by the Cyclopes. *The Geography of Strabo: An English Translation, with Introduction and Notes*, trans. Duane W. Roller (Cambridge: Cambridge University Press, 2014), p. 370.

8. *beyond fate*: Nietzsche gives 'über das Geschick' for Homer's *'hyper móron'*. See *Odyssey*, 5.436. '[. . .] and the great wave covered him. Then surely would unfortunate Odysseus have perished beyond fate [ὑπέρ μόρον], had not flashing-eyed Athene given him presence of mind.' Homer, *The Odyssey*, books 1–12, 2nd edn, Loeb Classical Library no. 104, trans. A. T. Murray, ed. George E. Dimock (Cambridge, MA and London: Harvard University Press and William Heinemann Ltd, 1995), p. 215, translation modified. The same expression appears twice at *Odyssey* 1.34–5. Similar expressions appear, for example, at *Iliad* 2.155 (ὑπέρμορα), 20.30 (ὑπέρμορον) and 20.336 (ὑπέρ μοῖραν).

9. *grieving unto death*: 'Rejoicing to heaven, grieved unto death, only in love can the soul draw its breath.' Johann Wolfgang von Goethe, *Egmont*, Act III, Scene 2, in *Five German Tragedies*, trans. F. J. Lamport (London: Penguin Classics, 1970), p. 148.

10. *starry worlds*: Franz Schubert, *Die Sternenwelten*, ('Starry Worlds'), D307, lyric by Johann Georg Fellinger after Urban Jarnik, 1815.

11. *raging demon*: 'I was once present when someone was asking the poet Sophocles about sex, and whether he was still able to make love to a woman; to which he replied, "Don't talk about that; I am glad to have left it behind me and escaped from a fierce and frenzied master [λυττῶντά τινα καὶ ἄγριον δεσπότην]." A good reply I thought then, and still do.' Plato, *Republic*, 2nd edn, trans. H. D. P. Lee, reissued with Further Reading by Rachana Kamtekar (London: Penguin Classics, 2003), (329c) p. 5.

12. *L'ordre du jour pour le roi*: the king's schedule.

13. *puffed-up old frog*: 'The Frog and the Ox'. See *Aesop's Fables*, trans. Laura Gibbs (London: Oxford University Press, 2002), p. 166. The frog's attempt to rival the ox by self-inflation causes it to explode.

14. *Whoever enters . . . a kindness* The ultimate source for this quote is Jules Janin, *Les petits bonheurs*, 2nd edn (Paris: Morizot, 1862), p. 234.

15. *being truly things apart*: literally 'these true in and of themselves
     [things]'. In English and German alike, one can signal that the
     preceding item is to be considered intrinsically or alone by adding
     'in and of itself'. Nietzsche nominalizes the German expression to
     suggest not that the individuals should be *considered* apart from
     anything else but that they are *in fact* apart from anything else.

16. *this is what I am*: Nietzsche is referring to Napoleon's remark,
     'I have a right to answer all your complaints with an eternal
     "this is what I am". I am apart from everyone and do not accept
     conditions from anyone.' *Mémoires de Madame de Rémusat,
     1802–1808*, vol. 1, 9th edn (Paris: Ancienne Maison Michel Lévy
     Frères, 1880), pp. 114–15 (translation mine).

17. *Corrupting the Text*: in German, 'Hinzu-Lügner', 'hinzugelo-
     gen'. The term here refers to interpolation in the sense of textual
     corruption. Interpolation in this sense is most commonly an issue
     for scriptural hermeneutics, because the purpose of inserting the
     passage is to gain authority for an otherwise questionable bit of
     doctrine, or to convey the impression of accuracy in a prophetic
     prediction by inserting references to later-known facts. Consider,
     for example, the claim (generally credited) that our oldest sources
     for the Gospel according to Mark contain everything in canon-
     ical Mark except an unambiguous account of the resurrection,
     which appears to have been interpolated by a later author. Though
     interpolation is especially objectionable to those who regard the
     scripture in question as authoritative, it is also of central concern
     to professional philologists (as Nietzsche himself was) attempting
     to determine the integrity of a text.

18. *the Aristotelian unities*: the doctrine, adhered to by seventeenth-
     century French neoclassical dramatists such as Racine and
     Molière, that a drama should display unity of action, place and
     time, inspired by Aristotle's remarks in the *Poetics*, books 7–9.

19. *as Socrates had once done*: see Plato, *Apology* 24b–26b, in *The
     Last Days of Socrates*, trans. Hugh Tredennick and Harold
     Tarrant (London: Penguin Classics, 2003), pp. 48–51.

20. *Historia abscondita*: secret history.

21. *Plaudite amici, comoedia finita est!*: 'Applaud my friends, the
     comedy is finished!' '*Plaudite, amici, commedia finita est!*' were
     in fact Beethoven's last words, not Augustus', though Augustus'
     last words (partly in Greek) convey much the same sense. 'On
     the day that he died, Augustus frequently enquired whether
     rumours of his illness were causing any popular disturbance. He
     called for a mirror, and had his hair combed and his lower jaw,

which had fallen from weakness, propped up. Presently he summoned a group of friends and asked, "Have I played my part in the farce of life creditably enough?", adding the theatrical tag:

> If I have pleased you, kindly signify
> Appreciation with a warm goodbye.

Then he dismissed them, but when fresh visitors arrived from Rome he wanted to hear the latest news of Drusus' daughter, who was ill. Finally he kissed his wife with "Goodbye, Livia; remember our marriage!", and died almost at once.' Suetonius, *The Twelve Caesars*, rev. edn trans. Robert Graves (London: Penguin Classics, 2007), pp. 100–101.

22. *qualis artifex pereo!*: 'Dead! And so great an artist!', ibid., p. 238.
23. *qualis spectator pereo!*: 'Dead! And so great a spectator!'.
24. *hoc est ridiculum, hoc est absurdum*: 'This is ridiculous, this is absurd.'
25. *the Wahhabi god*: Wahhabism is a branch of Sunni Islam, having its origins in eighteenth-century Arabia; its god is Allah. The Muslim declaration of faith is: 'There is no god but God, Muhammad is the messenger of God [*lā 'ilāha 'illā l-Lāh, Muḥammadur rasūlu l-Lāh*].'
26. *an astonished Englishman*: William Gifford Palgrave, who writes:

> So, putting on a profound air, and with a voice of first-class solemnity, he uttered his oracle, that 'the first of the great sins is the giving divine honours to a creature'. A hit, I may observe, at ordinary Mahometans, whose whole doctrine of intercession, whether vested in Mahomet or in 'Alee, is classed by Wahhābees along with direct and downright idolatry. A Damascene Sheykh would have avoided the equivocation by answering, 'infidelity.'
>
> 'Of course,' I replied, 'the enormity of such a sin is beyond all doubt. But if this be the first, there must be a second; what is it?'
>
> 'Drinking the shameful,' in English, 'smoking tobacco,' was the unhesitating answer.
>
> 'And murder, and adultery, and false witness?' I suggested.
>
> 'God is merciful and forgiving,' rejoined my friend; that is, these are merely little sins.

William Gifford Palgrave, *Personal narrative of a year's journey through Central and Eastern Arabia (1862–1863)*, 2nd edn (London: Macmillan, 1868), p. 282.

27. *real hardship*: for the sake of a more idiomatic translation, a cer-
     tain amount of wordplay is being sacrificed by translating 'Not'
     as 'hardship' and Notstände as 'crises', otherwise this could be
     rendered as 'Need itself is needed!', which echoes the use of
     'need' elsewhere in the aphorism.

BOOK II

1. *images of Saïs*: see note 4, Preface, above.
2. *the old earth-shaker himself*: Poseidon. The subsequent refer-
    ences to a bull, a labyrinth and a sailing ship are all reminiscent
    of the myth of Theseus (the son of Poseidon) and the Minotaur.
3. *action at a distance*: in physics, the idea that one body can
    influence another without mechanical contact, as in Newton's
    theory of gravitational attraction.
4. *an Athenian philosopher*: Xenocrates, who is reputed to have
    refused sums of money from Philip II, Alexander the Great, and
    also from Antipater, Alexander's general and later his regent. See
    Diogenes Laertius, *Lives of Eminent Philosophers*, books 1–5,
    Loeb Classical Library no. 184, trans. R. D. Hicks (Cambridge,
    MA and London: Harvard University Press and William Heine-
    mann Ltd, 1925), pp. 382–3.
5. *Vivat comoedia*: long live comedy.
6. *A little woman is never beautiful*: 'small people can be neat and
    well proportioned, but not beautiful'. Aristotle, *The Nicoma-
    chean Ethics*, trans. J. A. K. Thomson, rev. Hugh Tredennick
    (London: Penguin Classics, 2004), pp. 93–4.
7. *Rossini's or Bellini's*: Gioachino Rossini (1792–1868), Italian com-
    poser, best known for his opera *Il barbiere di Siviglia* (*The Barber
    of Seville*); Vincenzo Bellini (1801–35), Italian opera composer.
8. *Gil Blas*: *L'Histoire de Gil Blas de Santillane* (1715–35), a novel
    by Alain-René Lesage.
9. *pity and fear*: Aristotle's theory of tragedy held that the effect of
    tragedy was due to the emotions of pity and fear. As he says,
    'Tragedy is an imitation of an action that is admirable, complete
    and possesses magnitude; in language made pleasurable, each of
    its species separated in different parts; performed by actors, not
    through narration; effecting through pity and fear the purifica-
    tion of such emotions.' Aristotle, *Poetics*, trans. Malcolm Heath
    (London: Penguin Classics, 1996), p. 10. Although Nietzsche's
    earlier account of tragedy in *The Birth of Tragedy* differed from

Aristotle's in numerous respects, like Aristotle he did locate its distinctive characteristics in its emotional effects. Here, as is typical of his middle period, he distances himself from his former approach by emphasizing tragedy's rhetorical aspects.

10. *recitativo secco*: 'dry recitative', one of the forms of solo singing which attempts to approximate ordinary speech.

11. *asked a geometer*: Nietzsche's source for the anecdote appears to be Schopenhauer. See Arthur Schopenhauer, *The World as Will and Representation*, trans. and ed. Judith Norman, Alistair Welchman and Christopher Janaway, 2 vols (Cambridge: Cambridge University Press, 2010 and 2018), vol. 1, p. 213. Schopenhauer speaks of a 'French mathematician' and a performance of Racine's *Iphigénie*. There are many versions of this anecdote, the earliest of which appears to be in a letter from Diderot to Mme Volland dated 31 August 1760: 'D'Alembert, at the close of the French Academy, delivered a discourse on poetry, strongly condemned by some, highly praised by others. I was told that the *Iliad* and the *Aeneid* were there treated as boring and insipid works, and that *Jerusalem Delivered* and the *Henriade* were championed as the only two epic poems which were readable. It reminds me of the cold geometer who, tired of hearing Racine praised, whom he knew only by reputation, finally decided to read him. At the end of the first scene of *Psyche*: "Well," he said, "what does that prove?"' Denis Diderot, *Œuvres complètes*, ed. J. Assézat and Maurice Tourner, 20 vols (Paris: Garnier Frères, 1876), vol. 18, p. 441 (translation mine). According to Diderot's editors, the reference to *Psyche* is a slip of the pen, there being no such play by Racine.

12. *Est res magna tacere*: it's a great achievement to hold your tongue. Martial's full epigram (§ 80 of Book IV) reads: 'You declaim in a fever, Maron. If you don't know that this is lunacy, you're not sane, friend Maron. A sick man, a semi-tertian, you declaim. If you can't raise a sweat any other way, it makes sense. "Ah, but it's a great achievement." You err. When fever is burning up your insides, it's a great achievement to hold your tongue, Maron.' Martial, *Epigrams*, Loeb Classical Library no. 94, rev. edn trans. D. R. Shackleton Bailey, 3 vols (Cambridge, MA: Harvard University Press, 1993), vol. 1, p. 321.

13. *brushing away the dust from the wings of a butterfly*: the colour of a butterfly's wings is due to microscopic scales which come off to the touch like a coloured powder or dust. Since the scales are necessary for the butterfly's survival, touching its wings usually

will suffice to kill it. Nietzsche's simile is complex: the translator is 'dusting off' something old, making it clean and new, but 'verwischen' (brushing away) can also mean to smudge something, blurring its outlines and thereby rendering it indistinct: figuratively, to obscure its true nature. By making the moment a butterfly, Nietzsche suggests the fleeting nature of time. By making the dust of the past a butterfly's wing-dust, Nietzsche suggests that the translator, in brushing off the dust, is removing that which gives the past its life and colour, thereby destroying its distinctiveness, beauty and vitality.

14. *Horace ... Theocritus*: Quintus Horatius Flaccus (65–8 BC), Roman poet; Alcaeus of Mytilene (*c.*620–sixth century BC), Greek poet; Archilochus (*c.*680–*c.*645 BC), Greek poet; Sextus Propertius (*c.*50–45–*c.*15 BC), Roman poet; Callimachus (*c.*310–305–240 BC), Greek poet; Philetas of Cos (*c.*340–*c.*285 BC), Greek poet; Theocritus (*c.*270 BC), Greek poet.

15. *the power of discharging the emotions, of purging the soul*: these phrases allude to Aristotle's doctrine of catharsis in the *Poetics*.

16. *Terpander ... Damon*: Terpander, a Greek poet of the first half of the seventh century BC; Empedocles, a Greek philosopher of the fifth century BC; Damon of Athens, a Greek musicologist of the fifth century BC.

17. *Bards lie about many things*: in Greek, 'πολλὰ ψεύδονται ἀοιδοί'. The ironies here are multiple. Nietzsche quotes a poet in support of the thesis that one ought not to quote poets in support of theses because they are often mistaken; and yet the attribution to Homer would not only be a self-referential paradox – it is itself mistaken, as Nietzsche must have known. The maxim is generally attributed not to Homer but to Solon (640–558 BC). See Ron Owens, *Solon of Athens: Poet, Philosopher, Soldier, Statesman* (Brighton, Portland, OR and Toronto: Sussex Academic Press, 2010), p. 255.

18. *Manfred*: the eponymous character of a poem by Lord Byron. Manfred, like Faust, is a Romantic rebel figure. Nietzsche composed *Manfred-Meditation*, a duet for piano, in 1872.

19. *betel-chewing*: the areca nut, wrapped in betel leaves, is chewed in India and South-East Asia for its stimulative effects, which resemble those of tobacco.

20. *Here is a musician*: Richard Wagner. This section was subsequently reused in *Nietzsche contra Wagner* with slight changes. See *Nietzsche contra Wagner* in *The Portable Nietzsche*, pp. 662–4.

21. *Alfieri*: Count Vittorio Alfieri (1749–1803), Italian dramatist and poet. His memoirs, *La Vita di Vittorio Alfieri da Asti scritta da esso*, were published posthumously in 1806.

22. *War is the father of all good things*: an allusion to 'war is the father of all things', 'πόλεμος πάντων μεν πατήρ εστι', fragment 53 of Heraclitus (*c.*535–*c.*475 BC), pre-Socratic Greek philosopher. See *Fragments*, trans. Brooks Haxton (London: Penguin Classics, 2003), p. 29.

23. *Giacomo Leopardi, Prosper Mérimée, Ralph Waldo Emerson and Walter Savage Landor . . . masters of prose*: Giacomo Leopardi (1798–1837) was an Italian poet, philosopher, essayist and philologist. The bulk of the prose to which Nietzsche refers may be found in *Zibaldone: The Notebooks of Leopardi*, ed. Michael Caesar and Franco D'Intino (London: Penguin Classics, 2013). Prosper Mérimée (1803–70) was a French writer, primarily known for his novellas *Colomba* and *Carmen*, the basis for the opera of the same name by Georges Bizet. Walter Savage Landor (1775–1864) was an English writer and poet whose *Imaginary Conversations* consists of 147 dialogues between a variety of figures both historical and mythical, and was published in five volumes from 1824 to 1829.

24. *Fontenelle*: see note 4, Book I, above.

25. *Chamfort*: pen name of Sébastien-Roch Nicolas (1741–94), French writer.

26. *Mirabeau*: Honoré Gabriel Riqueti, Count of Mirabeau (1749–91), a leader of the French Revolution.

27. *Ah! Mon ami* etc.: 'Ah! My friend! I am finally leaving this world, where the heart must either break or turn to bronze', quoted in Stahl's Preface, in Chamfort, *Pensées, maximes, anecdotes, Caractères et dialogues* (Paris: Michel Lévy Frères, 1857), p. 50. Chamfort had attempted suicide in September of 1793 by shooting himself in the face with a pistol and died after several months of intense pain from the wounds caused by the attempt.

28. *I'll know his humours* etc.: *Julius Caesar*, Act IV, Scene 3. Nietzsche appears to be paraphrasing or misquoting Schlegel's translation; he has 'Kennt er die Zeit, *so kenn' ich seine Launen* – fort mit dem Schellen-Hanswurst!' where Schlegel has 'Kennt er die Zeit, so kenn' ich seine Laune. Was soll der Krieg mit solchen Schellennarren? Geh fort Gesell!' *Julius Cäsar*, trans. A. W. Schlegel, in *William Shakespeare's saemmtliche dramatische Werke übersetzt im Metrum des Originals in einem Bande*

(Vienna: J. P. Sollinger, 1826), p. 505. The Shakespeare reads:
'I'll know his humour, when he knows his time: What should the
wars do with these jigging fools? Companion, hence!' My translation of the paraphrase or misquote of Schlegel closely follows
Nietzsche's, adapting Shakespeare's language.

29. *all causes are only the occasional causes* etc.: 'With respect to
the begetter, procreation is only an expression, a symptom of his
decisive affirmation of the will to life: with respect to the begot-
ten, procreation is not the ground of the will that appears in
him, since the will in itself recognises neither ground nor conse-
quent; rather it, like all causes, is only an occasional cause for
the appearance of this will at this time in this place.' Schopenhauer, *The World as Will and Representation*, vol. 1, p. 354, and
quoted in Philipp Mainländer, *Die Philosophie der Erlösung*, 2
vols (Berlin: Verlag von Theobald Grieben, 1876), vol. 1, p. 537,
from which Nietzsche appears to have copied it.

30. *the will to life is present in every being*: Schopenhauer, *Parerga
and Paralipomena*, trans. and ed. Christopher Janaway, Sabine
Roehr and Adrian del Caro, 2 vols (Cambridge: Cambridge
University Press, 2015–16), vol. 2, p. 201, quoted in Mainländer,
vol. 1, p. 477.

31. *all lions are at bottom only one lion*: Nietzsche is quoting 'all
living lions are at bottom only one lion' (Mainländer, vol. 1, p. 480),
which is the latter's gloss on Schopenhauer's 'For instance, lions that
are born and die are like the drops of the waterfall; but the *leonitas*,
the *Idea* or form of the lion, is like the unmoving rainbow above.'
The World as Will and Representation, vol. 2, p. 499.

32. *the multiplicity of individuals is an illusion*: 'the plurality of
individuals an illusion', Mainländer, vol. 1, p. 476; the phrase
'the multiplicity of individuals' occurs at Schopenhauer, *The
World as Will and Representation*, vol. 1, p. 358.

33. *Lamarck's idea*: the inheritance of acquired characteristics,
propounded by the French naturalist Jean-Baptiste Lamarck
(1744–1829), about which Schopenhauer says: '[It] is an error
of genius that despite of all its absurdity still does him honour'.
Schopenhauer, *On Will in Nature*, trans. David E. Cartwright
and Edward E. Erdmann, in *On the Fourfold Root of the
Principle of Sufficient Reason and Other Writings*, ed. Christopher Janaway (Cambridge: Cambridge University Press, 2012),
p. 359, paraphrased in Mainländer, vol. 1, p. 486.

34. *in aesthetic intuition*: Nietzsche is paraphrasing Schopenhauer's
'this is precisely how someone gripped by this intuition is at the

same time no longer an individual: the individual has lost himself in this very intuition: rather, he is the *pure*, will-less, painless, timeless *subject of cognition*'. *The World as Will and Representation*, vol. 1, p. 201, quoted in Mainländer, vol. 1, pp. 500–501.

35. *the subject, being entirely absorbed into the intuited object*: 'This includes in itself and in the same way both object and subject, since these constitute its only form: but they both have equal weight in the Idea; and just as even here the object is nothing but the representation of the subject, so the subject also, being entirely absorbed into the intuited object, has become this object itself, so that its entire consciousness is no longer anything but this object's clearest image.' Schopenhauer, *The World as Will and Representation*, vol. 1, p. 202, quoted in Mainländer, vol. 1, p. 501.

36. *the nonsense about pity*: Schopenhauer's doctrine that compassion is due to an insight that, behind the veil of appearances, we are all one. Nietzsche is writing in light of Schopenhauer's remarks from *On the Basis of Morals*, in *The Two Fundamental Problems of Ethics*, ed. and trans. Christopher Janaway (Cambridge: Cambridge University Press, 2009), p. 200, which are quoted in Mainländer, vol. 1, pp. 568–9. Schopenhauer also refers to 'the source of all morality' on p. 205. Nietzsche's reference to 'breaching of the *principii individuationis*' appears to be due to his misreading Mainländer's 'Durchschauung [seeing through]' of the *principii individuationis* as 'Durchbrechung [breaking through]' of the *principii individuationis* on p. 568.

37. *dying is certainly to be seen as the true purpose of existence*: 'Dying is certainly to be seen as the true purpose of life.' Schopenhauer, *The World as Will and Representation*, vol. 2, p. 653. Nietzsche is again most likely misreading Mainländer's 'dying is the real aim of life' at vol. 1, p. 604.

38. *the possibility cannot outright* etc.: 'The possibility cannot outright be denied *a priori* that a magical effect of the kind described above might not also come from somebody already dead.' Schopenhauer, *Parerga and Paralipomena*, vol. 1, p. 268. Nietzsche follows Mainländer, vol. 1, p. 605, who omits the 'of the kind described above'.

39. *Be a man, and do not follow me* etc.: Goethe had added a poem to the second edition of *The Sorrows of Young Werther* in 1775 which concluded with this line, to dissuade readers from emulating the protagonist and committing suicide; the poem was removed from subsequent editions.

40. *Richard Wagner in Bayreuth*: Friedrich Nietzsche, *Unzeitgemässe Betrachtungen, Viertes Stück: Richard Wagner in Bayreuth*, 2nd edn (Schloss-Chemnitz: Verlag von Ernst Schmeitzner, 1876), pp. 94–5.

41. *in usum Delphinorum*: for the use of the dauphins, i.e. for the use of the kings. The allusion is to the Delphin Classics, a set of Latin classics created in the 1670s for the use of Louis of France (1661–1711), the eldest son of Louis XIV.

42. *The knights looked on boldly*: from 'The Minstrel', a poem in Goethe's novel *Wilhelm Meister* (1795–6). See Goethe, *Selected Verse*, ed. and trans. David Luke (London: Penguin Classics, 1982), p. 83.

43. *their meeting in Teplitz*: Goethe and Beethoven met in what is now Teplice in the Czech Republic in July 1812. In a letter to Carl Friedrich Zelter dated 2 September 1812, Goethe subsequently referred to Beethoven as 'an utterly untamed personality'. Johann Wolfgang von Goethe, *Briefwechsel zwischen Goethe und Zelter in den Jahren 1799 bis 1832*, ed. Edith Zehm et al., *Sämtliche Werke nach Epochen seines Schaffens: Münchner Ausgabe*, 33 vols (Munich: Carl Hanser Verlag, 1991), vol. 20.1, pp. 281–3.

44. *the pre-eminent German statesman ... his imperial mouthpiece*: Otto von Bismarck (1815–98), founder of the modern state of Germany, Chancellor of Germany (1871–90); and Wilhelm I (1797–1888), King of Prussia (1861–88) and first German Emperor (1871–88).

45. *As an aesthetic phenomenon existence is still bearable to us*: ten years before, Nietzsche had said, 'for it is only as *an aesthetic phenomenon* that existence and the world are eternally *justified*'. *The Birth of Tragedy Out of the Spirit of Music*, trans. Shaun Whiteside (London: Penguin Classics, 1993), p. 32. The question of what we are to do with existence remains, but the question of 'justification', a moral (and ultimately, theological) concern, has been quietly dropped. In the next and subsequent sections, Nietzsche will return to the question, albeit less quietly.

BOOK III

1. *After the Buddha died*: one of the earlier mentions of this story in Europe is in Max Müller, *Chips from a German Workshop*, 5 vols (London: Longmans, Green & Co., 1867), vol. 1, p. 273.

See also his *Buddhism and Buddhist Pilgrims: A Review of M. Stanislas Julien's 'Voyages des Pèlerins Bouddhistes'* (Edinburgh: Williams and Norgate, 1857), pp. 37–9.

2. *God is dead*: this is the first instance of this signature phrase in Nietzsche's published writings, though it appears in 1881 in his notebooks and is more often associated with its striking appearance in the Prologue to *Thus Spoke Zarathustra*. However, this phrase first appears in German in a poem by Gottfried Wilhelm Sacer (1635–99) titled 'At the grave of Jesus'; see *Die geistliche Dichtung von Luther bis Klopstock*, ed. Julius Klaiber (Stuttgart: Adolph Becher, 1864), pp. 437–8. Though it is seldom considered in connection with Nietzsche, the phrase's prior use generally refers to Jesus, regarded as the God Incarnate, dying on the cross and remaining dead for three days. And despite Nietzsche's recasting of the notion for his own ends, the Christian echoes in the phrase are still discernible, especially in § 125 below, where the madman's emphasis on humanity's responsibility for the death of God is reminiscent of Christian sermonizing about humanity's guilt in general, and guilt for the death of Jesus in particular. As Nietzsche will later say, 'God has died of his pity for man'; *Thus Spoke Zarathustra*, trans. R. J. Hollingdale (London: Penguin Classics, 1961), p. 114. While the slogan is generally understood to refer to the historical moment at which belief in God is no longer possible, its implications for Nietzsche are often misunderstood. First, Nietzsche is not saying that there can be no normative judgements at all unless they are backed by God's authority, thus confronting us with a stark choice between theism and nihilism. Nor is he claiming that the effects of belief in God were an unqualified boon, and the effects of disbelief will be an unqualified disaster. Rather, he is saying that in so far as we have used the notion of God as a source of normative authority, we now face a difficult task of re-envisioning normativity and putting it on a new foundation. Similarly, in so far as Christianity's legacy is a mixed one, we now face the prospect of emancipation from its more questionable effects, as well as the difficult task of sorting out just what normative commitments we wish to have. Most of all, Nietzsche thinks that the death of God demands a *response*, and Nietzsche's response in *Zarathustra* is to 'teach the superman', to urge us to organize our culture around the pursuit of personal excellence, the vision of which will serve to replace the image of God as the source of all that is good.

3. *our solar system . . . the Milky Way* etc.: the phrase translated as 'our solar system' is 'unserer Nachbar-Sterne' or 'our neighbour-stars', but based on Nietzsche's use of 'Stern' elsewhere, and his description in terms of 'cyclical movement', there is little doubt that he is referring to planets and not stars. At the time Nietzsche was writing, it had not yet been confirmed that the stars of the Milky Way generally also follow cyclical paths.

4. *the whole music box perpetually repeats* etc.: the eternal recurrence (see § 341 and the Introduction, pp. xvii–xx).

5. *the god of the Eleatics*: the concept of being as a changeless unity, espoused by the pre-Socratic philosopher Parmenides and his school.

6. *tables of goods*: 'Gütertafeln', a coinage of Nietzsche's which also barely occurs outside discussions of Nietzsche subsequently. Since the compound word is invariably associated with evaluation in Nietzsche, and each of its components is *plural*, the metaphor seems to be a commercial one: printed tables containing the prices of commodities. Such things enable one to determine at a glance what something is worth.

7. *Ariston of Chios*: ancient Greek Stoic philosopher (third century BC). Nietzsche's primary source of information about him was Diogenes Laertius, *Lives of Eminent Philosophers*; see books 6–10, Loeb Classical Library no. 185, trans. Hicks, p. 263.

8. *deprecating*: reading 'verbitternd' (embittering) as 'verbittend' (deprecating).

9. *he described it* etc.: 'nothing more excellent or more useful has been given by the Creator to mankind, if we except only the knowledge and true worship of himself, than these studies, which not only lead to the ornament and guidance of human life, but are applicable and useful to every particular situation; in adversity consolatory, in prosperity pleasing and honourable; insomuch that without them we should be deprived of all the grace of life and all the polish of society.' Leo X (1475–1521), quoted and translated in William Roscoe, *The Life and Pontificate of Leo the Tenth*, 4th edn, rev. Thomas Roscoe, 2 vols (London: Henry G. Bohn, 1846), vol. 1, p. 421. It is notable that the example of science under discussion here is philology; Leo was commissioning Philippus Beroaldus (1453–1505), a professor at the University of Bologna, to produce an edition of Tacitus' *Annals*.

10. *in so great a patron of them*: among the artists Leo supported was Raphael.

11. *'God Himself cannot do without wise men', said Luther*: quoted in Emerson's 'Nature'. See Ralph Waldo Emerson, *Essays*, 2nd series (Boston: James Munroe and Company, 1845), p. 203. The quote appears to be spurious.

12. *crimen laesae majestatis divinae*: high treason, an offence against the dignity of a sovereign (literally, 'the crime of treason against divine majesty'). In English the expression is usually the French *lèse-majesté* rather than the Latin phrase. Nietzsche's use involves some subtle wordplay in that in its ordinary use 'divine majesty' refers to a monarch, not to God; Nietzsche is suggesting that there is something peculiar in treating a god like a monarch, but its original sense implies that one should treat a monarch like a god.

13. *If I love you etc.*: Nietzsche is quoting Goethe: 'Wenn ich dich liebe, was geht's dich an?' See *From My Life: Poetry and Truth, Parts 1–3 (Goethe: The Collected Works)*, ed. Thomas P. Saine and Jeffrey L. Sammons, trans. Robert R. Heitner (New York: Suhrkamp Publishers, 1987), p. 459.

14. *Do not flatter your benefactor*: an attribution of a similar phrase to the Buddha can be found in Robert Hammerling, 'Über die Kunst zu schenken', in *Heimgarten* (Graz: Leykam-Josefsthal, 1881), vol. 5, p. 198.

15. *superhuman beings*: the expression Nietzsche uses here is 'Übermenschen'; the *Übermensch* or superman will play a central role in Nietzsche's next and most famous book, *Thus Spoke Zarathustra*.

16. *Ulfilas*: a fourth-century AD Gothic bishop and advocate of Arianism, who translated the Bible into the East Germanic language of Gothic (the so-called 'Wulfila Bible' or 'Gothic Bible') from the Greek translation of the Bible (the Septuagint). The word 'Deutsch' is derived from the Proto-Germanic **þeudō*, meaning 'people', 'nation' or 'folk'. Nietzsche's argument is as follows. The Hebrew word *goy* in the Old Testament has a similar meaning to **þeudō* but is also used there pejoratively (in the King James translation of the Bible it is rendered as 'heathen'). The word *goy* was subsequently translated into *ethnē* in the Septuagint and then from Greek to Gothic as *þiuda*. *Piuda*, like the German *deutsch*, is also derived from the Proto-Germanic **þeudō*. Therefore *deutsch* had at one time a pejorative connotation, just as 'heathen' does.

17. *Here I stand! I cannot do otherwise!*: Martin Luther is said to have uttered this phrase to the Holy Roman Emperor Charles V on 16 April 1521 at the Imperial Diet of Worms, which led to

the emperor issuing the Edict of Worms, outlawing Luther. Transcripts of the event do not agree on whether he said this or not. Nietzsche is suggesting that atheism is a natural outcome of the Protestant Reformation; in other places he suggests that the Protestant Reformation represented a major retrenchment of Christianity. One could say that these are 'Catholic' and 'Protestant' views of the Reformation, respectively; Nietzsche seems to adhere to both, apart from the question of his evaluation of Christianity itself.

18. *as Schopenhauer would have it*: specifically, in 'On Man's Need for Metaphysics', ch. 17 of *The World as Will and Representation*, vol. 2.

19. *as Horace demands*: in his *Ars Poetica*, Horace says, 'If you want your play to be called for and given a second performance, it should not be either shorter or longer than five acts. No god should intervene unless some entanglement develops which requires a deliverer to unravel it.' *Classical Literary Criticism*, rev. edn, ed. and trans. Penelope Murray, trans. T. S. Dorsch (London: Penguin Classics, 2000), p. 103. Nietzsche is suggesting that no *deus ex machina* is available to resolve a plot in which the central event is the killing off of every *deus*.

20. *tragic resolution . . . comic resolution*: Nietzsche's account of the structure of a play appears to follow Gustav Freytag's influential five-act account in terms of exposition, rising action, climax, falling action and resolution in *Die Technik des Dramas* (Leipzig: S. Hirzel, 1863); Nietzsche mentions Freytag briefly in his notebooks in the years he was formulating the ideas which would appear in *The Birth of Tragedy* (1872). Since 'man the poet' is both author and protagonist, Nietzsche is suggesting that the conclusion of the human drama will either be a nihilistic catastrophe or a 'comic' ending, which is suggestive of the idea of the 'joyousness' Nietzsche hopes to promote. Clearly this section echoes the announcement of God's death in § 125 above, and anticipates § 342 below, '*Incipit Tragoedia*' (the tragedy begins).

21. *what the Romans meant by the word mentiri*: lie, from *mens, mentis* (mind).

22. *Murat*: Joachim-Napoléon Murat (1767–1815), successively Marshal of France and Admiral of France, Prince Murat, Grand Duke of Berg and King of Naples under Napoleon.

23. *Les souverains rangent aux parvenus*: sovereigns belong with the upstarts.

24. *Fit secundum regulam*: done according to rule.

25. *The Music of the Best Future*: the expression 'music of the future' was associated with Wagner, though not exclusively, and was initially more used by his critics than his supporters. Nietzsche would subtitle his later book *Beyond Good and Evil* 'Prelude to a Philosophy of the Future'.

26. *we are all workers*: 'From Turin it is reported that the King of Portugal said to a deputation of workers' societies that greeted him, "We are all workers; some are workers of ideas; others, workers of justice, of religion, of agriculture, of industry, of commerce. Even the kings, when they do their duty, are working."' *Bamberger Zeitung*, 23 November 1865, p. 2.

27. *Hic niger est*: here he is black. Nietzsche is quoting Horace's *Satires*: 'The man who traduces a friend behind his back, who won't stand up for him when someone else is running him down, who looks for the big laugh and wants to be thought a wit, the man who can invent what he never saw but can't keep a secret – he's the blackguard [*hic niger est*]; beware of *him*, O son of Rome!' *The Satires of Horace and Persius*, rev. edn, trans. Niall Rudd (London: Penguin Classics, 2005), p. 18.

28. *brother by milk*: the German expression is 'Milchbruder'; two children are 'Milchbrüder' when one is being breastfed by a wet-nurse and the other is the natural child of the wet-nurse, who is also being breastfed by her at the same time. Although 'foster brother' once had the same meaning in English, its association with nursing, and thus Nietzsche's suggestion of brood parasitism, has largely been lost.

29. *Who has ears to hear, let him hear*: cf. Matthew 13:9, 13:43.

30. *Cerberus*: monstrous three-headed dog guarding the gates of Hades.

31. *Suum cuique*: to each his own.

32. *flying fish*: in a letter dated 8 December 1881 to his friend Heinrich Köselitz, Nietzsche says: 'I live strangely as on the crests of the waves of existence – a kind of flying fish. They are always *present* to me, my dear friend!'

33. *sit venia verbo*: pardon the expression.

34. *Sub specie aeterni*: under the aspect (or species) of what is eternal, an allusion to '*sub specie aeternitatis*', under the aspect (or species) of eternity. Spinoza himself does not use either phrase, instead saying 'under a certain species of eternity [*sub quadam aeternitatis specie*]'. Benedict de Spinoza, *Ethics*, trans. Edwin Curley, with an Introduction by Stuart Hampshire (London: Penguin Classics, 2005), p.60. However, '*sub specie aeternitatis*'

is widely associated with him and has become a common phrase in subsequent philosophy.

BOOK IV: SANCTUS JANUARIUS

1. *Sanctus Januarius*: Januarius I of Benevento (third century AD), Bishop of Benevento and patron saint of Naples. A sample of his blood is kept as a relic in a sealed glass ampoule in Naples Cathedral; three times a year it is said to miraculously liquify. See Introduction, p. xvii. Nietzsche quotes the poem which follows in his autobiography *Ecce Homo*, in his description of *The Joyous Science*, which I produce in my own translation on pp. 301–2.

2. *Sum, ergo cogito; cogito, ergo sum*: I am, therefore I think; I think, therefore I am. The allusion of course is to Descartes' Second Meditation, though the formulation 'I think, therefore I am' (*cogito ergo sum*) is not Descartes' own. 'Thus, having weighed up everything adequately, it must finally be stated that this proposition "I am, I exist" is necessarily true whenever it is stated by me or conceived in my mind.' René Descartes, *Meditations and Other Metaphysical Writings*, trans. Desmond M. Clarke (London: Penguin Classics, 1999), p. 24.

3. *Amor fati*: love of fate.

4. *every hair on our heads*: cf. Matthew 10:30, Luke 12:7, 'the very hairs of your head are all numbered'.

5. *the slope of Vesuvius*: Mount Vesuvius, an active volcano located on the Gulf of Naples in south-west Italy which erupted in AD 79, destroying the Roman cities of Pompeii and Herculaneum.

6. *Excelsior!*: 'Excelsior', which is Latin for 'onwards and upwards', is the name of a poem by Henry Wadsworth Longfellow, about a youth who attempts to climb a mountain in the Swiss Alps, despite various temptations. In the end he is discovered by St Bernard dogs, frozen to death, having never given up. Nietzsche refers to the poem in a letter to Erwin Rohde dated 14 April 1876.

7. *your seven solitudes*: Nietzsche also refers to the 'seven solitudes' or the 'seventh solitude' below at § 309, in a letter to Resa von Schirnhofer of June 1885, in the Foreword to *The Anti-Christ* and in the poems in *Dionysus Dithyrambs* (1888) titled 'The Fire Sign' and 'The Sun Sinks', as well as numerous times in his notebooks. Achard of St Victor (1100–72), in his treatise *On Self-Denial*, a commentary on the temptation of Christ in the wilderness, writes

of the seven deserts of the soul as a trope for seven degrees of self-renunciation. One of the Latin terms for desert is *solitudinem*.

8. *the eternal recurrence of war and peace*: an allusion to the doctrine of the eternal recurrence, discussed in § 341 and the Introduction, pp. xvii–xx.

9. *Alas, if you are still stones or animals* etc.: 'With songs such as these the Thracian minstrel bewitched the forests, entranced the beasts and compelled the rocks to follow behind him.' Ovid, *Metamorphoses*, trans. David Raeburn (London: Penguin Classics, 2004), p. 422.

10. *the wanderer to his shadow*: Nietzsche's book of 1880 was titled *The Wanderer and His Shadow*.

11. *The moral earth is also round*: like Columbus, Nietzsche embarks on a voyage of discovery.

12. *a new world*: another reference to Columbus, who was born in Genoa.

13. *I ask God to make me free of God!*: Meister Eckhart, *Selected Writings*, trans. Oliver Davies (London: Penguin Classics, 1995), p. 207.

14. *particles of aether*: Nietzsche is alluding to the notion that light propagates in waves through a luminiferous aether composed of particles, just as sound propagates in waves through the air, which is also composed of particles.

15. *Prometheia*: a trilogy of plays about Prometheus, traditionally attributed to Aeschylus. Only the first instalment, *Prometheus Bound*, and quoted fragments from the others survive.

16. *a foolish little riddle* etc.: after Homer asked the fishermen what they had caught, they replied: 'We have what we did not find; what we did find we left behind,' that is to say, they had been picking lice off themselves with only partial success. Homer, distracted by his inability to solve the riddle, slipped in the mud and later died. See Daniel B. Levine, 'Poetic Justice: Homer's Death in the Ancient Biographical Tradition', *The Classical Journal*, vol. 98, no. 2 (December 2002–January 2003), pp. 141–60.

17. *placitum*: decree.

18. *the ʿĪsāwiyya*: a Sufi mystical order founded in Morocco but present thoughout north-west Africa, noteworthy for its ritual trance music. Most nineteenth-century European reports emphasize its self-mortification practices, as Nietzsche does here. Ironically, the practices of the ʿĪsāwiyya probably more closely resemble Nietzsche's notion of the 'Dionysian' than they do Stoicism.

19. *trier of the hearts and reins*: 'Oh let the wickedness of the wicked come to an end; but establish the just: for the righteous God trieth the hearts and reins.' Psalm 7:9.

20. *Seventh Solitude*: see note 7, Book IV.

21. *gardens of Armida*: Armida is a character in Torquato Tasso's epic of the Crusades, *Jerusalem Delivered* (1581). She abducts the Christian knight Rinaldo and takes him to the aforementioned gardens, where he becomes infatuated with her and forgets the Crusade. His fellow knights Carlo and Ubaldo find him and, by showing him to himself in a mirror, disenchant him with his current condition and induce him to return to the Crusade. It may also be significant that Rinaldo is able to convert Armida in the end, thus reconciling them. The tale subsequently became the basis of many paintings and operas.

22. *The kingdom of heaven is at hand*: 'From that time Jesus began to preach, and to say, Repent: for the kingdom of heaven is at hand.' Matthew 4:17.

23. *Oliver Cromwell*: leader of the 'Roundheads' or Parliamentarians in the English Civil War (1642–51), which led to the execution of King Charles II and the establishment of the Commonwealth, over which Cromwell held the title 'Lord Protector'. His death in 1658, probably from malaria, was sudden and unexpected.

24. *In media vita*: in the middle of life.

25. *otium*: leisure.

26. *bellum*: war.

27. *quando etiam sapientibus cupido gloriae novissima exuitur*: 'for the last of all human infirmities to be shed, even by a philosopher, is a longing for glory'. Tacitus, *The Histories*, trans. Kenneth Wellesley (London: Penguin Classics, 1995), p. 212.

28. *Non ridere, non lugere, neque detestari, sed intelligere*: not to laugh, or mourn, or curse, but only to understand. The larger context of the quote reads: 'To investigate the matters pertaining to this science with the same freedom of spirit we're accustomed to use in investigating Mathematical subjects, I took great pains not to laugh at human actions, or mourn them, or curse them, but only to understand them.' *The Political Treatise*, in *The Collected Works of Spinoza*, 2 vols, trans. Edwin Curley (Princeton, NJ: Princeton University Press, 1985 and 2016), vol. 2, p. 505.

29. *know thyself*: a maxim of Apollo's oracle at Delphi, referred to in several of Plato's dialogues. For discussions, see Plato, *Early Socratic Dialogues*, reprinted with a new Preface and revised Bibliography, ed. Trevor Saunders (London: Penguin Classics,

2005), pp. 192–6; *Protagoras and Meno*, trans. Adam Beresford (London: Penguin Classics, 2005), p. 51; *Phaedrus*, trans. Christopher Rowe (London: Penguin Classics, 2005), p. 6; *Philebus*, reissued with a new Chronology, trans. Robin H. Waterfield (London: Penguin Classics, 2006), p. 56; *The Laws*, reprinted with a new Preface, Further Reading and minor revisions, trans. Trevor Saunders (London: Penguin Classics, 2004), p. 423.

30. *intellectual conscience*: cf. § 2, Book I.

31. *categorical imperative*: the notion that morality is based on an unconditional command derived from practical reason itself, with the implication being that immoral actions are in some sense irrational. See Immanuel Kant, *Groundwork of the Metaphysics of Morals* (1785), in *Practical Philosophy,* trans. and ed. Mary J. Gregor (Cambridge: Cambridge University Press, 1996), pp. 37–108.

32. *God, the soul, freedom and immortality*: Kant offers 'practical' proofs of the immortality of the soul and the existence of God in *Critique of Practical Reason* (1788). See *Practical Philosophy*, pp. 238–453.

33. *as I judge, so must everyone judge*: Kant's test of 'universalizability', one account of the categorical imperative, which reads 'act in accordance with a maxim that can at the same time make itself a universal law'. See *Groundwork*, in *Practical Philosophy*, p. 86.

34. *Vita femina*: female life.

35. *we ought to offer a cock to Asclepius*: as reported in Plato's *Phaedo'*. See Plato, *The Last Days of Socrates*, rev. edn, trans. Hugh Tredennick and Harold Tarrant (London: Penguin Classics, 2003), p. 198.

36. *Incipit Tragoedia*: the tragedy begins. Section 342, *'Incipit Tragoedia'*, of *The Joyous Science* is identical to the first section of the prologue to *Thus Spoke Zarathustra*, Nietzsche's next book, with the exceptions of reading 'the lake of his home' instead of 'Lake Urmi' and omitting the title *'Incipit Tragoedia'*.

37. *Zarathustra*: the Iranian prophet Zoroaster, founder of Zoroastrianism. In *Thus Spoke Zarathustra* Nietzsche imagines the prophet teaching Nietzsche's philosophy rather than Zoroastrianism, and, most importantly, the doctrine of the eternal recurrence, the very doctrine just introduced above in § 341. Thus Nietzsche is suggesting that the argument of *The Joyous Science* as a whole culminates in the doctrine of the eternal recurrence, and a transformation of Nietzsche's relationship to his audience from 'free spirit' to prophet-legislator. Nietzsche explains his choice of mouthpiece in *Ecce Homo* as follows:

I have not been asked, as I should have been asked, what the
name Zarathustra means in precisely my mouth, in the mouth
of the first immoralist: for what constitutes the tremendous
uniqueness of that Persian in history is precisely the opposite of
this. Zarathustra was the first to see in the struggle between
good and evil the actual wheel in the working of things: the
translation of morality into the realm of metaphysics, as force,
cause, end-in-itself, is *his* work. But this question is itself at
bottom its own answer. Zarathustra *created* this most fateful of
errors, morality: consequently he must also be the first to
recognize it. Not only has he had longer and greater experience
here than any other thinker – the whole of history is indeed the
experimental refutation of the proposition of a so-called 'moral
world-order' –: what is more important is that Zarathustra is
more truthful than any other thinker. His teaching, and his
alone, upholds truthfulness as the supreme virtue – that is to say,
the opposite of the *cowardice* of the 'idealist', who takes flight in
the face of reality; Zarathustra has more courage in him than all
other thinkers put together. To tell the truth and *to shoot well
with arrows*: that is Persian virtue. Have I been understood? The
self-overcoming of morality through truthfulness, the self-
overcoming of the moralist into his opposite – *into me* – that is
what the name Zarathustra means in my mouth.

Friedrich Nietzsche, *Ecce Homo: How One Becomes What
One Is*, trans. R. J. Hollingdale, reprinted with an Introduction
by Michael Tanner (London: Penguin Classics, 1992), pp. 97–8.

38.   *Lake Urmi*: Lake Urmia, a salt lake in Iranian Azerbaijan, near
the Iranian-Turkish border. According to medieval Arab sources,
Urmia was the birthplace of Zoroaster.

BOOK V: WE FEARLESS ONES

1.   *Carcasse, tu trembles?* etc.: 'You tremble, carcass? You would
tremble much more if you knew where I was leading you.' Henri
de La Tour d'Auvergne, Vicomte de Turenne (1611–75), Marshal General of France under Louis XIV. Nietzsche's source for
the quote is Ximénès Doudan, *Mélanges et lettres*, 4 vols (Paris:
Calmann Lévy, 1878), vol. 3, p. 347.

2.   *polytropoi*: many-turned, i.e. much wandering, an epithet of
Odysseus: 'Sing to me of the man, Muse, the man of [many]

twists and turns driven time and again off course, once he had plundered the hallowed heights of Troy.' Homer, *The Odyssey*, trans. Robert Fagles (London: Penguin Classics, 1996), p. 77. However, Plato interprets it in the *Hippias Minor* to mean 'complex', as in 'shifty, versatile, wily', which is clearly how Nietzsche takes it here. See *Early Socratic Dialogues*, pp. 276–83.

3. *in an individual case*: Paul Rée, author of *The Origin of the Moral Sensations* (1877), which can be found in his *Basic Writings*, trans. Robin Small (Urbana-Champaign, IL: University of Illinois Press, 2003), pp. 85–165.

4. *demonstration of power*: the notion that a belief must be true because believing it has beneficial effects on the believer. The biblical source for the phrase Nietzsche uses is 1 Corinthians 2:4. 'And my speech and my preaching *was* not with enticing words of man's wisdom, but in demonstration of the Spirit and of power'.

5. *Parisian naturalisme*: the literary style pioneered by Émile Zola and others.

6. *la vérité vraie*: the honest truth.

7. *nihilism of the St Petersburg variety*: Nietzsche mentions no names (other than a passing reference to Mikhail Bakunin in 1873) anywhere in his writings which one might associate with Russian Nihilism as a revolutionary political movement. The only person he mentions by name when using St Petersburg metonymically in this way is Leo Tolstoy, in *The Antichrist*, § 7. See *The Twilight of the Idols and the Anti-Christ: or How to Philosophize with a Hammer*, reissued edn, trans. R. J. Hollingdale with an Introduction by Michael Tanner (London: Penguin Classics, 1990), p. 131.

8. *Spinoza . . . self-preservation*: 'Each thing, as far as it can by its own power, strives to persevere in its being.' Spinoza, *Ethics*, p. 75.

9. *deformed, something scarce half made up*: an allusion to the self-description of Shakespeare's Richard III:

> I, that am curtail'd of this fair proportion,
> Cheated of feature by dissembling nature,
> Deformed, unfinish'd, sent before my time
> Into this breathing world, scarce half made up,
> And that so lamely and unfashionable
> That dogs bark at me as I halt by them.

William Shakespeare, *Richard III*, reissued edn, ed. Peter Holland (London: Penguin Classics, 2017), p. 6.

10. *the quiet fanaticism of the Moravian Brethren*: 'Herrenhuter-Fanatismus'. Herrnhut is a German town in Saxony, associated with the members of the Unitas Fratrum (Unity of the Brethren) founded by Jan Hus in the fifteenth century, who dwell there and are popularly known as the Moravian Brethren or the Moravian Church. The movement extolled the virtues of a Christ-like life over questions of doctrine.

11. *Genius of the Species*: the expression appears to have its origin in Schopenhauer, where it refers to sexuality. The irony of Nietzsche's appropriation of the expression is that Schopenhauer uses it to stress the way that the sexual impulse makes a mockery of all social niceties when they conflict with its imperatives, whereas here it is a social phenomenon which appears to have the upper hand. See Schopenhauer, *The World as Will and Representation*, vol. 2, pp. 565–75.

12. *This philosopher*: Plato.

13. *Graeculus histrio*: little Greek actor.

14. *ironwood*: also known as *Sideroxylon*. The double entendre here is that *Sideroxylon* really is a genus of trees, and thus a kind of wood out of which one might build things. But it is also an expression which both is and refers to an oxymoron, a contradiction in terms. This use of the expression in philosophy appears to date back to Schopenhauer in 1819, from whom Nietzsche presumably derived it. Because in German the vernacular expression 'hölzernen Eisen' is almost exclusively used to refer a contradiction in terms, while the Greek *Sideroxylon* is used almost exclusively to refer to actual trees, it is unclear whether Nietzsche intended the double entendre. Schopenhauer uses both expressions. See *The World as Will and Representation*, vol. 1, pp. 52, 298 and 554, and vol. 2, p. 20. The British philosopher F. H. Bradley appears to be one of the few authors to have used the expression in English. 'It is a standing contradiction, a barbarous sideroxylon.' F. H. Bradley, *The Presuppositions of Critical History* (Oxford: James Parker and Co., 1874), p. 44.

15. *Eduard von Hartmann*: Karl Robert Eduard von Hartmann (1842–1906), a German philosopher influenced by Hegel and Schopenhauer.

16. *the era of financial speculation in the early 1870s*: literally 'the Age of Foundations', a boom period which ended with the stock market crash of 1873. The first volume of Eduard von

Hartmann's book *Philosophie des Unbewussten* appeared in 1869; Nietzsche here likens his philosophy to a speculative investment which, by 1873, was revealed to be worthless. It is in 1873 that Nietzsche's notebooks begin to contain this assessment, which he makes public in 1874, in *On the Uses and Disadvantages of History for Life*, the second of the *Untimely Meditations*. See Friedrich Nietzsche, *Untimely Meditations*, 2nd edn, trans. R. J. Hollingdale, with an Introduction by Daniel Breazeale (Cambridge: Cambridge University Press, 1997), pp. 108–16.

17. *Bahnsen . . . Mainländer*: Julius Bahnsen (1830–81), a German philosopher influenced by Hegel and Schopenhauer; Philipp Mainländer, born Philipp Batz (1841–76), German poet and philosopher also influenced by Schopenhauer.

18. *Deutschland, Deutschland, über Alles*: a famous line from the 'Deutschlandlied' (Song of Germany), music by Joseph Haydn, lyrics by August Heinrich Hoffmann von Fallersleben. It was the unofficial anthem of the unsuccessful Revolution of 1848 and, then and since, an expression of German nationalism, and did not become Germany's official national anthem until 1922. The song was banned in 1945 after the Second World War, but a single stanza was reinstated as the German national anthem in 1952 and is still in use today.

19. *sub specie speciei*: 'under the aspect (or species) of the species', a play on Spinoza's *sub specie aeternitatis*, 'under the aspect (or species) of eternity'. See note 34, Book III.

20. *repudiating faith in the inspiration of the Councils*: in Martin Luther's treatise *On the Councils and the Church* (1539), in *The Annotated Luther*, ed. Paul W. Robinson, 6 vols (Minneapolis, MN: Fortress Press, 2016), vol. 3, pp. 317–443.

21. *Napoleon . . . wanted one Europe*: Napoleon's advocacy of European unification appears to have been at best a retroactive justification for his wars. Nietzsche's advocacy of European unification and the re-emergence of a Napoleonic Era sensibility, however, is a consistent feature of his thought throughout his mature writings, and a theme insufficiently explored in the secondary literature.

22. *not merely a betrothal of herself, but a full bestowal of herself*: in this phrase 'Hingebung' is rendered as 'betrothal' and 'Hingabe' as 'bestowal' in order to capture something of the auditory echo. Nietzsche has unaccountably reversed the terms in the later sentence, where he is still clearly using 'Hingabe' to

characterize something feminine. Therefore in this sentence (and in the final sentence of the section) we are reading 'Hinge-bung' as 'Hingabe' to preserve the contrast as he had initially laid it out.

23. *so-called elective affinity*: Goethe's notion that love between people resembles the affinities certain chemicals have for combining with others, as he presented it in his novel *Elective Affinities*, trans. R. J. Hollingdale (London: Penguin Classics, 1971).

24. *the worst society lets you feel*: 'The worst society lets you feel that you are a man with men.' Johann Wolfgang von Goethe, *Goethe's Faust. Erster und zweiter Theil. Text und Erläuterung in Vorlesungen*, ed. Alexander von Oettingen (Erlangen: Verlag von Andreas Deichert, 1880), p. 153 (translation mine).

25. *litteris et artibus*: arts and letters.

26. *The Cynic Speaks*: Nietzsche reused this section in *Nietzsche contra Wagner*, with some modifications. See *Nietzsche contra Wagner*, in *The Portable Nietzsche*, pp. 664–6.

27. *What Is Romanticism*: a rough draft of the portion of this section which begins 'With regard to all aesthetic values' and ends with 'Wagner's music' can be found in Nietzsche's notebooks, and was later published as § 846 in *The Will to Power* (1901). See Friedrich Nietzsche, *The Will to Power*, ed. R. Kevin Hill, trans. R. Kevin Hill and Michael Scarpitti (London: Penguin Classics, 2017), pp. 476–7. The portion of § 370 which runs from the beginning to the phrase 'principal distinction' was extensively revised by Nietzsche for the section of *Nietzsche contra Wagner*, titled '*We Antipodes*'. See *Nietzsche contra Wagner* in *The Portable Nietzsche*, pp. 669–71. The most substantial modification is the insertion of the sentence 'to understand this emotion we have but to look closely at our anarchists.'

28. *some gross errors and exaggerations*: contained in Nietzsche's *The Birth of Tragedy* (1872).

29. *Condillac and the Sensualists*: Étienne Bonnot de Condillac (1714–80), a French philosopher and disciple of John Locke; Sensualists refers to Empiricists.

30. *Epicurus, the opposite of a Dionysian pessimist*: note the shift from a favourable attitude towards Epicurus in § 45, Book I, first published in 1882, to the more critical portrait here, published in 1887.

31. *my proprium and ipsissimum*: my distinguishing characteristic and own very self.

32. *the cold realm of 'ideas'*: the allusion to Plato is unmistakable, and the 'dangerous Southern island' might even be an allusion to Sicily, where, according to the Seventh Letter, Plato became embroiled in the dynastic politics of Syracuse. See *The Collected Dialogues of Plato, Including the Letters*, new impression edn, ed. Edith Hamilton and Huntington Cairns (Princeton, NJ: Princeton University Press, 2005), pp. 1574–98.

33. *Sirens' music*: an allusion to the episode in which Odysseus has himself tied to the mast of his ship so that he can hear the music of the Sirens, which is said to lure sailors into shipwreck. Odysseus' crew avoided this fate by stopping up their ears with wax. See Homer, *The Odyssey*, reprint edn, trans. Robert Fagles (London: Penguin Classics, 1999), pp. 271–85. Although Nietzsche seems to identify with Odysseus, thus placing Plato, who would then be likened to one of the crew, on a lower level, a subtler reading would suggest that because Plato *did* expose himself to the *praxis* of political life on the 'dangerous Southern island' of Sicily, he (narrowly) escaped 'shipwreck' anyway. This would make *Plato* into Odysseus (and Spinoza the modern into one of the crew members who must stop up his ears), wary of the music of the senses but self-disciplined enough to not have to stop up his ears. In his notebooks, Nietzsche asks: 'is Plato's integrity unimpeachable?' (*The Will to Power*, p. 254), suggesting that he may have more in common with wily Odysseus than one might think. See the discussion of *polytropoi*, the Homeric expression which Nietzsche uses in § 344, in note 2, Book V.

34. *amor intellectualis dei*: the intellectual love of God. Spinoza discusses it in the *Ethics*, pp. 175–7.

35. *self-examination of the intellect*: as suggested by Kant. See Immanuel Kant, *Critique of Pure Reason*, ed. and trans. Marcus Weigelt (London: Penguin Classics, 2008). Nietzsche's arguments against the possibility of a preliminary self-examination of the intellect recall those of Hegel. See G. W. F. Hegel, *Phenomenology of Spirit*, rev. edn, trans. A. V. Miller, with an analysis of the text and Foreword by J. N. Findlay (Oxford: Oxford University Press, 1977), pp. 46–57.

36. *fermata*: a pause in music.

37. *gaya scienza*: 'joyous science' in Provençal and the subtitle of this book. See Introduction for a fuller explanation.

38. *Chinesery*: the German word is 'Chineserei', which Nietzsche seems to be using as a disparaging expression meaning 'to act Chinese'. It is related to the French borrowed word 'Chinoiserie',

which usually refers to an artistic style in the decorative arts inspired by Chinese models, but that does not appear to be the way that Nietzsche is using it here.

39. *Saint-Simonian*: pertaining to Henri de Saint-Simon (1760–1825), a utopian socialist.

40. '*The Wanderer' Speaks*: Nietzsche's 'free spirit' trilogy consisted of *Human, All Too Human*, *Dawn* and *Joyous Science*. He subsequently published two additions to *Human, All Too Human* titled *Mixed Opinions and Maxims* and *The Wanderer and His Shadow*, which in the second edition were combined to form vol. 2 of *Human, All Too Human*.

41. *thoughts on moral prejudices*: the subtitle to Nietzsche's book *Dawn*.

42. *untimeliness*: Nietzsche's second book was titled *Untimely Meditations*.

43. *Diu noctuque incubando*: by incubating it day and night. Newton appears never to have said this; rather, it is a maxim attributed to the painter Peter Paul Rubens by Eugène Fromentin. See Eugène Fromentin, *Les Maîtres d'autrefois: Belgique-Hollande* (Paris: Plon-Nourrit, 1877), p. 128. Nietzsche may have been thinking of the following anecdote about Newton reported by Jean-Baptiste Biot, who says that 'car un jour, comme on lui demandait de quelle manière il était parvenu à ses découvertes, il répondit: "En y pensant toujours"' (one day, when he was asked how he had come by his discoveries, he replied: 'By thinking about them always'). *Biographie universelle, ancienne et moderne*, 83 vols (Paris: Michaud, 1811–53), vol. 31 (1822), p. 156.

44. *drive away the crickets*: a German idiom that means 'to chase away the blues'.

45. *the singer's curse*: the title of a poem by Ludwig Uhland (1787–1862).

APPENDIX: 'SONGS OF THE OUTLAW PRINCE'

The Appendix 'Songs of the Outlaw Prince' was added in the second edition of 1887. Nietzsche had previously published eight poems under the title *Idylls from Messina* in 1882. From these he selected six (omitting 'The Little Brig, Called *The Little Angel*' and 'Pia, Caritatevole, Amorosissima', set separately on pp. 297–9 of the current volume), and added to them 'To Goethe', 'These Uncertain Souls',

'The Fool in Despair', 'Rimus remedium', 'What Luck!', 'Towards New Seas', 'Sils-Maria' and 'To the Mistral Wind'.

1. *Outlaw Prince*: the phrase 'Outlaw Prince' renders 'Prinz Vogelfrei'; 'vogelfrei' literally means 'free as a bird', but since at least the eighteenth century it has referred to someone who has been completely ostracized as legal punishment for some serious offence. Earlier usage suggested independence. Nietzsche clearly intends to suggest both the negative and positive usages, as well as the avian imagery, much of which is lost in translation.

2. *The timelessly foolish*: a reference to Goethe's 'timelessly feminine' from the conclusion of his *Faust*, which this poem parodies:

> All that's impermanent
> Is but a simile;
> The insufficient
> Turns into reality;
> As the ineffable
> Here is enacted;
> The timelessly feminine
> Draws us all upward.

Johann Wolfgang von Goethe, *Goethe's Faust*, p. 364 (translation mine). The same themes are developed at length in the contemporaneous *Zarathustra* II, 'On the Poets', which also criticizes Goethe, contains extensive allusions to the conclusion of *Faust*, and even repeats in its first sentence almost exactly the same remark as the first line of this poem: 'und alles das "Unvergängliche" – das ist auch nur ein Gleichniss' (and all the 'permanent' – that is also only a simile). See *Thus Spoke Zarathustra*, pp. 149–52.

3. *Poet's Vocation*: originally titled 'Judgement of the Bird' in *Idylls from Messina*. In its revision for *Joyous Science*, Nietzsche has replaced the words 'Thus spoke' in the final line of the second stanza with 'Chirped' and has added four stanzas which repeat the final couplet of the second stanza. In his *Natural History*, Pliny the Elder mentions that some woodpeckers were used for taking auguries. Nietzsche's echo of Edgar Allen Poe's 'The Raven' is intentional.

4. *In the South*: originally titled 'Outlaw Prince' in *Idylls from Messina*. It is also the poem appended to *Joyous Science* which

most differs from its earlier version: not only did Nietzsche add the final stanza, he substantially redrafted the rest of it as well.

5. *Pious Beppa*: Originally titled 'The Little Witch' in *Idylls from Messina*. The revisions to the poem are slight. Provisional titles included 'The Pious Witch' and, significantly, 'Juanita', suggesting a female version of Byron's Don Juan. Byron himself had said that his *Don Juan* (1819) was to be a 'a poem in the style and manner of *Beppo*' (See *Byron's Letters and Journals*, ed. Leslie A. Marchand, 12 vols [London: John Murray, 1973–82], vol. 6, p. 67), an earlier poem of his, and since both of those poems contain considerable autobiographical elements, this suggests that Nietzsche's fictional 'Beppa' was intended to be something of a female Byron.

6. *The Mysterious Boat*: originally titled 'The Nocturnal Mystery' in *Idylls from Messina*.

7. *Declaration of Love*: originally titled 'Bird Albatross' in *Idylls from Messina*. Nietzsche's albatross does not carry with it the strong association in English derived from Coleridge of a terrible burden. A very large and powerful predatory bird of elegant appearance, the albatross instead suggests nobility. It is also notable in its capacity for dynamic soaring, which involves the exploitation of layers of air masses of differing velocity, thus enabling the bird to travel over great distances with relatively little effort. The albatross' ability to travel far from land and nest makes it an unusually good trope for Nietzsche's conception of the free spirit. In the original version for *Idylls from Messina*, Nietzsche's identification with the bird is heartfelt and unqualified. However, by altering the title as he has he suggests that this identification is false and foolish: his feet on the ground, he gazes upwards at something at a height he cannot attain, and, not looking where he is going, falls into a ditch. This calls to mind both the biblical caution about the blind leading the blind (Matthew 15:14), as well as Plato's remark about Thales, the first philosopher, 'how he was looking upwards in the course of his astronomical investigations, and fell into a pothole, and a Thracian serving girl with a nice sense of humour teased him for being concerned with knowing about what was up in the sky and not noticing what was right in front of his feet'. Plato, *Theaetetus*, trans. Robin Waterfield (London: Penguin Classics, 1987), pp. 69–70. Although a philosopher should take to the heights and look down, it's not clear that a philosopher is anything more than a poet, one of the blind leading the blind.

8. *Song of a Theocritean Goatherd*: originally titled 'Song of the Goatherd (To my neighbour Theocritus of Syracuse)' in *Idylls from Messina*; the two versions differ only with regard to spelling and punctuation. Theocritus was a Hellenistic pastoral poet of the third century BC, noteworthy for *The Idylls*; Nietzsche's identification with him is evident not only here but in the title *Idylls from Messina* for the earlier collection of some of these poems.

9. *the seven evils*: this expression comes from Martin Luther's *Tessaradecas consolatoria* (1520), and refers to (1) the evil within us, the wicked heart, (2) the evil before us, the future, (3) the evil behind us, the past, (4) the evil below us, hell, (5) the evil to our left, our enemies, (6) the evil to our right, the suffering of friends, (7) the evil above us, the suffering of Christ on the cross.

10. *Rimus remedium*: remedy of rhyme.

11. *brazen bull*: a method of execution used by Phalaris of Akragas, an ancient Sicilian tyrant. The condemned were placed inside the bronze bull, and a fire was lit under it. Not only were the condemned roasted to death, but the head of the bull was designed in such a way as to convert their screams into a more pleasing sound.

12. *San Marco*: Piazza San Marco, or St Mark's Square, in Venice.

13. *Campanile*: the bell tower of St Mark's Basilica.

14. *Towards New Seas*: in 1882, Nietzsche began developing a poem on the theme of Columbus which went through several drafts. A version from the autumn of 1884 titled 'Yorick-Columbus' added a third and fourth stanza to the previous two, and it was this later pair of stanzas which were ultimately developed into the text of 'Towards New Seas'.

15. *my Genoese sailing ship*: an allusion to Christopher Columbus.

16. *Sils-Maria*: a Swiss Alpine village in the Upper Engadine between Lake Sils and Lake Silvaplana, where Nietzsche spent all but one of his summers between 1881 and 1888.

17. *My friend*: Nietzsche is addressing Lou Andreas-Salomé, with whom he experienced an intense but fleeting friendship in 1882. Nietzsche's first written reference to Zarathustra, who would become the focus of his next work, *Thus Spoke Zarathustra*, was in a fragment dated Spring–Autumn 1881; Nietzsche's first published reference to Zarathustra is in the first edition of *Joyous Science* (1882), § 342.

18. *Mistral Wind*: a strong north-westerly wind that blows through southern France in general and Provence in particular (the title

of the book, 'The Joyous Science', refers to the art of poetry especially as practised in Provence; see Introduction, pp. xxi–xxii).
The word 'Mistral' derives from the Occitan language and means
'masterly'. The effect of the Mistral Wind is to maintain the
sunny, dry and clear climate of Provence, qualities Nietzsche
treasured and with which he tried to imbue his prose. Nietzsche
included an earlier draft of 'To the Mistral Wind' in a letter to
Heinrich Köselitz dated 22 November 1884.

EXCERPTS FROM *IDYLLS FROM MESSINA*

1. *The Little Brig*: a sailing vessel with two square-rigged masts.
2. *The Little Angel*: a Genoese sailing ship which was christened
   Angiolina in remembrance of a girl who had committed suicide
   out of lovesickness.
3. *Pia, caritatevole, amorosissima*: pious, charitable, most loving.
   This poem, also known as 'Campo Santo di Staglieno', 'Staglieno'
   or 'On the Campo Santo', was composed in 1882, in Genoa. The
   occasion for the poem was a grave marker Nietzsche saw during
   one of his visits to the Monumental Cemetery of Staglieno in
   Genoa, on which was depicted a girl with a lamb, and the inscrip-
   tion 'Pia, Caritatevole, Amorosissima'.

THUS SPOKE ZARATHUSTRA

Friedrich Nietzsche

'Yes! I am Zarathustra the Godless'

Nietzsche was one of the most revolutionary and subversive thinkers in Western philosophy, and *Thus Spoke Zarathustra* remains his most famous and influential work. It describes how the ancient Persian prophet Zarathustra descends from his solitude in the mountains to tell the world that God is dead and that the Superman, the human embodiment of divinity, is his successor. With blazing intensity and poetic brilliance, Nietzsche argues that the meaning of existence is not to be found in religious pieties or meek submission, but in all-powerful life force: passionate, chaotic and free.

Translated and edited with an Introduction by R. J. Hollingdale

ISBN: 978 0 14 044 118 5

BEYOND GOOD AND EVIL

Friedrich Nietzsche

'That which is done out of love always takes place beyond good
and evil'

Beyond Good and Evil confirmed Nietzsche's position as the
towering European philosopher of his age. The work dramatically
rejects traditional Western thought with its notions of truth and
God, good and evil. Nietzsche seeks to demonstrate that the Christian world is steeped in a false piety and infected with a 'slave
morality'. With wit and energy, he turns from this critique to a
philosophy that celebrates the present and demands that the
individual impose their own 'will to power' upon the world.

Translated by R. J. Hollingdale
With an Introduction by Michael Tanner

ISBN: 978 0 14 044 923 5

THE WILL TO POWER

Friedrich Nietzsche

'This world is the will to power – and nothing besides! And even
you yourselves are this will to power – and nothing besides!'

One of the greatest minds of modernity, Friedrich Nietzsche
smashed through the beliefs of his age. These writings, which did
much to establish his reputation as a philosopher, offer some of
his most powerful and troubling thoughts: on how the values of
a new, aggressive elite will save a nihilistic, mediocre Europe, and,
most famously, on the 'will to power' – ideas that were seized
upon and twisted by later readers. Taken from Nietzsche's unpublished notebooks and assembled by his sister after his death, *The
Will to Power* now appears in a clear, fluent new translation, with
previous errors corrected in light of the original manuscripts.

Translated by R. Kevin Hill and Michael A. Scarpitti
With an Introduction and Notes by R. Kevin Hill

ISBN: 978 0 14 119 535 3